QUESTIONS & ANSWERS:
Family Law

QUESTIONS & ANSWERS: Family Law

Multiple-Choice and Short-Answer Questions and Answers

Second Edition

MARK STRASSER
Trustees Professor of Law
Capital University Law School

LexisNexis

ISBN: 978-1-4224-9337-3

> **NOTE TO USERS**
>
> To ensure that you are using the latest materials available in this area, please be sure to periodically check the LexisNexis Law School web site for downloadable updates and supplements at www.lexisnexis.com/lawschool.

Editorial Offices
121 Chanlon Rd., New Providence, NJ 07974 (908) 464-6800
201 Mission St., San Francisco, CA 94105-1831 (415) 908-3200
www.lexisnexis.com

MATTHEW⬥BENDER

(2011–Pub.3183)

Dedication

To my mother, Pearl Strasser, and the memory of my late father, Louis Strasser.

About the Author

Mark Strasser has a B.A. from Harvard College, an M.A. and Ph.D. from the University of Chicago, and a J.D. from Stanford Law School. He is the Trustees Professor of Law at Capital University in Columbus Ohio, where he teaches Family Law, Constitutional Law, and Torts. He has written extensively in Family Law, Constitutional Law, Torts, and Law and Sexual Minorities.

Preface

Traditionally, family law is a matter of state rather than federal concern, and it is course true that family law is not uniform across the states. Nonetheless, there is significant overlap in the family law context both with respect to how issues should be approached and with respect to the substantive law. This book does not focus on the law of a particular jurisdiction but, instead, explores some of the similarities and differences that might be found when considering the various laws across the nation.

There are two types of questions here — short-answer and multiple-choice. Most of the questions involve fact scenarios in invented jurisdictions, and those using the book will consider and explore some of the similarities and difference in family law across the country. Because our society is extremely mobile, these questions focus on both jurisdictional and substantive issues.

The areas covered here include a wide range of issues that might be covered in family law courses. The book aims to improve test-taking skills and, in addition, enhance the understanding of family law by highlighting some of the obvious and non-obvious points that will help resolve some of the issues that might arise in the family law context.

Professor Mark Strasser
mstrasser@law.capital.edu
Columbus, Ohio
April, 2011

Table of Contents

QUESTIONS

Alice Adams, age 16, and Billy Binghamton, age 18, live in the state of Old Jersey, which does not permit minors to marry without parental permission. They are in love and want to marry. However, Alice's parents are inalterably opposed to the union, Alice's pregnancy notwithstanding. Alice and Billy go to the neighboring state of Old Hampshire, which permits pregnant minors who have reached age 16 to marry even without parental permission. Alice and Billy marry and go back to live in Old Jersey in Billy's studio apartment. Three months later, their child, Cary, is born. One month after the birth, Billy's grandmother dies. She has provided in her will for all of her grandchildren and for any great grandchild born into a lawful marriage. Billy consults an attorney to find out whether Cary can take under the will.

1.   The attorney should say:

   (A)   Because Alice and Billy married legally in Old Hampshire, Old Jersey must recognize the marriage, which makes Cary a child born into a lawful marriage.

   (B)   Even though Alice and Billy married legally in Old Hampshire, Old Jersey need not recognize the marriage if it treats minor marriages as void. Assuming that the provision providing only for those grandchildren born into a lawful marriage does not itself violate public policy, whether Cary can take under the will depends upon whether Old Jersey law treats minor marriages as void or voidable.

   (C)   Cary can take under the will only if Alice's parents ratify Alice's marriage by withdrawing their objections to it.

   (D)   Because Alice and Billy cannot marry under Old Jersey law, Cary was not born into a legal marriage and thus cannot take under the will. However, assuming that Alice and Billy remain together, Cary will be able to take under a similar will if the testator dies after Alice attains majority.

Assume the same facts as stated in Question 1. It is now three years later and Alice and Billy are still living together with Cory. However, Alice deeply regrets having married Billy and now wishes to sever the relationship. She consults an attorney to explore her options.

2.   The attorney should say:

   (A)   Even if Old Jersey treats minor marriages as voidable, Alice can file a motion to have the marriage declared void, because she was a minor when the marriage was celebrated.

   (B)   Even if Old Jersey treats minor marriages as void, Alice must still seek a formal dissolution of the marriage, because she continued to live with Billy after she had attained majority.

(C)   Regardless of whether Old Jersey treats minor marriages as void or voidable, Alice and Billy were living together when each had attained legal age, so their marriage is valid and must be formally dissolved.

(D)   Assuming that minor marriages in Old Jersey are merely voidable rather than void, the parties living together after each has attained majority ratifies the marriage and Alice must seek a formal dissolution of the union.

Samuel Smith, aged 19, wishes to marry his second cousin, Teresa Thomas, aged 12, and secures Teresa's parents' permission to do so. He marries her and they have a child together, Wanda. He is charged with sexual assault and pleads his marriage as a defense.

3.   What result?

(A)   Had Teresa and Samuel not married, he would have been subject to prosecution. However, because he married Teresa with her parents' consent, he is immune from prosecution.

(B)   Absent evidence of coercion or duress, there will be no basis for a conviction. The sexual relations between Samuel and Teresa, a married couple, will be presumed to be consensual.

(C)   Because Samuel's imprisonment would harm both Teresa and Wanda, Samuel is immune from prosecution. However, had Teresa and Samuel not had a child together, Samuel would have been subject to prosecution, notwithstanding the marriage with parental consent.

(D)   States permitting minors to marry with parental consent tend not to allow such a young minor to marry with that consent, and most states would not recognize the marriage as a defense to rape in this case.

Edward Ellington, age 17, and Frieda Frederickson, also age 17, are prohibited from marrying in their domicile, Minihio, unless their parents consent to the union. One day, Edward and Frieda travel to the neighboring state of Tenntucky, lie about their age to a Justice of the Peace, and marry. They return home and tell their respective parents what they have done. As anticipated, Frieda's parents are furious and forbid her from seeing Edward. On his 18th birthday, Edward is given a very valuable family heirloom by his grandmother. He goes out drinking with some friends to celebrate and, on the way home, is in a fatal car accident. Edward's father consults with an attorney to see if he can have the marriage annulled before Frieda reaches her 18th birthday, because he fears that otherwise Frieda will inherit the heirloom under the laws of intestacy, since Edward had never made a will.

4.   What should the attorney tell Edward's father?

(A)   Because Edward and Frieda had not ratified the marriage by living together after both had attained majority, the marriage never became valid and Frieda is not entitled to inherit.

(B)   If Minihio treats minor marriages as voidable and Minihio intestacy law gives priority to spouses, then the marriage will be treated as valid and Frieda will be entitled to inherit at the very least a substantial share of the heirloom. Once one of the spouses to a voidable marriage has died, the marriage's validity can no longer be challenged.

(C)   The marriage will not be recognized by Minihio. Frieda's parents had not approved of the marriage before and cannot now complain if the state refuses to recognize its validity.

(D) The marriage will be recognized because Edward's father failed to challenge it before Edward had reached age 18. At this time, only Frieda's parents can challenge the validity of the marriage.

Gregory and Harriet are juniors in high school. Neither will be eighteen until another year has passed. They want to marry but their domicile, Orego, preclude minors from marrying without parental permission, and both Gregory and Harriet's parents oppose the union. Gregory and Harriet go to the neighboring state, Washorado, and marry in accord with local law. They come back to Orego, deciding to wait for the most propitious time to tell their parents.

A week after they return, Gregory meets Ida, who has just moved to Orego from Washorado. For Gregory, it is love at first sight, and he no longer wants anything to do with Harriet. Gregory and Ida date for a month, while he and Harriet have nothing to do with each other. Two years later, Harriet is asked by Joseph to marry him. Harriet consults an attorney to find out if she is free to marry.

5. What should the attorney say?

ANSWER:

John Johnson, age 19, and Karen Kingston, age 17, have been dating for several years. Karen is pregnant, and she and John wish to marry. However, Karen has heard that the state in which she lives, South Califano, does not permit minors to marry, and she consults an attorney to find out whether there is some way that she and John can marry before their child is born.

6. What should the attorney say?

ANSWER:

Mary Martin married Ned Newton, whom she later discovered was a violent, abusive man. Before long, she left him. Recently, she has been dating Oliver Owens. She and Oliver never discussed her previous relationships and she does not know how to broach the subject now that Oliver has asked her to marry him. Especially because she is quite confident that Ned must be dead by now, she agrees to marry Oliver, notwithstanding her knowing that she never formally ended her relationship with Ned. She and Oliver live happily together for several years as husband and wife when Oliver dies suddenly.

Within days of his death, Oliver's estranged brother, Peter, shows up with documentary proof that Ned Newton had not died until a year after Oliver and Mary had celebrated their marriage. Peter claims that Mary's marriage to Oliver was bigamous and thus void, making Peter the sole surviving heir of Oliver. May seeks advice from an attorney.

7.   What should the attorney say?

    (A)   Because Mary knew that she had never formally divorced Ned, she knew or should have known that there was a good chance that she would be contracting a bigamous marriage when marrying Oliver. She has dirty hands and cannot complain when her marriage is treated as bigamous.

    (B)   Because Mary believed in good faith that Ned was dead and that there was no bar to her marrying Oliver, her marriage to him was at worst voidable and cannot now be challenged.

    (C)   Whether or not Mary had the good faith belief that Ned was dead and thus that she was free to marry Oliver, her marriage was bigamous and thus void ab initio. Separate questions involve whether her belief that she was free to marry was in good faith or whether state law affords protections to someone who had a good faith belief in the validity of her marriage.

    (D)   Because Mary was free to marry Oliver once Ned had died and the impediment had been removed, Mary's marriage to Oliver will be viewed as valid.

Roberta Robinson and Sid Smith marry. For the first few years, all goes well. Then, they start to have some horrible fights. In one of their daily arguments, Roberta says that she will seek a divorce unless Sid agrees to go to marriage counseling. Sid responds that there is no need for counseling, because they do not have a valid marriage anyway. He explains that he had never gotten a formal divorce from his first wife, who had left him when they had started to argue frequently. Roberta is shocked and consults an attorney the very next way to find out whether she has a valid marriage and, if not, how she can protect her interests.

8.   The attorney should say:

    (A)   Even if Sid had a wife living when he and Roberta had married, Roberta had had no reason to know this. Her marriage will be treated as valid.

(B)   If Roberta wishes to be married to Sid, he must divorce his first wife and Roberta and Sid can then celebrate their nuptials. If she does not wish to be married to him, then she does not need to do anything, because their marriage was void from the beginning. However, she has no hope for any support or property settlement, because there was never a valid marriage.

(C)   If Roberta wishes to end her relationship with Sid, she should seek a divorce. Depending upon the state, she may well be able to get support or a property division, the invalidity of their marriage notwithstanding.

(D)   There is nothing that Roberta can do. She should just start over.

Wally and Terry Wainwright have been married for several years. Wally has a fatal accident at work and Terry seeks Workmen Compensation benefits. However, the Bureau denied her claim, because there is proof that at the time that Wally and Terry married, Wally was legally married to someone else, who has since died. Terry consults an attorney to explore her options.

9.   What should the attorney tell her?

ANSWER:

Larry lives in the state of Kanaska next to his eldest brother, Richard, whose daughter, Martha, is Larry's age. While Larry and Martha have always been best friends, they realize during a vacation in Connachusetts that they have romantic rather than platonic feelings for each other. Being of age, they go to a local Justice of the Peace in Connachusetts and marry in accord with local law. When they get home, they do not tell everyone what they have done, wanting instead to consult an attorney before making any announcements. Larry calls Alice Attorney for advice.

10.   What should Alice tell them about the validity of their marriage?

   (A)   Because Connachusetts treats uncle-niece marriages as valid, Kanaska will also recognize the marriage.

   (B)   If a marriage cannot legally be celebrated within a state, then it will not be recognized by that state merely because it was validly celebrated elsewhere. If Larry and Karen cannot legally marry within Kanaska, then Kanaska will not recognize the marriage even if validly celebrated elsewhere.

   (C)   Some marriages that cannot be celebrated within the domicile will nonetheless be recognized if validly celebrated elsewhere. As to whether an uncle-niece marriage validly celebrated elsewhere by Kanaska domiciliaries will be recognized in Kanaska, is a matter that is left up to Kanaska.

   (D)   Because Larry and Martha validly celebrated their marriage in Connachusetts, the marriage will only be valid if Connachusetts intended the marriage to have extraterritorial effect.

Assume the same facts as described in question 10, except this time Larry and Martha are first cousins rather than uncle and niece.

11.   Will their marriage be treated as valid?

   (A)   Because Connachusetts recognizes the marriage, Kanaska will recognize it as well.

   (B)   Assuming that Kanaska treats first-cousin marriages, like uncle-niece marriages, as void because incestuous, then Kanaska will not recognize the marriage, just as it would not have recognized an uncle-niece marriage.

   (C)   If first-cousin marriages are expressly prohibited by statute in Kanaska, then Kanaska will not recognize the marriage even if validly celebrated in Connachusetts.

   (D)   Even if Kanaska treats first-cousin marriages and uncle-niece marriages as void, the state might nonetheless recognize a first-cousin marriage validly celebrated elsewhere.

Zeke and Yolanda are living together without benefit of marriage with Zeke's son, Wayne. Upon reaching his twenty-second birthday, Wayne moves out of the house. Yolanda realizes that she has romantic feelings for Wayne. She calls him and finds out that he feels the same way. She leaves Zeke. Months later, she consults an attorney to find out whether her marriage to Wayne would be considered valid.

12.   What should the attorney say?

ANSWER:

Alvin and Beverly are engaged to marry. One day, while riding horseback, Alvin is thrown, resulting in his being paralyzed from the neck down. Alvin and Beverly marry despite the accident. After a few years, Beverly files for a divorce. In his counterclaim, Alvin sought an annulment, arguing that the union was never consummated, and thus that Beverly was not entitled to a property division and support.

13. What result?

    (A) Because Alvin and Beverly never had sexual relations, the marriage was never consummated and will be annulled.

    (B) Even if nonconsummation is a ground for annulment as a general matter, it may well not be in this case, because it was known before the marriage that some kinds of sexual relations would be impossible.

    (C) While nonconsummation is a basis for annulment, a suit seeking an annulment on this basis will not be granted if the marriage can be ended in another way, e.g., by granting a divorce based on incompatibility.

    (D) Because Alvin is seeking the annulment based on nonconsummation, the claim will be rejected. However, Beverly would have been granted an annulment on this basis.

Carol and David Donaldson have been trying to have a child for several years. They have been tested and find out that David cannot father a child. David wishes to adopt, but Carol does not. Eventually, after arguing about this constantly, they decide to end their marriage. David files for divorce based on incompatibility and Carol in her counterclaim seeks to annul the marriage based on David's impotence.

14. Who, if anyone will succeed?

    (A) Carol will succeed because David has been independently verified to be impotent.

    (B) David will succeed because Carol is being unreasonable in refusing to consider adoption a viable alternative.

    (C) David is more likely to succeed because many states interpret their impotency ground for annulment as requiring nonconsummation rather than infertility.

    (D) Carol will succeed as long as she can establish both his infertility and her fertility. If she is also unable to have a child, then she will not be able to get an annulment.

Fred and Georgina Hendricks had rather dissatisfying sexual relations on their wedding night and have never tried again, his frequent requests notwithstanding. Five years later, Fred seeks an annulment, claiming nonconsummation.

15.   Will Fred be successful? Why or why not?

ANSWER:

Nancy and Oscar are married in the state of Marryton by a Justice of the Peace after having had a whirlwind romance. One week later, Nancy falls into a deep depression and voluntarily commits herself for 72 hours for observation in a private sanitarium. Tragically, due to the gross negligence of sanitarium personnel, a violent inmate escapes from a secure ward and kills Nancy. Oscar sues the sanitarium for wrongful death and, in defense, the sanitarium contends that Oscar is not Nancy's widower because she was not competent to consent to the marriage at the time of the ceremony due to her mental illness.

16.   What result?

    (A)   Some states treat marriages involving someone incompetent because of mental illness as void, whereas others states treat such marriages as voidable. Regardless of the position taken by the state of Marryton, the hospital will not be permitted to challenge the marriage because it was not a party to it.

    (B)   If Marryton treats marriages involving someone who was arguably incompetent due to mental illness as merely voidable, then the hospital will likely not be permitted to challenge the marriage, because one of the parties to it has died. However, if such marriages are treated as void by Marryton, then even a third party can challenge the marriage, even after one of the parties to the marriage has died.

    (C)   Because Nancy and Oscar were married by a Justice of the Peace, their marriage is presumed to be valid and, at this point, is not subject to challenge by anyone.

    (D)   Because a person who is not competent as a result of mental illness simply cannot consent to marry, no state treats such a marriage as valid, even if the person who later becomes competent does not disapprove of the match. Instead, such a person, while competent, would be free to contract a marriage and thereby enter into a relationship that the state will recognize.

Yves and Zelda are finally celebrating their marriage after years of waiting. Yves is so excited that he cannot sleep the night before the wedding and, perhaps unwisely, has a few shots of whiskey before the ceremony to calm his nerves. He becomes quite inebriated, because he had had so little sleep the previous night. The ceremony proceeds as planned, although Yves needs some help walking down the aisle. Regrettably, the marriage is not a happy one and Yves seeks to have it annulled after six months, claiming that he was not competent to contract it.

17.   Will Yves be able to have the marriage annulled?

    (A)   Yes, because Yves was noticeably drunk when saying "I do" and thus was not competent to marry.

(B) No, as long as Yves was sober enough to understand what he was doing when consenting to marry Zelda. Further, even if he was not competent during the ceremony, he later ratified the marriage when, while sober, he continued to live with his wife, Zelda.

(C) Yes, because Yves' sleeplessness the previous night explains why a few shots of whiskey might have made him so drunk that he would not have understood what he was doing.

(D) No. If Yves was able to walk done the aisle, even with help, he was obviously competent to marry.

Assume the same facts in Question 17 except that witnesses testify that Yves was so drunk that he did not seem to understand where he was or what he was doing.

18.   What result?

(A) Because marriage is so important both for society and for the individuals themselves, Yves having said the correct words at the right time suffices to make the marriage valid.

(B) Because marriage is so important both for society and for the individuals themselves, the marriage must be considered void when one of the parties does not understand what he is doing when contracting the marriage.

(C) Because Yves was not competent at the time of the ceremony due to his extreme drunkenness, his consent was of no effect and thus the marriage is void.

(D) Even if Yves did not understand where he was or what he was doing while at the ceremony, that will likely be viewed by the state as making the marriage voidable rather than void. Yves having lived with Zelda for six months after the wedding will likely be construed as a ratification of the marriage.

Alice and Ben live in Nevarado. They have been dating for awhile and have discussed marriage, but neither believes that their marrying would be a good idea. One day, after consuming several pitchers of margaritas, they decide to give marriage a shot. They awaken a Justice of the Peace, who officiates at the ceremony with his wife as witness. Regrettably, their reservations about marrying were justified. Despite their best efforts, it was clear after a few months of living together that they could not remain married. Because the only no-fault provision in Nevarado requires that they live separate and apart for a year before they can get a divorce on that ground, Ben seeks to have the marriage annulled.

19.   What result?

ANSWER:

Oscar and Ophelia Orrington are married, although they have not lived together for several years. Oscar has been living with Penelope Prynne for the past two years, whom Oscar has promised to marry as soon as he divorces his wife. Penelope no longer believes that Oscar will get a divorce, so she threatens to leave him unless he promises to continue to support her in the style to which she has become accustomed, even if they should later decide to end their relationship. Oscar signs the agreement. Three years later, Oscar and Ophelia reconcile, and Oscar moves back into the Orrington home. Penelope seeks to enforce her agreement with Oscar for support.

20. Will Penelope be successful?

   (A) Penelope will not be successful because the agreement was not signed voluntarily — Oscar signed it under duress because Penelope threatened to leave him unless he signed the agreement.

   (B) Penelope will be successful, assuming that the agreement is not construed as void because based upon meretricious considerations.

   (C) Penelope is unlikely to be successful. While Oscar's signing it will be viewed as voluntary, this agreement is likely to be viewed as unenforceable as a violation of public policy, even though cohabitation agreements may be enforceable if not based on meretricious considerations and not based on fraud or duress.

   (D) Penelope will not be successful. This agreement, like all cohabitation agreements, will be held unenforceable as a violation of public policy, because such agreements tend to undermine marriage.

Sarah Samuels and Ted Thomas are thinking about getting married, but they are of different religions and Ted will only marry Sarah if she signs an agreement specifying that their children will be raised in his religion. Sarah signs the agreement in large part because she does not anticipate having any children. Sarah and Thomas wed. They have twins and all goes well until it is time to start educating the children about religion. Sarah and Thomas start to fight constantly about this and eventually divorce with Sarah being awarded custody of the children. Thomas seeks to enforce the prenuptial agreement to prevent Sarah from teaching the children religious views with which he disagrees.

21. Will Thomas's attempt to enforce the prenuptial agreement be successful?

   (A) Thomas will not be successful in his attempt to enforce the prenuptial agreement because as a general matter prenuptial agreements are unenforceable as a violation of public policy.

   (B) Thomas will be successful, because the agreement was made voluntarily and because Sarah knew that Thomas would only marry her (and have children with her) if he knew that they would be raised in his faith.

(C) Thomas is very unlikely to be successful. While prenuptial agreements as a general matter do not violate public policy as long as they are voluntary and do not involve fraud, duress, misrepresentation or overreaching, many courts will not enforce a stipulation that children receive a particular kind of religious training.

(D) Thomas will be successful because Sarah was willing to have the children raised in Thomas's religion when the agreement was made and she will not be allowed to change her mind now when he has detrimentally relied on her willingness to have the children receive that training.

Gregory George and Hilary Hendrickson were working out the details of their prenuptial agreement. Each had a previous marriage end with a very nasty custody fight, and each wished to avoid a bitter custody fight if at all possible. They each agreed that should they divorce, Gregory would have custody of any male children and Hilary would have custody of any female children. Two children were born of the marriage, Ida and John. Regrettably, when Ida was 10 and John was 8, Gregory filed for divorce, seeking custody of John following the prenuptial agreement or, in the alternative, custody of both children. Hilary sought custody of both children, arguing that the prenuptial agreement was unenforceable because it violated public policy.

22. Who will be awarded custody of Ida and John?

(A) Pursuant to the agreement, Gregory will likely be awarded custody of John and Hilary will be awarded custody of Ida. The agreement was voluntary and there was no coercion or duress involved.

(B) Hilary will likely be awarded custody of both children. Because Gregory only wants custody of both children if the prenuptial agreement will not be enforced, he obviously does not really want custody of Ida. Because a parent who does not want custody of a child should not be awarded custody of that child and because it would not be in the best interests of the children to be separated, Hilary should be awarded custody of both children.

(C) Gregory will likely be awarded custody of both children. Gregory clearly wants custody of both children but wants to honor the agreement that he made, whereas Hilary is refusing to honor an agreement that she freely made. Individuals should not be allowed to profit by refusing to honor their agreements, so Hilary should not be awarded custody of either child.

(D) This provision of the prenuptial agreement is unenforceable if contrary to the interests of the children. Custody of each child should be determined in light of which parent would best promote the interests of that child, where one of the factors to be considered is that it might well be in the interest of the children not to be separated.

Carole and David Donaldson are having marital difficulties. Carole wants to divorce but David wants to remain married to Carole. Carole says that she will give the marriage another try, but only if David agrees to give her a valuable piece of property in case their attempted reconciliation is unsuccessful. David agrees. Carole and David stay together for another six months, but ultimately decide to divorce. David contests the validity of the postnuptial agreement, contending that such agreements violate public policy as a general matter or, in the alternative, that this agreement should be struck because made under duress.

23. What result?

(A) The postnuptial agreement will be declared void and unenforceable, because such agreements promote divorce.

(B) The postnuptial agreement will be upheld. They are not against public policy as a general matter. Here, the agreement was made voluntarily without duress and Carole's giving the marriage another try should be viewed as consideration for the agreement.

(C) The postnuptial agreement should be struck down in this case because it was made under duress. David was simply trying to save his marriage and he should not in effect be punished for having done so in the only way that he could.

(D) The postnuptial agreement will be upheld. As long as the parties understood the terms of the agreement, it will be enforceable.

Assume the same facts in Question 23. However, in this example, Carole filed for divorce as soon as David signed the post-nuptial agreement, admitting that she had known all along that she would be filing for divorce but just wanted to get a more advantageous property division.

24. What result?

(A) The postnuptial agreement will be upheld. The agreement was clear, voluntary, and not unconscionable.

(B) The postnuptial agreement is unenforceable, because it allows Carole to receive property to which she otherwise would not have been entitled.

(C) The postnuptial agreement is enforceable. David signed the agreement, understanding that there were no guarantees that the marriage would survive. Basically, he tried to increase the likelihood that the marriage would survive and that effort ultimately failed.

(D) The postnuptial agreement is unenforceable because it was not made in good faith, although it likely would have been enforceable had Carole made a genuine effort to give the marriage another chance.

Ellen and Frank's wedding is to begin the following day. Shortly before the rehearsal dinner, Ellen asks Frank whether he has signed the prenuptial agreement yet. Frank says that his attorney has said that it is fair, but Frank wants to look it over one more time. The following day, twenty minutes before the ceremony, Ellen goes up to Frank with the prenuptial agreement in hand. She says that she will not go through with the wedding unless he signs it. Frank is shocked but cannot imagine telling all of the guests that they must come back another time for the wedding. He signs the agreement. Ellen and Frank remain married for several years. However, when Ellen files for divorce, Frank seeks to have the prenuptial agreement declared void because he signed it under duress.

25. Will Frank be able to have the agreement declared void and of no legal effect?

(A) Yes, because it was signed under duress. By insisting shortly before the ceremony that it be signed, she in effect forced him to sign it.

(B) No, unless there is another ground upon which to invalidate it, e.g., that Ellen had hidden some of her assets.

(C)   Yes, because Frank obviously thought something was wrong with the agreement, notwithstanding his attorney having approved it. Because Frank would not have signed it but for Ellen's having insisted, it is unfair to have it enforced against him.

(D)   No. As long as he signed it and had had it long enough that he was able to have his attorney check it, he cannot now complain if he does not like the agreement that he made.

Henrietta and Joseph, both very successful attorneys, sign a prenuptial agreement that assures that neither will have to support the other should the marriage end in divorce. There is no duress or coercion involved and each has a good understanding of the other's assets. They marry. Regrettably about six years into the marriage, Joseph is diagnosed with cancer. He undergoes aggressive treatment, which forces him to stop practicing law. Around this time, Henrietta files for divorce. Joseph seeks spousal support and Henrietta seeks to enforce the prenuptial agreement.

26.   Is the prenuptial agreement enforceable?

(A)   Yes, because Joseph signed it voluntarily, with a full and accurate understanding of Henrietta's finances.

(B)   No, because Joseph did not know that he would be diagnosed with cancer, and thus it was signed without full information.

(C)   Yes, because there was no fraud, duress, mistake, misrepresentation, or nondisclosure of material fact. Further, it was fair when signed, and everyone understands that unfortunate circumstances may arise in the future.

(D)   While this would depend on the state, such an agreement would not be enforceable in many states because it would be unconscionable at the time of enforcement, even if reasonable at the time it was signed.

Nancy and Peter are living together. Peter wants to get married if only because it would mean so much to his parents. Nancy does not want to marry because she believes marriage is an outdated institution. They reach a compromise. Nancy will go through a ceremony to please Peter's parents but Peter will sign a document stating that the marriage is only for show and should not be understood to have any legal effect. Four years later, Nancy and Peter decide to divorce. Peter seeks support and a division of marital property and Nancy produces the writing to show that property should not be divided and that she should not be required to pay spousal support.

27.   Is their agreement to treat the marriage as a nullity enforceable?

(A)   The agreement between Nancy and Peter will be enforced. They entered the agreement voluntarily and it was done for the benefit of Peter.

(B)   The agreement will not be enforced. Individuals cannot by private agreement modify the law of the state that would otherwise govern the distribution of assets upon divorce.

(C)   The agreement will be enforced. Individuals can order their relations in any way that they see fit as long as the agreement is informed, voluntary, and backed by consideration.

(D)   The agreement will not be enforced. To go through the formalities of contracting a marriage but allegedly make it invalid by private agreement would be to nullify existing law by private contract.

Randi and Steven each have children from previous marriages. They sign a prenuptial agreement specifying that in the event of divorce neither will be required to pay either spousal or child support. After several years, they divorce. Randi, who is awarded custody of the one child born of the marriage, seeks spousal and child support.

28.   What kind of support, if any, will Randi be awarded?

(A)   While many states permit spousal support to be waived in a prenuptial agreement assuming no fraud, coercion, duress, misrepresentation, or unconscionability, they do not permit child support to be waived, so that provision at the very least will be struck down.

(B)   Most states would treat both waivers of support as unenforceable because a violation of public policy.

(C)   Assuming no fraud, duress, coercion, misrepresentation, or unconscionability, the agreement to waive spousal and child support will be enforceable.

(D)   Agreements to waive child support are enforceable as long as they can plausibly be construed to have been in the child's best interests, e.g., by guaranteeing that the parent who will promote the child's best interests will in fact be awarded custody or, perhaps, by assuring that the child will be able to stay in the home in which he or she had been raised.

Paul Peterson and Rachel Roberts have each gone though bitter divorces. They accept the possibility that their upcoming marriage might also end in divorce and wish to reduce the likelihood that their union might end bitterly. In their prenuptial agreement, they specify that:

(1)   Rachel will have custody of any children born of the marriage.

(2)   The religious training of any children born of the marriage will be determined by the parties jointly, and

(3)   Neither party will pay spousal support.

After spending several years together and producing two children, Paul and Rachel end their marriage. The enforceability of the prenuptial agreement is at issue.

29.   Which conditions of the agreement, if any, are enforceable?

ANSWER:

Abigail Adams and Bertrand Bottomsley sign a cohabitation agreement whereby Abigail promises to provide reasonable support to Bertrand for ten years should their relationship end, while Bertrand promises to provide all of the care and comfort that a paramour should. They stay together for several years but eventually part ways. While Bertrand and Abigail can agree about what kind of support would be reasonable in the circumstances, they disagree about whether the agreement is enforceable.

30.   Will Abigail be required to support Bertrand?

(A) Because their agreement is like an agreement to provide spousal support for a fixed term and because there does not seem to be any difficulty in determining what would constitute reasonable support in this case, the agreement is enforceable.

(B) The agreement is unenforceable for lack of consideration. Abigail would be providing money to Bertrand but Bertrand would not be providing anything to Abigail.

(C) The agreement is enforceable, assuming that it was made voluntarily, did not involve duress or coercion, there was no misrepresentation, and it was not unconscionable at the time it was signed or when it was to be enforced.

(D) The agreement may well be held unenforceable because based on meretricious considerations if the paramour services are construed as essentially sexual in nature.

In anticipation of their moving in together Robin Roberts and Kim Kennedy have entered into an agreement to combine their efforts and earnings and share equally in property accumulated during their relationship. Robin's consulting business will be conducted mostly from the home where Robin in addition will have primary child-raising duties with respect to Paul, a child born of Kim's previous relationship. Robin and Kim maintain their relationship for several years but then end it. Robin seeks a share of the property accumulated during the relationship but Kim argues that distributing property produced during a non-marital relationship would violate public policy.

31. Will Robin be awarded a share of the property?

ANSWER:

Colleen Collins has discovered that her husband Carl has committed adultery. Rather than seek a divorce, Colleen says that she will remain married to Carl if he signs a postnuptial agreement specifying that she will receive certain property that he owns separately if he is found by a court to have committed adultery after the agreement was made. A few years later, Carl and Beverly divorce because of Carl's post-agreement infidelity. Beverly seeks to enforce the postnuptial agreement and Carl argues that the adultery exception is unenforceable.

32. What result?

(A) Carl is likely to prevail. Because the agreement only specifies what will happen if he commits adultery but says nothing about her committing adultery, it violates public policy and cannot be enforced.

(B) The agreement will likely be held enforceable, assuming that there is no other ground upon which to invalidate the agreement.

(C) The agreement will be held unenforceable because it lacked consideration.

(D) The agreement will be enforceable because it specified that she would receive property if he committed adultery. However, no state would have enforced the agreement if, instead, it had specified that the adulterer would lose any support to which he or she would otherwise have been entitled.

Heidi and Henry are dating. Heidi mentions that her wealthy grandmother is very ill and that Heidi is greatly saddened by her grandmother's imminent demise, expectation of significant inheritance notwithstanding. On a different occasion, Heidi talks about her very sick uncle, who had always treated Heidi as if she were his only daughter. Henry, who had always wanted to marry someone wealthy, proposes. Heidi accepts. Not long after they marry, Henry discovers that Heidi has only poor relations and that her financial prospects are even less rosy than his. Henry seeks to have the marriage annulled. Heidi contests the annulment.

33.   What result?

    (A)   The annulment will not be granted. Because Heidi never stated that she had wealth and only implied that she might inherit money someday in the future, her statements were not sufficiently clear and unambiguous as to be the basis of an annulment action.

    (B)   The annulment will be granted as along as Henry can establish that he married her because he thought that she would inherit a lot of money.

    (C)   The annulment will not be granted because this is not the kind of fraudulent claim that most states would permit to be the basis of an annulment action.

    (D)   The annulment will be granted if Henry can establish that Heidi made the fraudulent claim precisely because she knew that he would thereby be induced to propose to her.

Joseph Jones and Karen King are members of Campus Pure, a national organization that promotes chastity until marriage for college students. They find that they have a lot in common and start dating. After several months, Karen proposes marriage and Joseph accepts. Several months into their marriage, Karen discovers that Joseph was not a virgin when they had married. Karen seeks to have the marriage annulled on the basis of fraud.

34.   Will Karen be able to have the marriage annulled on the basis of Joseph's unchasity?

    (A)   The marriage will likely be annulled. Joseph knew that chastity before marriage was important to Karen by virtue of her having joined Campus Pure. By having joined Campus Pure as well, Joseph communicated to Karen that he, too, was chaste and believed in its importance before marriage.

    (B)   The marriage will likely not be annulled on this basis. Joseph did not expressly mislead Karen; she merely assumed that he, too, was chaste.

    (C)   The marriage will likely be annulled. Not only has Joseph failed to reveal his having engaged in sexual relations when he knew that this was important to Karen, but by hiding something so significant at the start of the marriage, he has destroyed the possibility of trust, which is an essential element of any successful marriage.

(D)   The marriage will likely not be annulled. His lack of chastity, without more, will likely not be held an essential of marriage.

Ned and Mary Martin have been married for several years but have never had children. Mary is beginning to worry that they will never have children unless they act quickly but Ned says that he does not want to have children now and, further, would not mind if they never had children. Mary is astonished because she had always assumed that Ned wanted to have children as much as she did. Mary seeks an annulment, claiming that Ned deceived her into believing that he, too, wanted children.

35.   What result?

(A)   The annulment will not be granted. Because there are many happily married couples without children, not wanting to have children obviously does not go to the essence of marriage.

(B)   The annulment will be granted. Traditionally, the willingness to have children goes to the essence of marriage and Ned's having failed to manifest his wanting not to have children constitutes fraud.

(C)   The annulment will not be granted. Because it is not even clear that Mary and Ned can have children and because Mary has never before complained that the marriage is unbearable notwithstanding having been married to Ned for several years, Mary cannot now claim that the fraud somehow goes to the essence of her marriage.

(D)   The unwillingness to have children will likely be viewed as going to the essence of marriage. However, for Mary to be successful in her attempt to have the marriage annulled, she must show that Ned has wanted not to have children since before their marriage began rather than has only recently adopted that view.

John meets Joanna, who is the embodiment of his prayers. She is everything he ever wanted in a wife and he proposes to her within six weeks of their meeting. They live happily together for several years when she dies unexpectedly in an industrial accident at work. Within a few weeks, Ken Kensington presents proof to John that Ken and Joanna had been married and had never divorced.

36.   As the innocent, defrauded spouse in a bigamous marriage, does John have any recourse? Explain.

ANSWER:

Bob and Carol are in love. Bob tells Carol that he very much wants to have children and does not believe in using contraception. Carol says she agrees with him wholeheartedly. However, after they marry, Carol refuses to have marital relations with Bob unless they use contraception. Carol says that she would love to adopt a child. However, Bob does not want to adopt and instead seeks to have the marriage annulled.

37.   What result?

ANSWER:

Pam Price and Quentin Quick marry and honeymoon as part of a wonderful vacation package on Fantasy Island. They then return to live in their domicile, Oklanagon, which recognizes common law marriage. One day, Pam reads an expose in the paper that the person who had pronounced them husband and wife had not been qualified to do so and thus that their marriage is not recognized by the state. Pam and Quentin decide that they better participate in another ceremony. However, they must delay getting married again because Pam requires surgery immediately. Fortunately, the surgery is successful, but the insurance company refuses to pay because it claims that Pam is not Quentin's lawful spouse and thus is not covered under the policy.

38. Will she be able to establish that she is Quentin's wife and thus covered under the policy?

    (A) No, because they never went through a marriage ceremony with a qualified person officiating.

    (B) Yes, because Pam and Quentin entered into the marriage in good faith.

    (C) No, because they were on notice that they were not legally married and did not rectify matters before the surgery was performed.

    (D) Yes, she may well be able to establish that they have a common law marriage, assuming that they lived together, there was no bar to their marrying, they treated each other as husband and wife, and they had the reputation in the community of being husband and wife.

Alice is married to Alvin, whom she detests. One day, she summons up her courage and moves to Washego, which recognizes common law marriages, to live with her sister, Betty. Alice meets Carl, with whom she falls in love. They start to live together, treating each other as husband and wife and holding themselves out to the community as husband and wife. They have been together for several years when Alice is informed that Alvin has died and that she is entitled to $1000 as his widow. With that money, she buys Carl a ring, giving it to him and telling him that they now really are husband and wife. The next day, Carl gets a ring for Alice and gives it to her, echoing the sentiments that she had expressed when giving him the ring. Three months later, Carl dies in a car crash. Alice seeks her intestate share as his widow, but Carl's son, David, claims to be Carl's sole surviving legal heir.

39. Will Alice be recognized as Carl's widow and thus be entitled to a share of Carl's estate?

    (A) No. Alice was legally precluded from being Carl's wife when they began living together, because she was still legally married to Alvin.

    (B) Yes, because for a long time Alice and Carl had considered themselves to be husband and wife and had been known in the community as husband and wife.

    (C) No, because Alice and Carl failed to go through a ceremonial marriage once Alvin had died and Alice was free to marry.

(D) Yes, because the impediment to their marrying had been removed when Alvin had died and because they had recognized the new circumstances when exchanging rings after his death.

Greg Gregorian and Hannah Havorford live together. They treat each other as husband and wife and are known in the community as husband and wife. However, they have never had a ceremonial marriage. South Florina does not recognize common law marriage but does recognize common law marriages if validly celebrated elsewhere. Greg and Hannah frequently vacation in West Tenntucky, which does recognize common law marriage, but they have never been domiciled anywhere other than in South Florina. Greg must establish that he is married to Hannah in order to be covered under her insurance policy.

40.   Will Greg be able to establish that he is married to Hannah?

(A) Assuming that there is no bar to their marrying, the marriage will be recognized. They meet all of the requirements of common law marriage, and even if South Florina does not recognize such marriages, other states do.

(B) The marriage is unlikely to be recognized. Greg and Hannah could have celebrated a ceremonial marriage but did not, their knowing that the state does not recognize common law marriage notwithstanding.

(C) That depends upon whether they met West Tenntucky's common law marriage requirements and whether West Tenntucky would recognize the marriage even though Greg and Hannah had not been domiciled in the state but, instead, had only visited there. If West Tenntucky would recognize the common law marriage and South Florina recognizes common law marriages validly celebrated elsewhere even by those domiciled in South Florina at the time the marriage is contracted, then Greg is likely to be able to establish that he is married to Hannah.

(D) The marriage cannot be recognized, because they were never domiciled in a state recognizing common law marriage.

Tess Thompson and Walter Williams have lived together for a long time. They treat each other as husband and wife and are known in the community as husband and wife. Even though the state in which they live, New Caledonia, recognizes common law marriage, Tess wants to go through a ceremonial marriage with Walter. Walter's steadfast refusal to have a ceremonial marriage has been gnawing at Tess, and she ultimately decides to leave him. Several months later, Tess meets Fred Feigel, whom she marries in a beautiful wedding. They live happily together until Fred's untimely death a decade later. The validity of the marriage between Fred and Tess is challenged by Fred's brother, Zeke.

41.   What result?

(A) Because Tess and Walter never had their common law marriage recognized and because in any event a ceremonial marriage trumps a common law marriage, the marriage between Fred and Tess will be recognized.

(B) Assuming that Walter and Tess met the requirements for contracting a common law marriage in New Caledonia and that their marriage was never formally dissolved, the marriage between Fred and Tess will likely be viewed as void as long as Walter is still living.

(C) Because Tess obviously rejected her relationship with Walter and because Walter was unwilling to have their relationship formally recognized, the relationship between Walter and Tess will be considered invalid and the marriage between Tess and Fred will be recognized.

(D) The marriage between Fred and Tess would not be recognized if Walter were challenging it. However, Zeke, who was not a party to either of the relationships at issue here, will not be permitted to challenge the validity of the marriage between Fred and Tess.

Yolanda Yellowstone and Zachary Zoolander have been living together for years in Alalina, which recognizes common law marriage. They treat each other as husband and wife and are known in the community as husband and wife. Zachary seeks to assert the privilege not to testify against his wife, Yolanda. If Yolanda and Zachary have a common law marriage, he will not be forced to testify. However, to Zachary's surprise, it was revealed at trial that Yolanda's first husband, Theodore, had died only twelve months earlier and that Yolanda and Theodore had never formally dissolved their union.

42.   What result?

ANSWER:

Jim and Hank have entered into a civil union in New Vermshire in accordance with local law. After several years, Jim and Hank fall out of love. Jim disavows the relationship in front of all of their friends. Jim later meets Matthew, and enters into a civil union with him. Matthew is injured in an auto accident and Jim brings a loss of consortium claim against the careless driver. The careless driver challenges the validity of Jim's relationship with Matthew.

43.   What result?

    (A)   Because civil unions are merely a creature of state law permitting individuals to have their relationships afforded legal recognition, they have no implications for tort actions such as for loss of consortium.

    (B)   Jim ended his relationship by publicly disavowing it, so his relationship with Matthew will be recognized and the loss of consortium claim can proceed.

    (C)   Because Jim and Hank's civil union status was never formally ended, Jim's civil union with Matthew will likely be treated as void and Jim will not be able to pursue the loss of consortium claim by virtue of his civil union with Matthew.

    (D)   Jim formally ended his civil union with Hank by voluntarily and knowingly entering into a civil union with Matthew, which means that there will be no bar to the loss of consortium claim proceeding.

Joanne and Kimberly have entered into a civil union in New Vermshire. Joanne had received a wonderful employment opportunity in Connachusetts, and she and Kimberly are wondering whether their relationship will be recognized in the new state. She consults Alice Attorney to find out what effect their moving would have on their legal relationship?

44.   What should Alice say?

ANSWER:

Bernard and Bobbi Sue have been married for years in Louisabama. Bernard is very kind and considerate when he is sober, but is sometimes violent when he drinks. Bernard has tried both Alcoholics Anonymous and an anger-management program without success. Bernard has just lost his job and gone on a bender. When he gets home, he starts throwing furniture against the wall. Without saying a word, Bobbi Sue takes two suitcases that have already been packed and rushes to her car. Bobbi Sue goes to stay at her mother's home and refuses to go back to Bernard. Bobbi Sue sues Bernard for constructive desertion and Bernard countersues Bobbi Sue for desertion. Louisabama affords an advantage in property distribution to the innocent party in a fault-based divorce, so it is important to determine who is at fault here.

45.   What result?

   (A)   Because Bobbi left the home and Bernard is still living there, she will likely be found to have deserted him.

   (B)   Because Bobbi had already packed her bags, she was obviously planning to leave and thus cannot claim that Bernard somehow forced her to leave. Bobbie Sue will likely be found to have deserted Bernard.

   (C)   Because "constructive desertion" involves a refusal by one spouse to have marital relations with the other spouse without just cause, Bobbi Sue will be unsuccessful. However, Bernard will be successful because Bobbi Sue deserted the marital home with no intention of coming back.

   (D)   Bobbi Sue may well be successful because of Bernard's making it impossible for her to stay within the home without risking life and limb.

Ronni is sure that her husband, Samuel, is having an affair. Not only has he started to dress better and to bathe more frequently, but he has stopped insisting that they have marital relations every day. He denies that he is having an affair but she does not believe him. Ronni consults an attorney to find out what kind of proof she needs to establish that he is committing adultery.

46.   What should the attorney say?

   (A)   This is a matter of state law. However, because this is such a serious charge, many states require that the charging spouse witness the affair.

   (B)   This is a matter of state law. However, because this is such a serious charge, many states require that the offending spouse admit the affair.

   (C)   This is a matter of state law. However, because this is such a serious charge, many states require that the adulterous acts be both witnessed and corroborated by disinterested third parties.

(D)   This is a matter of state law. However, because this is such a serious charge, many states require at the very least that there be both opportunity and the disposition to commit the act.

Oscar and Ophelia are married but have found that they no longer love each other and simply no longer have anything in common. They both want a divorce. The state in which they live, Blissfulvania, requires couples to live separate and apart for fifteen months before they can get a no-fault divorce. Because Oscar and Opehlia do not have much money, they cannot afford to live in two different households. They divide up their apartment, including different times for use of the kitchen, so that they see each other as rarely as possible. Fifteen months later, Oscar files for divorce. Each will testify that the couple has not had marital relations for over two years.

47.   Will the dissolution of their marriage be granted?

(A)   The dissolution will likely be granted because they have not had marital relations for over fifteen months and because each has testified that they will never again have marital relations with each other.

(B)   The dissolution will likely not be granted. States that will grant a dissolution of a marriage based on the couple's having lived separate and apart require that they not live together and that they not have marital relations. While they have refrained from having sexual relations during the required period, they nonetheless have lived under the same roof and thus will not be found to have lived apart from each other.

(C)   The dissolution may well be granted. Some jurisdictions do not require that the individuals live in separate households as long as the individuals can establish that they are living their lives separately, even if they happen to live under the same roof.

(D)   The dissolution is unlikely to be granted. That they can live together for this long and cooperate with each other suggests that the relationship is salvageable and thus should not be dissolved by the state.

Herbert and Henrietta Henderson are married but have been living in different houses for the past two years in Divorca. They both feel that there is no substance to their relationship anymore, although they still enjoy having sexual relations with each other and do so frequently. Herbert files for a dissolution of their marriage based on their living separate and apart, reasoning that they can still sleep together whether or not they are married. Henrietta does not oppose the dissolution of the marriage, because in her view that marriage has been over for a longtime. Divorca follows the majority rule with respect to when a couple will have met the requirements for living separate and apart.

48.   What result?

(A)   Because they have living separately for the statutorily required period and no longer have a real marriage worthy of the name, it is likely that they will be able to have their marriage dissolved.

(B)   The dissolution will likely not be granted. Once they had marital relations once, they had to start the clock over again.

(C)   The dissolution will likely be granted. Because they are no longer sharing one roof, they will not have the reputation in the community of being a married couple so there is no reason to perpetuate the myth that they are married.

(D)   The dissolution will likely not be granted. Living separate and apart means that they are not continuing to have marital relations regularly, and their having continued to do so frequently will likely be interpreted to mean that their marriage might still be salvageable.

Robert and Roberta Robinson have fallen out of love and would like to divorce. Neither has committed a marital fault, and neither wishes to pretend to commit such a fault just to escape a currently loveless marriage. They have one child, Richard, and they agree that Roberta should have custody and Robert should have liberal visitation.

49.   Will they be able to dissolve their marriage?

(A)   While each state has its own form of no-fault, they should not assume that they can secure a no-fault divorce immediately. Some states require that a married couple live separate and apart for a period of time before their marriage can be ended.

(B)   A no-fault divorce is only open to couples who are entirely blameless. However, individuals do not simply fall out of love with their marital partners, so this option will not be open to them.

(C)   While no-fault divorce is certainly an option, both parties must understand that when a marriage is dissolved on that basis, there can be no award of spousal support.

(D)   No-fault divorce is not an option when a child has been born of the marriage.

Ellen and Edward Ellickson are legally separated. It is clear to both of them that they will never again live together as a married couple. Ellen has started to date Fred, and has sometimes stayed overnight in his apartment. Edward accuses Ellen of adultery. Ellen consults an attorney to find out whether her dating Fred could have any effect on her divorce.

50.   What should the attorney say?

(A)   Because Ellen and Edward are living separately anyway, her dating Fred can have no effect on her divorce from Edward.

(B)   Because Ellen and Edward are still married in the eyes of the law, her dating Fred must be treated as a factor contributing to the breakdown of the marriage.

(C)   Because she and Edward are going to divorce anyway, she should be pleased, because this may speed up when the divorce is actually granted.

(D)   Her dating Fred after the separation may affect spousal support or the distribution of marital assets depending upon whether fault is permitted to affect those and whether the marriage will be found by the court to have been irretrievably broken before the adultery occurred.

Alice and Bob Cartwell live in Minnegan. They are having marital difficulties and they decide that it would be best if Bob takes a job in nearby Pennigan in the town of Pennio. Minnegan law requires couples to live separate and apart for 18 months before they can file for divorce, whereas Pennigan law requires couples to live separate and apart for 12 months before they can file for divorce. Thirteen months after Bob moves to Pennigan, Alice files for divorce in Pennio on the no-fault ground of having lived separate and apart for more than twelve months. Bob contests the divorce, claiming that the divorce cannot be granted because Alice is a Minnegan domiciliary.

51.   Which of the statements below is correct?

   (A)   Alice cannot file for divorce in Pennigan, because she is not a Pennigan domiciliary.

   (B)   While Alice can file for divorce in Pennigan, she can only secure a divorce based on having lived separate and apart for eighteen months, which is the amount of time required in Minnegan, her domicile.

   (C)   Because there is personal jurisdiction over both parties, the divorce can be granted.

   (D)   Unless an applicable statute says otherwise, because at least one of the parties has met the residency requirement and at least of the parties is a domiciliary of the state, the divorce can be granted as long as the Pennigan statutory requirement for living separate and apart has been met.

Zelda and Yevgeny Wainwright, who live in Divorca, have been fighting constantly and both have serious reservations about continuing their marriage. They agree that Yevgeny should go live with his brother for a year in Peacefulvania, so that they can have some time apart to see if they want to remain together. Yevgeny does so, making sure that Zelda has all of the relevant contact information.

Twelve months later, Zelda publishes a notice in the local paper to give Yevgeny constructive notice of her seeking a divorce. She files for divorce, saying that she and Yevgeny have been living separate and apart for at least twelve months and that there is no hope of reconciliation. The divorce is granted, because the statutorily required period of separation has been met. Two months after the decree becomes final, Zelda is killed in an auto accident. Zelda's sister, Tess, claims to be Zelda's sole surviving relative, which is important because Zelda died intestate. Yevgeny, who returned to the state one week after the auto accident, claims to be Zelda's widower and seeks his share of her estate.

52.   What result?

   (A)   Yevgeny ceased to be Zelda's husband when the decree became final and will not receive anything.

   (B)   Because Yevgeny received constructive notice of the divorce and because the statutorily required period of living separate and apart had been met, Yevgeny has no basis for claiming that he was married to Zelda at the time of her death.

   (C)   Because the required period for living separate and apart in Peacefulvania is two years and because Zelda and Yevgeny had not been apart that long, the divorce is invalid and he was still her husband at the time of her death.

   (D)   Because Zelda knew where Yevgeny was living, her published notice in the local paper will not meet the notice requirement and the divorce will not be considered valid. Yevgeny may well be found to be Zelda's husband.

Georgina and Herbert Isaacs are living separate and apart from each other. Fifteen months have gone by and Herbert publishes in the local paper that he is filing for divorce, even though he has Georgina's address. He is granted the divorce. After the decree is final, he meets Ida, whom he eventually marries. Karen, Georgina's former best friend, runs into Herbert and asks about Georgina. Herbert replies that he and Georgina are no longer married and that last he had heard Georgina had gone to live with her sister in another part of the state. Karen calls Georgina's sister, saying that it is very important that Georgina come back to town.

Georgina comes back to town just in time to see Herbert on the evening news for having won one million dollars in the Instant Lottery. On the way back from the T.V. station, Herbert is robbed and killed. Herbert has left no will, and Georgina and Ida each claim to be entitled to the estate.

53. What result?

(A) Because Herbert only gave Georgina constructive notice of the divorce when he could have given her actual notice, the divorce will be declared invalid and she will be entitled to her share of the estate. Because Ida had married Herbert when he had not validly divorced Georgina, her marriage to Herbert will be treated as void and she must receive nothing.

(B) Because Georgina had constructive notice of the divorce, the requisite period of living separate and apart had been met, and Herbert and Ida had married in good faith, Georgina will not be entitled to anything because she is not his lawful widow.

(C) Because Georgina did not receive adequate notice, she will be viewed as Herbert's legal wife. However, as long as Ida had no reason to suspect that her marriage to Herbert was invalid, she may well be entitled to a share as a putative spouse.

(D) Because Georgina sat on her rights by remaining out of town, she will not now be entitled to challenge his marriage to Ida now.

Sarah and Thomas Vinson are married and have one child, Abigail. Sarah has felt extremely lonely for years and has recently met someone, David, whom she believes is her soulmate. So far, the relationship has been platonic but she wonders what she would stand to lose if she has a romantic relationship with David. She asks her attorney about the possible legal effects of her having a romantic relationship with David before she leaves Thomas.

54. What should the attorney say?

(A) Because Sarah is not getting anything out of her relationship with Thomas and is considering divorce anyway, her exploring a relationship with David can have no adverse legal effects.

(B) Her having an affair might affect her chances of getting custody, but it cannot have an effect on either spousal support or the distribution of marital asserts.

(C) While her having an affair will not affect custody because that is evaluated in light of what will best promote the interests of the child, it might affect spousal support or the distribution of marital assets.

(D) Her having an affair might affect the distribution of marital assets, the likelihood of her getting custody, whether she receives spousal support, or how much support she might receive.

Lynn, a male-to-female transsexual, has been dating John. Lynn and John are considering marriage and John helps pay for Lynn's sex reassignment surgery. Lynn and John marry in Marryvania. After several years, Lynn and John become estranged. Lynn files for divorce. In his response, John argues that they were never legally married in the first place, because Marryvania does not recognize same-sex marriage.

55.   Will Marryvania treat the marriage as void?

   (A)   Because John knew of Lynn's transsexual status and married her anyway, he was obviously not defrauded and the state will recognize the marriage.

   (B)   Because Marryvania does not recognize same-sex marriage, it cannot recognize Lynn and John's marriage.

   (C)   The state may recognize the marriage if it defines the sex of post-operative transsexuals in terms of their self-identified rather than their chromosomal sex.

   (D)   The court will hold the marriage void because transsexuals are not permitted to marry anyone.

Joanne T. and Kim G. wish to marry in Restrictafornia, which defines sex in terms of an individual's chromosomes and precludes same-sex couples from marrying. Kim is a male-to-female transsexual who plans on going through sex reassignment surgery with Joanne's support. Kim and Joanne are married by a Justice of the Peace before Kim has undergone the surgery.

56.   Will Restrictafornia recognize the marriage?

   (A)   No, because transsexuals cannot marry anyone.

   (B)   Yes, the state may well recognize the marriage, assuming that Joanne has XX chromosomes and Kim has XY chromosomes.

   (C)   No, because Kim plans sometime in the future on having sex-reassignment surgery.

   (D)   Yes, because they were married by a Justice of the Peace.

Fred and Frieda Frederickson are married but are having marital difficulties. Fred is always berating Frieda for not having a higher paying job and Frieda is always berating Fred for not maintaining a clean and orderly home. Finally, Frieda decides that she has had enough abuse and files for divorce claiming mental cruelty as a ground.

57.   Will the divorce be granted on this ground?

   (A)   Yes. The marriage is not thriving and Fred's constant chiding of Frieda is obviously taking a toll; else, she would not have filed for a divorce on this ground.

   (B)   No, because each is doing something that the other does not like, neither can be described as being cruel to the other.

(C) Yes, because each is casting aspersions upon the other's performance of a core function in a marriage — being a good provider or adequately maintaining the home.

(D) No, it is unlikely that a divorce will be granted upon this ground because complaining that one's spouse is not a good provider is unlikely, without more, to be thought sufficiently cruel to justify granting a divorce.

Jack and Jill Johnson have been living separate and apart for the last year. They get together for one last dinner before they file for divorce. Each is genuinely fond of the other, although each is certain that the marriage cannot be sustained. They have too much to drink and end up spending the night together. The next morning, each apologizes to the other, each admitting that the night only confirms that they should divorce. Jack consults his attorney to find out whether they must wait another year before they can divorce.

58. What should the attorney say?

(A) Because they slept together, they obviously have not been separate and apart for the requisite year. No state would grant a divorce under these circumstances.

(B) Because they both are committed to getting a divorce, it does not matter that they had sexual relations during their separation — the important consideration is that they are not living together.

(C) They will not be able to get a divorce, because they still get along so well together. Even had they not had martial relations, they would not have been manifesting the required degree of enmity to obtain a divorce.

(D) While this is a matter of state law and thus might require further research, many states permit couples to divorce based on the ground of living separate and apart, even if they have had sexual relations once during the relevant period.

Peter and Penny Pennington have decided to get a divorce. Knowing that he soon will be free, Peter accepts a job in Singlevania, where he buys a condominium, registers to vote, and changes his driver's license, all within one month. The next month he files for divorce. Penny challenges his right to do so, claiming that he had not met the local residency requirement, while Peter argues that because he has established domicile in Singlevania he of course is a resident there as well.

59. What result?
ANSWER:

Sarah and Stewart Sunington are vacationing for the summer in Divorca. Stewart is having a wonderful time and so is surprised one morning when he receives notice that Sarah has filed for divorce in Divorca after they have been there long enough to meet the local residency requirement.

Rather than contest the divorce in Divorca, he decides that he would prefer to challenge it in their domicile of Marryvania, which has more stringent divorce requirements. Sarah is granted the divorce. After their (separate) vacations are over, Sarah and Stewart both return to their respective jobs in Marryvania, where Stewart files to challenge the validity of the divorce.

60.   What result?

ANSWER:

Jack and Jill Johnson have one last fling before they are going to file for divorce based on their living separate and apart for a year, despite having been told by their attorney that they would have to wait another year if they had sexual relations again during the relevant period. They discuss the situation and decide that they are unwilling to wait another year and that they will have to find another way to end their marriage. They flip a coin. Jill "wins," and so she invites a co-worker, Tom, to go out for drinks with her. When Tom has had a few too many, she invites him home for a nightcap. Before too long, Tom and Jill are in the bedroom with their clothes off. A little while later, Jack opens the bedroom door with cell phone in hand and takes a picture of them in flagrante. Jack files for divorce, claiming adultery.

61.   The scenario above is an illustration of:

   (A)   recrimination, because Jack is conspiring with Jill to do something that could be subject to criminal penalty.

   (B)   condonation, because Jack obviously approves of Jill's feigning adultery so that they can get a divorce.

   (C)   collusion, because Jack and Jill planned together for her to commit a marital fault.

   (D)   ingenuity, because this would be one of the few ways that they could get a divorce.

Gertrude and Henry are married but have lived separate lives for years. They each have a paramour, and Gertrude finally decides that it is time to end their sham of a marriage. She files for divorce, claiming irreconcilable differences. Henry also wants the divorce, but he charges that Gertrude has been having an affair. This way, Henry may receive a more favorable distribution of the marital assets. Gertrude consults with her attorney to find out what if anything she should do. She wants a divorce but does not want to receive an unfavorable distribution of the marital assets.

62.   What should Gertrude's attorney tell her?

ANSWER:

Mary and Norman are married and living in Forgivahoma. Mary has an affair. She admits her mistake to her husband, promises never to stray again, and decides to tell her paramour, Oscar, that she does not want to see him ever again. Oscar becomes extremely upset when Mary tells him that they must stop seeing each other. She tries to comfort him and, regrettably, ends up having sexual relations with him again. When she gets home, she is extremely upset. She explains that she ended her affair with Oscar, and Mary and Norman have sexual relations that night.

Her having ended the affair notwithstanding, Norman no longer trusts Mary and wants to end their marriage, preferably on a fault-based ground. He consults an attorney to explore his options.

63.   What should the attorney tell him?

ANSWER:

Sandra and Thomas have a loveless marriage, and have been living separate and apart for over a year. Thomas files for divorce, falsely claiming not to know where Sandra lives. Sandra never has actual notice of the proceeding, although she would just as soon be free of Thomas anyway. Thomas eventually remarries and has a child with his new wife, Velina. Twenty years after their divorce, Thomas wins one million dollars in the lottery. Now Sandra seeks to have Velina's marriage to Thomas declared invalid, arguing that the divorce was void due to Thomas's failure to give Sandra actual notice of the divorce proceeding.

64.   What result?

    (A)   Sandra's having waited this long will be construed as condonation of Thomas's failure to respect her due process rights, and thus the marriage to Velina will be treated as valid.

    (B)   Sandra's having waited this long will be treated as connivance by her to induce him to contract a bigamous relationship and thus the marriage to Velina will be recognized.

    (C)   Sandra's having waited this long will itself be viewed as involving wrongdoing, and thus Velina and Thomas's marriage will be recognized based on the defense of recrimination.

    (D)   The marriage of Velina and Thomas may well be upheld because Sandra sat on her rights so long and thus Thomas might successfully argue laches.

Able and Brianna are married and live in Puritania, which imposes severe penalties on the guilty party in a fault-based divorce. Able no longer wishes to be married to Brianna but wants her to commit a marital fault so that he will get a more favorable distribution of marital assets. Able offers to pay Cain $1000 if he seduces Brianna and offers proof of the seduction. Cain seduces Brianna, secretly recording their escapade, and posts the recording on YouTube.

65.   Which defense does Brianna have to Able's charge that she has committed a marital fault?

    (A)   Condonation, because Able's paying Cain to seduce Brianna establishes that he did not disapprove of her adultery.

    (B)   Recrimination, because Able's bribing Cain to seduce his wife would be subject to civil and possibly criminal penalty.

    (C)   Connivance, because Able is acting to bring about his wife's committing a marital fault.

    (D)   Collusion, because Able and Cain colluded to bring about Brianna's committing a marital fault.

Michael and Michaela Moonington are married and live in Connsylvania. Their marriage is not a happy one and Michael wishes to end it, but he is unwilling to wait the two years of living separate and apart that is required under state law. He decides to start a new life and takes a job 1000 miles away in Divorca, which has a six-week residency requirement and will grant divorces based on irreconcilable differences without requiring that the couple live separate and apart for an extended period. When he has met the residency requirement, he files for divorce, claiming irreconcilable differences. Michaela has actual notice of the proceeding, but declines to go to Divorca to contest the divorce. Michaela then seeks to challenge the validity of the divorce in Connsylvania, claiming that the two-year separate and apart standard had not been met.

66. What result?

   (A) The divorce will be held void because Divorca did not have jurisdiction over Michaela.

   (B) The divorce will be upheld because Michael was a Divorca domiciliary who had met the residency requirement.

   (C) The divorce will be held invalid because the Divorca court should have applied Connsylvania law, which is where the marriage was contracted and where Michaela still lives.

   (D) The validity of the divorce will be upheld, because Michaela had an opportunity to fly to Divorca and challenge the divorce if she had wanted to do so.

Sarah and Sam Smith are married and live in West Mexico. Sam has been having an affair with Teresa Thomas. Sam decides to divorce his wife, Sarah, so that he can marry Teresa. While in West Texicana for business, he meets the state's one-month residency requirement and files for divorce. Sarah has notice of the divorce but chooses not to go to West Texicana to contest it. The divorce is granted based on Sam's claim of irreconcilable differences. When Sam finishes his business in West Texicana, he comes back to West Mexico and marries Teresa. Sarah challenges the validity of the divorce.

67. What result?

   (A) The divorce will be recognized as valid as long as West Texicana and West Mexico both recognize irreconcilable differences as a ground of divorce.

   (B) The divorce will not be recognized, because the West Texicana court should have applied West Mexico law to determine whether a divorce could be granted.

   (C) The divorce will be recognized as valid, because Sarah could have contested the divorce in West Texicana if she had had a valid basis for doing so.

   (D) The divorce will likely not be recognized, because Sam was not a domiciliary of West Texicana so that court did not have jurisdiction to grant the divorce.

Winston and Violet Jones are married and living in New Caledonia. Violet wishes to divorce her husband but wants to do so more quickly than the law would allow. Violet goes to Nevodu, which has a very short residency requirement for divorce filing purposes. She meets the requirement and files for divorce. Winston goes to Nevodu to contest the divorce, arguing that Violet is not a domicilary of the state and thus that the Nevodu court does not have jurisdiction to grant the divorce. The Nevodu court rejects Winston's claim and grants the divorce. Both Winston and Violet return to New Caledonia. Winston files in New Caledonia to challenge the validity of the divorce.

68. Will the Nevodu decree the recognized in New Caledonia?

(A) Because Violet has returned to New Caledonia, she obviously did not become domiciled in Nevodu. The divorce will be held invalid because the Nevodu court lacked jurisdiction to grant the divorce.

(B) The divorce will likely be given full faith and credit by the New Caledonia court. Because the Nevodu court correctly applied Nevodu divorce law, the divorce cannot be challenged collaterally.

(C) The divorce will be held invalid. Because Violet went to Nevodu precisely because their divorce requirements were less strict, she will be held to have been imposing a fraud on the New Caldeonia courts and the divorce will not be recognized.

(D) The divorce will likely be given full faith and credit. Winston had an opportunity to challenge the jurisdiction of the court in the Nevodu proceeding and he will not be given a second bite at the apple. He instead should have appealed the trial court decision in the Nevodu courts.

Anthony and Ann Adams are married in Calizona in name only. Each has a romantic partner. They decide to get a fast divorce by going to Divoricaria, another country, which has beautiful weather and a 72-hour residency requirement. They spend a few relaxing days on the beach and are awarded a divorce based on irreconcilable differences. They each marry their respective paramours. Ann and her new husband, Arthur, are quite happy and have two children. Regrettably, Anthony's marriage to Louisa does not work out as well. Louisa sues for divorce after three years and Anthony claims that they never had a valid marriage because his divorce from Ann was invalid.

69. Will Anthony's marriage to Louisa be held void?

(A) The Calizona court will recognize the divorce as a matter of full faith and credit.

(B) The Calizona court must recognize the divorce as a matter of comity.

(C) The Calizona court will treat the divorce as void because neither Anthony nor Ann was domiciled in Divoricaria at the time of the divorce proceeding.

(D) The Calizona court may treat the divorce as void or may estop Anthony from challenging the divorce's validity.

Monica and Albert are first cousins living in the state of Restrictavania, which prohibits first cousins from marrying. They decide to take a weekend trip to Laxivania, the neighboring state, where their marrying is permitted by law. They marry and return to their domicile to live. Four years later, Albert files for divorce, and Monica asserts that their marriage was never valid in the first place because Restrictavania does not permit them to marry.

70.   Will Restrictavania recognize their marriage?

(A)   The Restrictavania court will not recognize the marriage because it could not have been celebrated locally.

(B)   The Restrictavania court will recognize the marriage as long as it was valid where celebrated.

(C)   The Restrictavania court will declare the marriage void because the state has decided that individuals so closely related by blood should not be allowed to marry.

(D)   The Restrictavania court may recognize the marriage, even though it could not be celebrated locally, as long as such marriages are not thought to violate an important public policy of the state.

Assume the facts in Question 70 except that Monica and Albert were domiciled in Laxivania when they married and that they then moved to Restrictavania for a job opportunity.

71.   Will Restrictavania recognize their marriage?

(A)   Because the marriage was validly celebrated in the domicile, it is subject to full faith and credit guarantees and must be recognized.

(B)   Because such a marriage cannot be celebrated within the state, it will not be recognized even if validly celebrated in a sister domicile.

(C)   The state must treat the marriage in the same way as it would have been treated had they been domiciled in Restrictavania when celebrating the marriage in Laxivania.

(D)   While it is unclear whether the state will recognize the marriage, it is nonetheless true that some marriages that could not be celebrated by domiciliaries will nonetheless be recognized if celebrated by the parties while domiciled in a jurisdiction permitting the marriage.

Bob and Betty Binghamton live in the state of Bismarkania, which requires couples to live separate and apart for two years before they can be granted a dissolution of their marriage and which also will distribute marital assets more favorably to the innocent spouse in a fault-based divorce. Bob decides that he wants to get out of his loveless marriage but does not want to wait two years. During a business trip, he meets the

41

residency requirement of Dakatacut, a state hundreds of miles from Bismarkania. He files for divorce, making sure that Betty has actual notice of the proceeding. Bob is granted a divorce and he returns home, renting an apartment in which to live.

A few months after returning, he meets Aurelia, whom he starts to date seriously. He begins to spend several nights a week in Aurelia's home when Betty files for divorce, asserting his adultery as a ground.

72. What result?

ANSWER:

Stan and Susan Sallington live in Texarkana. They have one child, Celina. They decide to adopt a child, Bernardo, who is Celina's age. When Celina and Bernardo have each reached twenty one years of age, they go to the neighboring state of Nevarado, marry in accord with local law, and return to Texarkana.

73. Will the marriage of Celine and Bernardo be recognized?

ANSWER:

74. Which of the following is an example of dissipation of marital assets?

   (A) John uses marital assets to buy his wife, Joanne, an expensive car for her birthday. It is totaled in a terrible accident on the first day it is driven even before John has had a chance to have it insured.

   (B) Roberta uses marital assets to buy her husband an expensive painting that he hates and that can only be sold for one tenth of its original purchase price.

   (C) Zelda uses marital assets to buy stock in a publicly traded company. Because of financial mismanagement widely reported in the press, the stock can only be sold for pennies on the dollar.

   (D) Depressed because his wife has announced that she is filing for divorce, Walter treats himself to a gambling vacation where he loses his entire year's salary at a roulette table in a casino.

Myron and Myrna Mousekowitz live in the state of Muskegan. They both have secure jobs but have relatively little in the way of marital assets. Myron's aunt bequeathes to him alone her vacation cabin. Myron and Myrna start arguing about the cabin and soon divorce. Myrna wants to force Myron to sell the cabin and split the proceeds.

75. Will Myra be able to force Myron to sell the cabin and split the proceeds?

   (A) Yes, because not forcing him to do so would be inequitable to Myrna.

   (B) No, because separate property can never be reached when assets are being distributed pursuant to a divorce.

   (C) Because Myron inherited the cabin during the marriage, it will be treated as marital property and its value must be distributed.

   (D) Absent Myron's having done something such as dissipating marital assets, the cabin may well be treated as Myron's separate property and not subject to distribution.

Brad and Bobbi Joe Buttinski live in Boravania. They have decided to divorce and Brad goes on a gambling spree where he wastes several thousand dollars of marital assets, significantly reducing the assets subject to distribution. Bobbi Joe suggests that those assets lost in gambling should be accounted for on Brad's side of the ledger, whereas Brad argues that the remaining assets should be distributed equitably. After all, if he had won thousands of dollars gambling, those would have been subject to distribution.

76. How are the assets likely to be distributed?

ANSWER:

Assume the facts in Question 76 except also assume that Brad has lost so much gambling that Bobbi Joe would not get an equitable share of the marital assets (as they existed prior to the gambling spree), even if she were awarded all of the remaining asserts. Also assume that Brad owns separate property in Coloho, the neighboring state.

77.   What, if anything, can be done to achieve an equitable result for Bobbi Joe?

   (A)   Nothing, at least with respect to the separate property located in a different state.

   (B)   The court can transfer ownership of the property from Brad to Bobbi Joe.

   (C)   The court can order Brad to sell the property and split the proceeds or, in the alternative, order Brad to transfer title of the property to Bobbi Joe.

   (D)   The court can punish Brad by giving Bobbi Joe custody of the children, even if the children's interests would be best served by Brad being awarded custody.

Robin and Kim have been having marital difficulties for a long time. Each is confident that there has been an irreparable breakdown of the marriage and they are now living separate and apart from each other. Robin buys a lottery ticket and wins an eight-million dollar payout. Kim asserts that the lottery winnings are marital property, while Robin asserts that the lottery winnings are separate property and not subject to distribution.

78.   Will Kim be awarded a share of the lottery winnings?

   (A)   Because Robin and Kim were still legally married when Robin bought the ticket, the winnings may well be characterized as marital property subject to distribution.

   (B)   Because Robin and Kim were not living together at the time the lottery monies were won, the winnings are separate property and not subject to distribution.

   (C)   Only those winnings actually distributed before the divorce decree is final will be subject to distribution.

   (D)   If Kim and Robin had been living separate and apart for at least one half of the required period to establish the ground and if they ultimately divorce once they live separate and apart for the requisite period, then the winnings will be treated as separate; otherwise, they will be treated as marital.

Dick and Diane Dickerson are married with no children. Dick inherits an expensive statue from his aunt, which Diane hates. Diane buys a very expensive car with funds she receives in salary. Only Diane drives the car. The Dickersons decide to divorce. They can agree about all of the property characterizations except they disagree about whether the statue and car are marital or separate property. The way that these are characterized will help determine who receives a certain amount of cash.

79.   What are the proper characterizations of the car and the statue?

(A) Both the car and the statue are separate property, because Dianne is the only person to use the car and Dick is the only person to use (or enjoy) the statue.

(B) Both the car and the statue are marital property, because they were both acquired during the marriage.

(C) The car is marital because it was bought with marital funds, but the statue is separate property because it was inherited by Dick alone.

(D) The car is separate because Dianne is the only person to use it, but the statue is marital property because Dianne sees the statue frequently, dislike for it notwithstanding.

Juanita and Jose have been married for twenty years. Juanita has bought them each Rolex watches with monies earned during the marriage. Jose claims that Juanita's watch is marital property, whereas his watch is separate property. Juanita claims that his watch is marital property, whereas her watch is separate property.

80. How should these different watches be characterized?

(A) Because Juanita bought both watches with monies that she earned, both watches should be treated as separate property.

(B) Because only Jose wears one of the watches and only Juanita wears the other watch, each should be treated as the separate property of the person wearing it.

(C) Because both watches were bought with marital funds, they both should be treated as marital.

(D) This depends upon the intent of the parties and background state law. If Juanita expressly or impliedly made a gift of the watch to Jose, then it should be treated as his separate property. If Jose expressly or impliedly made a gift of his share of the watch to Juanita, then it should be treated as her separate property. If neither Juanita nor Jose expressly or impliedly made a gift of the watch to the other and background law does not include a presumption that gifts are separate property, then their watches should be treated as marital property and their value distributed.

Susan and Thomas Williams are married and have lived in the home in which Susan was raised, Susan having inherited the house before Susan and Thomas were married. Separate funds have been used to maintain the house for the past ten years, and no improvements have been made to the home since it was inherited by Susan. Susan and Thomas are now planning to divorce, and the only matter about which they cannot agree is whether the house should be treated as marital or separate.

81. How should the house be characterized?

(A) The house should be characterized as separate property unless, for example, it can be shown that Susan expressly or impliedly gifted an interest in the property to Thomas.

(B) The house should be characterized as marital property because Susan and Thomas lived in it for their entire marriage.

(C)   The house should be characterized as separate property, because it was inherited by Susan rather than by Susan and Thomas together.

(D)   The house should be characterized as marital, because both parties had their names on the mailbox.

Same facts as in Question 81, except that extensive improvements were made to the house during the decade in which the couple lived there, and those improvements were purchased with marital funds.

82.   How should the house be characterized now?

(A)   The house should be characterized as separate, because Susan alone inherited it.

(B)   The house may be characterized as marital, because substantial improvements were made to it, those improvements were paid for by marital funds, and there is no way to divide up the house into both marital and separate property.

(C)   Absent an express or implied gift of an interest in the house to Thomas, the house is Susan's separate property.

(D)   The house is marital property, because it had been the domicile for the duration of the marriage.

Carol and Donald Edwards are living in the house that Carol had bought before the marriage by putting $50,000 down with a $200,000 mortgage. At the time of their divorce, the mortgage had been reduced by $50,000 through the use of marital funds to make the mortgage payments. The only issue about which Carol and Donald cannot agree involves the extent to which Donald has an interest in the house.

83.   What is Donald's interest in the house?

(A)   Most jurisdictions would say that because mortgage payments were made with marital funds, the house has become a marital assert and Donald has a 50% interest in the house, although Carol must get a $50,000 credit for her down payment.

(B)   Because Carol bought the house in her own name and never made a gift of an interest in it to Donald, the house is separate property. The share of marital funds attributable to Donald that were used to pay down the mortgage will be viewed as a gift to Carol from Donald.

(C)   Because Carol put down the $50,000, the amount paid down on the mortgage was $50,000, and the remaining amount owed on the mortgage is $150,000, Donald has a one-fifth share of the house — the amount of the mortgage paid down divided by the total amount of the mortgage plus the down payment.

(D)   Because Carol put down the $50,000, the amount paid down on the mortgage was $50,000, and the remaining amount owed on the mortgage is $150,000, Donald has a one-tenth share of the house. The denominator is $250,000 and the numerator is one half of the amount that the mortgage was reduced. (The marital funds belong to both of them and should be distributed equally.)

Tom Thompson and Mary Martinson each own apartment buildings, although Mary has a management team take care of all aspects of the maintenance and improvement of the building with the team's fees plus all maintenance and improvement expenses being paid out of the rents paid by the tenants. Professionally, Mary is a doctor. Tom does not have another job. Instead, he works full-time managing and maintaining the apartment building he owns. When they divorce, neither seeks spousal support from the other. The only issue in contention is how to characterize the apartment buildings.

84. How should the apartment buildings be characterized?

(A) Assuming no express or implied gifts of an interest in either building, both buildings are separate property and neither party is owed any compensatory payments to make up for the expenditure of marital time and effort with respect to them.

(B) Both buildings are marital property because they were each owned for a substantial period during the marriage.

(C) Because Mary is a passive investor during the marriage investing neither marital time nor marital funds in the apartment buildings, that building remains separate and is not subject to distribution. However, because Tom was spending marital time and effort in maintaining the building, either Mary will be thought to have acquired an interest in the building or she will be entitled to receive some compensation for his having used martial time, energy, and funds to promote his separate business.

(D) Because Tom and Mary are each quite wealthy and because no children were born of the marriage, the judge will treat their ten-year marriage as if the couple had never married, i.e., neither will receive spousal support and neither will receive any property.

Don and Darla meet in college. Don is studying to be a nurse and Darla is pre-med. They marry the day after they graduate from college. Don works as a nurse to help put Darla through medical school, although Darla is able to secure some loans to help pay for her education.

While Darla is doing her residency, she meets and falls in love with one of the doctors in the hospital, Richard Bellaire. Don and Darla have virtually no tangible marital assets, in part because most of Don's salary has been used to pay for necessities like rent and food. When they divorce, Don claims that the medical degree is marital property, the expected value of which is subject to distribution. Darla claims that the degree is not property — it cannot be sold or transferred. She argues that Don is not entitled to any division of property or compensation to account for her having received a medical degree.

85. Will Don be entitled to property division or some sort of compensation for his sacrifice in helping put Darla through medical school?

(A) No. One always takes a chance when entering into a marriage and no jurisdiction would permit Don any sort of compensation on these facts.

(B) Yes. Don will receive a credit amounting to the opportunity costs incurred, i.e., a credit for half of what Darla would have made had she worked instead of going to medical school.

(C) No, because there is no way to assess the value of the degree, unless Don and Darla agreed before the marriage about how much Don would receive if they were to divorce.

(D) Yes, many jurisdictions will permit a spouse in Don's position to receive some compensation. However, they do not all treat a professional degree as marital property subject to distribution, and may instead use some other rationale to achieve an equitable result.

Lynn and Nat are married. Nat has always worked at Goodjob Corporation. Lynn has worked inside the home with primary responsibility for raising the couple's children. The youngest child has now reached age 18, and Lynn and Nat have decided to end the marriage. Nat is now age 70, and half of the years worked at Goodjob will have been while not married (20 years prior to the marriage) and half of the years will have been during the marriage. Lynn and Nat can agree about everything except about how the pension benefits should be distributed.

86.   What share, if any, should Lynn receive of Nat's pension benefits?

(A) No share. The pension benefits are separate property, because they will not be awarded until Nat and Lynn have divorced.

(B) Lynn should receive 50% of the benefits. The pension benefits are marital property, because at least half of the time at this particular employer was spent during the marriage.

(C) No share. Although the pension benefits are separate property, the court will make up for this inequitable result by awarding Lynn a greater proportion of the marital property, e.g., the house in which they have lived.

(D) Lynn should receive roughly 25% of the benefits. One half of the pension benefits are marital property and subject to distribution.

87.   Community property includes:

(A) the property that is acquired by gift or bequest during a marriage.

(B) the property that everyone in a family is permitted to use.

(C) all property acquired or purchased during a marriage.

(D) all property acquired during a marriage in a community property state that does not meet one of the statutory exceptions making the property separate.

88.   Quasi-community property includes:

(A) property that is partially separate property and partially community property.

(B) property that will become community property as soon as some additional community resources are invested in it.

(C) property that is jointly owned in a community property state by a non-marital couple.

(D) property that would be community property had it been acquired in a community property state but in fact was acquired in a common law state.

Bob and Bernice Bottomly live in Calidaho. They are having marital difficulties and Bob decides to take a job in Monoming, which is hundreds of miles away. After meeting the residency requirement, he files for divorce. Bernice has actual notice of the proceeding. The Monoming court not only grants Bob the divorce but divides some of the property located in Bob and Bernice's Calidaho home. While Bernice does not wish to challenge the divorce, she does want to challenge the property distribution. She consults an attorney to find out her options.

89. What should the attorney tell Bernice?

  (A) Because the Monoming court did not have jurisdiction over Bernice, it could neither grant Bob the divorce nor divide the marital property.

  (B) Because the Monoming court had jurisdiction to grant the divorce, the court had the power both to end the marriage and to divide the marital property.

  (C) While the Monoming court had jurisdiction to grant the divorce, it did not in addition have the power to distribute marital property located in Calidaho, and so that part of the decision is subject to challenge.

  (D) If Bernice had wanted to protect her property rights, she should have gone to the Monoming proceeding to make sure that she would receive an equitable distribution. She has now lost her chance to contest the distribution.

John and Karen King are married and living in New Carington. Karen accepts a job in East Virginton, which is over one thousand miles from their home. Karen anticipates that she and John will soon be ending their relationship. She meets the residency requirement and files for divorce. John has actual notice of the proceeding but decides that it is simply too far away to go. The East Virginton court not only grants Karen a divorce but awards her almost all of the property that she had with her in East Virginton. John consults an attorney because he wants to challenge the validity of both the divorce and the property distribution.

90. What should the attorney say?

  (A) Because the East Virginton court did not have jurisdiction over John, it could neither grant the divorce nor distribute marital property.

  (B) The court could grant the divorce because Karen was a domiciliary of East Virginton who had met the residency requirement and had afforded John actual notice of the proceeding. However, courts are split with respect to whether a court had the power to distribute marital property located in the forum under these circumstances.

  (C) If John had wished to contest the divorce or protect his property interests, he should have hired an attorney to represent his interests in East Virginton. He lost his opportunity to contest the decision when he decided not to go to East Virginton.

  (D) While the East Virginton court clearly had jurisdiction to grant the divorce, it did not have jurisdiction over Bob and thus clearly could not distribute any marital property under these circumstances.

Donna Derrickson has bought a home with a down payment of $50,000 and has taken on a mortgage of $100,000. She later meets and marries Edward Evans. She makes the mortgage payments from her salary. She is able to retire the mortgage because of an inheritance she receives from her aunt. As a way of expressing her love, she puts the property in both Edward's and her name. He thanks her but does not have her name placed on the deed of separate property that he owns. When Donna and Edward later divorce, they disagree about whether the home should be characterized as her separate property or as marital property.

91.   How should the home be characterized?

ANSWER:

Molly and Ned Owens have been married for several years but are now divorcing. They can agree about the proper characterization of all of their property except for a gift of a car from Molly to Ned and a gift of expensive jewelry from Ned to Molly.

92.   Which, if any, of these gifts should be characterized as separate property and which as marital property?

ANSWER:

93.   Which of the following is determined in light of the best interests of the child standard?

    (A) which parent, if either, is unfit.

    (B) how much child support should be paid.

    (C) whether a court should override a parent's decision with respect to the appropriate medical treatment for her child.

    (D) which parent should have custody of a child.

Some jurisdictions still use a tender years presumption when making custody decisions.

94.   What does the presumption involve?

    (A) an unrebuttable presumption that a child's mother should be awarded custody of the child if that child is below a certain age.

    (B) a presumption that parents of tender years, i.e., teenagers, should not be awarded custody of a child if another suitable (older) adult is available.

    (C) the express preferences of children of tender years with respect to who will have custody of them will be presumed not to be the product of careful deliberation and thus will be given little or no weight.

    (D) a rebuttable presumption that the mother should be awarded custody of a child below a certain age.

Pauline and Oscar Noonan are divorcing after fifteen years of marriage. They can agree about nothing. Each is a fit parent who loves Mary, the only child born of the marriage. However, neither thinks very much of the other's parenting abilities. Indeed, there is very good reason to think that Pauline, if awarded custody, would do her utmost to prevent Oscar from seeing Mary, although there is no reason to think that Oscar would prevent Pauline from seeing Mary were he awarded custody.

95.   How, if at all, would the relative willingness to promote visitation with the other parent affect who is awarded custody?

    (A) Not at all. The issue to be decided is which parent's having custody would be most likely to promote the best interests of the child, not whether one parent thinks well of the ex-spouse's parenting abilities.

    (B) Because it is important for the child to maintain contact with both parents, this factor will be dispositive.

(C) This factor is only considered as a tie-breaker.

(D) This is simply one factor to consider among many.

William and Yolanda Zickers are divorcing after seventeen years of marriage. They can agree about property issues but each seeks custody of their fifteen-year-old daughter, Miranda, who has expressed a decided preference to live with her father. Yolanda claims that Miranda wishes to live with her father because he does not discipline her and, further, has promised her a car when she turns sixteen if she comes to live with him.

96. What result?

(A) The test for custody is what will best promote the interests of the child rather than simply what the child wants, so a child's expressed preferences are irrelevant in any event.

(B) Because Miranda is fifteen years old and capable of making a deliberate and reasoned decision, her stated preference will be considered dispositive.

(C) A child's stated preference must be given substantial weight when the child has reached fifteen years of age, so William must be awarded custody as long as he is a fit parent.

(D) The stated preference of an older child is given significant weight in custody decisions unless there is reason to believe that following the preference of the child will not promote her interests. Unless the trial court believes that Miranda was bribed by her father or that his being awarded custody would inure to Miranda's detriment, her expressed preference would likely be given substantial weight.

Many states require a substantial or material change in circumstances before a motion for a modification of custody will be considered.

97. What does this standard involve?

(A) A material change in circumstances refers to a significant change in the ability of either parent to provide material support for the child.

(B) A material change in circumstances involves a development that the child subjectively feels is important.

(C) A material change in circumstances refers to any change in residence.

(D) A material change in circumstances involves important new facts that were unknown at the time custody was initially awarded.

98. When used in the context of parent-child relationships, parental alienation involves:

(A) a parent's deciding that he no longer wishes to be a parent and so is voluntarily surrendering his parental rights.

(B) the feelings of one parent towards his/her ex-spouse in a contentious divorce.

(C) a relatively short-lived feeling that parents sometimes have when they need to take a short break from their parenting responsibilities.

(D) one parent's taking affirmative steps to poison the well and alienate the child from the other parent.

Alice and Zachary Jacobson are married and live in Vermshire. They have two children, Doreen, age 6, and Jack, age 4. Alice and Zachary have decided to divorce. Alice will remain in Vermshire with custody of both children, while Zachary is moving to Oklexio, where he will start a new job. The children will see their father on certain holidays and stay with him for two months every summer.

By the time that Doreen has reached her ninth birthday, Zachary has already remarried. That summer, when the children have been staying with their father for the past five weeks, Zachary files for a modification of custody, claiming a substantial change in circumstances because of his remarriage and his receipt of a substantial increase in salary. Alice appears at the proceeding making all of the appropriate arguments.

99. What is the likely result?

(A) Unless Alice has also remarried in the interim, Zachary's request for a custody modification is likely to be granted.

(B) Zachary's request is unlikely to be granted, because Oklexio must give full faith and credit to Vermshire's initial custody determination.

(C) Zachary's request is likely to be granted as long as Oklexio's version of the Uniform Interstate Family Support Act permits modifications.

(D) Zachary's request is likely to be denied because Oklexio's version of the Uniform Child Custody Jurisdiction and Enforcement Act (UCCJEA) will likely establish that Vermshire rather than Oklexio has jurisdiction to modify custody.

Same facts as in Question 99 except that Zachary has never moved out of state and instead has always remained domiciled in Vermshire.

100. Will Zachary be awarded custody?

(A) Unless Alice has also remarried, Zachary is likely to have his request granted.

(B) Zachary's request is unlikely to be granted because Vermshire's version of the UCCJEA is unlikely to permit custody modifications under these circumstances.

(C) Zachary's request is likely to be granted unless Alice has also had a comparable salary increase.

(D) Zachary's request is likely to be denied unless he can show a material change in circumstances in the home environment provided by Alice that was adversely affecting the children and thus would justify a custody modification.

Winona and Thomas Smart are married and live in Delacut. They have two children, Susan and Richard. One night when Winona comes home from work unexpectedly, she discovers Thomas in bed with her best friend, Gladys. Winona and Thomas divorce with Winona awarded custody of the children, who will be with their father during certain holidays and for an extended period during the summer.

Thomas and Gladys move to West Marylania to start new lives. A few years later, Winona receives permission to move to Eastlandia for a wonderful job opportunity. One year later after the children have been with their father for a month during the summer, Thomas files for a modification of custody. He claims a substantial change in circumstances, noting his own remarriage to Gladys and that Winona and the children have moved to a new state. Winona contests the jurisdiction of the West Marylania court.

101. What result?

(A) On these facts, Thomas's request for a modification of custody cannot be heard in West Marylania. He must instead request a custody modification in Delacut, the jurisdiction initially making the custody award.

(B) On these facts, the West Marylania court has jurisdiction to decide the modification. Because none of the parties continues to have any contacts with Delacut, the state with the longest ongoing contact with members of the family, West Marylania, is where the custody modification request must be considered.

(C) On these facts, the state where the children have been domiciled for the past year, Eastlandia, is where the request for a custody modification must be filed.

(D) On these facts, no state has jurisdiction to consider the request for a custody modification. The children have been domiciled in Eastlandia for only a year rather than the required eighteen months, West Marylania was never the children's domicile, and Delacut is no longer the children's domicile.

Morris and Nancy Overton are divorced and living in Yorkylvania, with Nancy having custody of the couple's children. Nancy receives a wonderful job offer in Calington, which is 2000 miles away from Yorkylvania. Were she to accept the offer, she would be much nearer extended family and would be able to provide for her children in ways that simply are not possible in Yorkylvania. Nancy seeks court permission to move. Morris opposes the move because he would then be too far from the children to have frequent contact with them.

102. Will Nancy be permitted to move?

(A) No, because the move would impair the relationship between Morris and the children.

(B) Yes, because Nancy has the right to move wherever she wishes for any reason.

(C) No, unless she can show that Morris in only contesting the move out of spite.

(D) Yes, she is likely to have the move approved, providing that she can establish why the move would promote the best interests of the children.

When considering whether a parent's having committed adultery should affect whether that parent will be awarded custody, some states use a nexus test.

103. What is the nexus test is this context?

(A) The court examines the nexus between the (alleged) injustices attributable to the "innocent" spouse and the behavior of the adulterous spouse.

(B) The court examines how closely related in time were the discovery of the adultery and the filing for divorce.

(C) The court examines whether the adultery has had an adverse impact upon the child.

(D) The court examines whether the adultery occurred as a result of extenuating circumstances, e.g., depression from loss of a job or family member.

Wendell and Tania Sarasota are divorced. Wendell has custody of their child, Rory. Wendell has been seeing Jim for the past several months. Jim and Rory get along very well and Rory has mentioned in passing to Tania that Jim may be come to live with Rory and Wendell. Disapproving of the relationship between Wendell and Jim, Tania seeks a modification of custody.

104. What result?

ANSWER:

Jack and Jill Kantington are divorcing. They have been having marital problems for a long time and Jill has admitted that she has been having an affair. Each blames the other for the behavioral problems that their child, Josephina, has been experiencing, and each seeks custody. Jill has a warm relationship with Josephina, although Jack claims that this is because he has to be the disciplinarian.

105. Who will get custody of Josephina?

ANSWER:

Alex and Beverly Carrington are divorced and living in Massacut with Alex being awarded custody of the couple's two children, Donald and Edweena. Alex has since remarried, and Donald and Edweena are having some difficulty getting along with Heidi and Isabel, the children of Alex's new wife, Jezebel. Beverly has also remarried, and Donald and Edweena get along quite well with Sarah and Jimmy, the children of Beverly's new husband, Fred. Beverly seeks a modification of custody.

106. What result?

ANSWER:

Assume the same facts in Question 106 except that Beverly and Fred now live in Floramba. Donald and Edweena have spent six weeks with her during their summer vacation in accord with the established visitation arrangement and, pursuant to their request, Beverly files in Floramba for a modification of custody.

107. What result?

ANSWER:

Billie Jean Binghamton is living with Gertrude Gunningham. They are raising Frieda, a child born to Billie Jean though artificial insemination. Gertrude is Frieda's primary caretaker and, pursuant to local law, has adopted her. Billie Jean and Gertrude decide that they can no longer live together and each seeks custody of Frieda.

108. Who will be awarded custody of Frieda?

ANSWER:

Bob and Marley live together with Marley's child, Norman. Bob has helped raise Norman for the past several years, and the two have a very good relationship. However, Bob has never sought to adopt Norman, even though local law would have allowed him to do so. Bob and Marley have decided to split up and each seeks custody of Norman.

109. What result?

ANSWER:

In *Spouse v. Spouse*, the New Vermshire Supreme Court strikes down that state's tender years presumption because it employs a sex-based classification when presumptively awarding custody of a young child to the child's mother. Grant Gilman's attorney, Laura Lawyer, challenges the trial court's awarding custody of Bob Gilman to his mother, Greta Gilman, claiming sex discrimination and citing *Spouse v. Spouse*. Laura can show that in the vast majority of contested child custody cases, women rather than men are awarded custody of their children.

110. What result?

ANSWER:

Bob and Betty Burns live in Old Jersey. They have been trying to conceive for a long time but have never been successful. They decide to hire a surrogate, Samantha Smith, who will be artificially inseminated with Bob's sperm. Eventually, Samantha becomes pregnant. However, when she gives birth to Carl, she refuses to give up custody of the child. Bob sues Samantha to force her to relinquish custody of Carl per their agreement.

111. Will Samantha be forced to relinquish custody of Carl?

ANSWER:

Assume the same facts as in Question 111, although with the following modification. Assume that Bob and Betty acquired eggs from an egg donor, made use of in vitro fertilization using Bob's sperm, and then hired Samantha to be a gestational surrogate.

112. Would Samantha's having been a gestational surrogate have any effect on the ultimate disposition of this case?

ANSWER:

Alex and Amy Albertson have been married for several years. They have fallen out of love and wish to end their marriage but they live in Forevervania, which requires couples to live separate and apart for two years before they can end their marriages. Alex decides to go to the state of Easydivorce, which is in a sunny climate and has only a one-week residency requirement. He is granted a divorce. He then returns to Forevervania.

Alex meets and marries Barbara Bennett, a divorcee who has been receiving spousal support from her ex-husband, Carl, which was to continue until Barbara's death or remarriage. Alex buys a winning lottery ticket, which entitles him to two million dollars. Amy challenges the validity of the divorce, because she wants her share of the lottery winnings. Forevervania refuses to recognize the validity of the divorce because Alex was never domiciled in Easydivorce, which makes his marriage to Barbara void. Barbara seeks reinstatement of support payments from Carl, claiming that Carl is still obligated to make the support payments because her marriage to Alex was void from the beginning.

113. Will Carl be forced to continue paying Barbara spousal support?

   (A) Because Barbara was never remarried in the eyes of the law, Carl may well be forced to resume his support payments.

   (B) Carl will be forced to resume payments only if Amy and Alex reconcile.

   (C) No, because Alex can pay the support out of the lottery winnings.

   (D) No, because Amy should be forced to make up the difference from her share of the lottery winnings, since she should have challenged the validity of the divorce earlier, which would have saved everyone from all of these legal difficulties.

Keith and Linda Matherson live in East Caroda. They have been having marital difficulties for a long time. Linda has an affair with William. Keith is granted a divorce on the ground of adultery and Linda is ordered to pay Keith spousal support.

Not long after the divorce, Keith meets Karen, who seems to be perfect for him. In no small part because she has repeatedly expressed her desire to have a big family, Keith asks Karen to marry him. They marry, much to Linda's delight because she believes that she no longer has to pay Keith spousal support. Regrettably, Karen does not want to have a big family and she will only have sexual relations with Keith if they are using contraception. When it is clear to Keith that he and Karen will never have children, he seeks an annulment of the marriage, claiming that she had lied about something going to the essence of marriage. Further, because an annulment would mean that the marriage had never existed, he seeks to have Linda's support payments reinstated. Keith consults an attorney to find out whether he can get an annulment and a resumption of spousal support.

114. What should the attorney tell Keith?

(A) Because it is unclear whether Keith and Karen would have been able to conceive anyway, it is speculative whether they would have had a child even if they had tried and thus there is no basis for an annulment much less a resumption of Linda's spousal support obligation.

(B) While Keith is likely to be able to have the marriage annulled, Keith is unlikely to be able to get the support order reinstated, because his marriage to Karen is merely voidable rather than void ab initio.

(C) Keith is unlikely to be able to have the marriage annulled unless he explicitly stated that he would marry Karen precisely because she wanted to have children. If he is able to have the marriage annulled, then he will be able to have support reinstated.

(D) Keith's ability to have support reinstated will turn entirely on whether Linda has remarried since the divorce. If she has, there will be no reinstatement of support. If she has not, then she will be required to pay support again.

115. Rehabilitative spousal support involves:

(A) one spouse paying for the other spouse to receive psychological counseling that is intended to help the latter spouse recover from the former spouse's physical and emotional abuse.

(B) one spouse giving financial support to the other spouse pursuant to a divorce decree that allows the latter spouse to develop or improve job skills so that the latter spouse will be able to be self-sufficient.

(C) one spouse paying for the other spouse to receive physical therapy pursuant to a divorce decree so that the latter spouse can be self-sufficient.

(D) one spouse paying owed spousal support to the other so that child visitation might be resumed.

116. Spousal support pendant lite is:

(A) support for one of the spouses during the period in which the divorce or annulment proceeding is pending.

(B) temporary support designed to help one of the spouses gain needed training so that he or she will be able to enter the work force.

(C) support that has temporarily been suspended pending the outcome of divorce litigation.

(D) the term for spousal support that is ordered as part of a divorce decree.

Martin and Mary Moonington have been married for twenty-five years. Three children were born of the marriage, and the youngest has just turned eighteen. Mary has never worked outside of the home. Martin announces that he no longer loves Mary and wants a divorce. Mary consults an attorney to find out whether she is likely to get permanent spousal support. The attorney responds that several factors in the case make it very likely that she will receive permanent support.

117. Which of the following would be unlikely to be considered when determining whether Mary should be awarded permanent support?

(A)   the likelihood that even with training Mary would be unable to enter the job market.

(B)   the standard of living to which Mary had become accustomed.

(C)   the length of the marriage.

(D)   the ages of the couple's children.

Wayne and Zelda Young are divorcing after ten years of marriage. They both have good jobs. Zelda seeks custody of the couple's two children, Alex and Benita. Wayne has said that he will contest custody unless Zelda agrees that he will not have to pay either spousal or child support. Because she believes that Wayne would not be a good custodial parent, she is unwilling to take a chance that he will be awarded custody, so she agrees to his terms. Assume that the court will grant Zelda custody because her being the custodial parent would be best for the children.

118. How likely is it that the court will approve the non-support agreement worked out by Wayne and Zelda?

(A)   The court is likely to approve the agreement, absent evidence of fraud, duress or coercion, and Wayne's possibly seeking custody would not count as coercive, since that is something that he is entitled to do.

(B)   The court will not approve of either part of the agreement, assuming that Wayne makes significantly more than Zelda in salary.

(C)   While the court normally would award child support, it will enforce the agreement that there would be no child support in this case, provided that Zelda's salary is adequate to provide for the needs of the children.

(D)   Even assuming no evidence of fraud, coercion or duress, the court is unlikely to approve an agreement to waive child support, because that would not promote the interests of the children and, in any event, is not something that Zelda can bargain away in exchange for uncontested custody. However, the court is likely to approve the agreement that Zelda receive no spousal support.

Dennis and Edith Jacobsen live in New Floraco. They have two children, Alice and Linda. When working out their divorce, neither Dennis nor Edith thought about the college educations of their children, because the older daughter, Alice, was only nine years old at the time of the divorce. Now, Alice is a college junior and Linda is about to begin college. Edith has been helping Alice with her college education costs and now sees that she will simply be unable to help Linda, too, unless Dennis helps. Dennis has thus far been unwilling to help pay for either child's college education, so Edith consults with Laura Lawyer to find out whether Dennis can be forced to contribute.

119. What should Laura say?

(A)   If Dennis and Edith had worked this out at the time of their divorce, then Dennis could be forced to contribute. However, without such an agreement, no state would force Dennis to contribute at this point.

(B) Some states requires divorced parents to contribute to the college educations of their children as long as doing so would not impose an unreasonable burden on the parent. Laura will have to do some research to find out whether New Floraco imposes such an obligation.

(C) Because a college education is now viewed in the same way as a high school education was viewed a few generations ago, all states require divorced parents to the contribute to their children's college education costs as long as doing so would not impose an unreasonable burden.

(D) As long as Alice and Linda have reached age eighteen, Dennis will not be required to pay college support, because the children will have reached the age of majority.

As part of the divorce settlement with Nancy, Marty agrees to pay for the reasonable college expenses of their two twin children, Zeke and Yolanda, assuming that he has some say in the decision. However, when Zeke and Yolanda are in their senior year of high school, they both apply to and are accepted by Very Expensive College. They both are also accepted by Prestigious State School, which is located in a different state, and Very Good State University, which was the only school within the state to which they applied. They decide that they want to go to Very Expensive College, notwithstanding Marty's reservations about the cost and his advising them that Very Good State University provides a much better value, and inform their father that he will have to pay over $120,000 annually for the next four years so that they both can attend that college. Marty consults with an attorney to find out how much he can be forced to pay toward the twins' college expenses.

120. What should the attorney say?

(A) The attorney should reassure Marty that the agreement with Nancy is only aspirational and not enforceable, so Marty will only have to pay what he believes is appropriate under the circumstances.

(B) The attorney should explain that Marty will be responsible for the reasonable costs associated with their going to Prestigious State School, even though the costs of going there as out-of-state students were almost triple what it would have cost for them to go to Very Good State University.

(C) The attorney should explain to Marty that given his failure to specify that he would only pay for the reasonable costs associated with an in-state university, he may be responsible for the reasonable expenses associated with going to Very Expensive College, although there may well be case law in the jurisdiction suggesting that he will be responsible for in-state tuition, especially because he included as a condition that he have some say in the determination.

(D) The attorney should explain that because both parents are responsible for contributing to college education costs, Marty may well be responsible for half of the twins' reasonable costs associated with going to Very Expensive College.

Mario and Nona have been having difficulty conceiving. After they have been tested, they discover that Mario is sterile. They decide to make use of artificial insemination. Eventually, Nona becomes pregnant and has a child, Dorothy. Nona teases Mario about his inability to father a child to the point that Mario begins to hate both Nona and Dorothy. When Mario and Nona divorce, Mario and Nona can agree about the division of property and that there will be no spousal support. However, Mario also says that he does not want to pay child support for Dorothy, who is not biologically related to him anyway. Further, he does not seek visitation with her, since she represents all that he hates about himself and Marilyn.

121. What is the court likely to do?

(A) Because Mario and Dorothy are not biologically related, he will have no duty of support and would not be awarded visitation rights even if he had wanted them.

(B) Because Mario and Dorothy are not biologically related, he will have no duty of support. However, because as a general matter it is good for a child to have a relationship with two parents, he will be ordered to visit her on a regular schedule.

(C) Because Mario consented to the in vitro fertilization, he will be viewed as Dorothy's father, lack of biological connection notwithstanding, and will likely be ordered to pay child support because that would promote Dorothy's interests. However, it is unlikely that a visitation schedule will be imposed if his seeing her would be harmful to her.

(D) Because Mario consented to the in vitro fertilization, he will be viewed as Dorothy's father, lack of biological connection notwithstanding, and will likely be ordered to pay child support because that would promote Dorothy's interests. Because as a general matter it is good for a child to have a relationship with two parents, he will be ordered to visit her on a regular schedule.

John and Mary Smith have been trying to have a child for years without success. After undergoing tests establishing that John is sterile, they decide that Mary will be artificially inseminated. Shortly after the artificial insemination begins, Mary discovers that she is pregnant. Mary and John divorce soon after the birth of the child, Bob. John argues that he should not have to support Bob, who is biologically related to Mary's paramour, Wesley.

122. Will John be forced to pay child support for Bob?

(A) No, because John has no positive feelings for either the child or for Mary, he will neither be forced to pay child support nor be entitled to visitation.

(B) Yes, he already agreed to being responsible for a child not biologically related to him, and he cannot now complain just because Mary had a successful pregnancy.

(C) Yes, because it would be in Bob's best interests to receive support, John's desire not to do so notwithstanding.

(D) John would be unlikely to be ordered to pay support if the pregnancy had not resulted from artificial insemination. However, the answer is much less clear if it can be shown that the standard procedures for artificial insemination were followed, e.g., if they had used a doctor as an intermediary.

Larry and Kim have been married for several years. Two children have been born of the marriage, Carla and David. Larry has always assumed that he was the children's father and he has a very good relationship with each of them. He has just learned that Kim has been having an affair for a long time with William, who is the biological father of both children. Larry wants nothing to do with either Kim or the children.

123. In the judgment granting a divorce, is Larry likely to be ordered to maintain visitation or

pay child support?

    (A) Larry is likely to be ordered both to see them and to pay support, because he rather than William has functioned as their father for the past several years.

    (B) No, because he was defrauded into believing that he was their father, no jurisdiction would now force him to pay child support.

    (C) Yes, because it is not the fault of the children that Larry was deceived, they should not be penalized by losing his financial and emotional support.

    (D) Jurisdictions vary with respect to whether a husband who had been helping to raise children in the good faith belief that he was biologically related to them would be ordered to pay child support when the truth about their parentage became known.

Same facts as in Question 123, although assume now that Larry wishes to continue to have a relationship with the children but Kim seeks to prevent him from paying any support or having any contact with them.

  124. Assuming that Kim is awarded custody, will Larry be awarded visitation rights or support obligations?

    (A) Because the custodial parent is presumed to know what is in the best interests of the children, Larry will have no right of visitation or duty of support if Kim thinks that such an arrangement would best promote the interests of the children.

    (B) Because Kim led Larry to believe that he was their biological father, he may well be recognized as their legal father or, in the alternative, she may well be estopped from denying his paternity now. Larry is likely to have a duty of support imposed and a right of visitation recognized.

    (C) If indeed Larry is not biologically related to the children, then he will have neither a duty of support nor a right of visitation.

    (D) Because Kim believes that it would be better for the children never to see Larry, he will likely be denied a right of visitation. However, because it would be better for the children to receive support from him (if only so that the dollars can be put in a college fund), Larry will be ordered to pay child support.

Jimmy and Sarah have been dating for awhile. Sarah would love to have a child but Jimmy always insists that contraception be used before any sexual relations take place. One day, Sarah announces that she is pregnant and that Jimmy is the father. She notes that no contraception method is foolproof. After giving birth to Abigail, Sarah seeks child support from Jimmy. When Jimmy finds out that Sarah had lied and had not been using any contraception whatsoever, he contests paying child support.

  125. Will Jimmy be forced to pay child support, Sarah's deception notwithstanding?

    (A) Had Sarah been using contraception, Jimmy would have had a duty to pay support. Because she was not using any, however, he will not have to pay any support.

(B)   Usually, even when no contraception is used, the biological father is responsible for child support. However, because Sarah affirmatively misrepresented that contraception was being used, she will be estopped from seeking child support.

(C)   Because Jimmy knew that contraception was not foolproof and because the support would benefit Abigail, Jimmy is likely to be ordered to pay support.

(D)   Jimmy will only be ordered to pay child support if his salary is higher than Sarah's.

Alex and Melinda are married and have one child, Zeus. When Alex and Melinda divorce, Melinda is awarded custody. Alex is ordered to pay child support, even though Melinda's salary is significantly higher than Alex's. Alex is quite resentful, especially because he never bonded with Zeus anyway. Alex quits his job and then seeks a child support modification, because he simply no longer has any earnings that can be used for child support. Melinda opposes the support modification.

126.   Is Alex's request to modify support likely to be granted?

(A)   Yes, because Alex has no earnings, he will not have to pay anything in support. When Alex gets a new job, the support obligation will be reinstated.

(B)   Yes, because Alex is no longer receiving a salary. However, Alex will still be required to pay something if he has an income stream from other sources such as dividends, rents, or other payments.

(C)   No, once a support order is made, it can only be changed under extraordinary circumstances.

(D)   No, because Alex quit his job in order to avoid having to pay support, his support obligation will likely not be modified.

Roni and Steve have one child, Terri. Pursuant to the divorce decree, Steve is awarded custody and Roni is ordered to pay support. Roni marries Verne, and they have twins. While Roni is continuing to work, her salary has not kept pace with her increased responsibilities associated with having two children. She seeks a child support modification because she is having great difficulty in paying support and providing for the twins.

127.   Will her request be granted?

(A)   No. Roni married Verne, already knowing that she had an obligation to pay child support for Terri. Roni's taking on new obligations should not be allowed to undercut the pre-existing obligation to help support Terri.

(B)   Yes, Roni's support obligation may be reduced to some extent, provided that her having twins was not reasonably foreseeable.

(C)   No, because Verne also has a responsibility to support the twins, Roni's support obligation to Terri is unlikely to be reduced. However, if Verne were unable to help support the twins, then Roni's support obligation would likely be modified.

(D) Yes, Roni's support obligation is likely to be modified, because Roni has a legal obligation to support the twins, which will be included in the calculation determining her support obligation with respect to Terri.

Same fact scenario as in Question 127. However assume that Roni has decided to quit her job so that she can stay home with the twins and then seeks to modify her support obligation.

128. Is Roni's request to modify support likely to be granted? Why or why not?

ANSWER:

Beatrice and Colby are married and live in New Vermshire, where they have one child, Daniella. When Beatrice and Colby divorce, Beatrice is ordered to pay support. She gets a new job in Massecticut and moves there. For awhile, everything is fine. However, because of a terrible downturn in the economy, Beatrice loses her job. She files for a support modification in Massecticut, which Colby opposes. Massecticut and New Vermshire each have their own versions of the Uniform Interstate Family Support Act (UIFSA), which basically mirror each other and the Uniform Act.

129. What is the likely result of Bernice's attempt to reduce her support obligation?

(A) Because there is ample evidence that Bernice has been trying on good faith to get another job and that she was not at fault when losing her prior job, her request will likely be granted.

(B) Because it is not Daniella's fault that Bernice lost her job and because Daniella would not be benefited by a reduction in Bernice's support obligation, Bernice's request is unlikely to be granted.

(C) Her request will likely be granted. As a matter of equity and common sense, an individual without a job should not and cannot be forced to make support payments when she does not have the money to do so.

(D) Bernice is unlikely to be successful because under UIFSA Massecticut does not have jurisdiction to grant her request.

Henrietta and Irwin are married and live in New Vermshire. When they divorce, Henrietta is ordered to pay spousal support. She gets a new job in Massecticut and moves there. For awhile, everything is fine. However, because of a terrible downturn in the economy, Henrietta loses her job. She files for a support modification in Massecticut. Irwin appeared in Massecticut to oppose her request. Massecticut and New Vermshire each have their own versions of the Uniform Family Support Act (UIFSA), which basically mirror each other and the Uniform Act.

130. What result?

(A) Henrietta is likely to be successful. Because Irwin appeared in Massecticut, the court will have jurisdiction and there is no dispute about whether there has been a substantial change in the circumstances.

(B) Henrietta is unlikely to win. Unless Irwin is making substantially more than he was before, he will still need the support, and he should not be punished merely because Henrietta was laid off.

(C)   Henrietta is likely to be successful, because she did nothing wrong to cause the layoff and she needs any available funds to pay her own expenses.

(D)   Henrietta is likely to be unsuccessful, because under UIFSA Massecticut would be unlikely to have subject matter jurisdiction to modify spousal support in this case.

Wylie and Winona Williams grew up in and married in Texarkana, where they lived for the first few years of their marriage. They then moved to Oklexico for a job opportunity. After a few years there, Wylie sent Winona back home to Texarkana where most of her family lived. He said that he needed some time to decide whether he was committed to remaining in the marriage. By the time that Winona had met the local residency requirement, she had learned that Wylie had been having an affair. She filed for divorce, seeking spousal support. While Wylie did not oppose the divorce, he claimed that Texarkana would not order him to pay spousal support because the court did not have jurisdiction over him, because he was not domiciled in the state.

131.   Does the Texarkana court have jurisdiction to order spousal support?

(A)   While the Texarkana court has jurisdiction to grant the divorce because Winona is domiciled there and has met the residency requirement, the court does not have jurisdiction to order spousal support because Wylie is not domiciled there.

(B)   Because Wylie is not domiciled in Texarkana, the court neither has jurisdiction to grant the divorce nor jurisdiction to order him to pay spousal support.

(C)   Lack of jurisdiction over Wylie notwithstanding, the Texarkana court has jurisdiction to grant both the divorce and spousal support.

(D)   Assuming that Winona is domiciled in Texarkana and that the Texarkana court has jurisdiction over Wylie via the state long-arm statute, the court can both grant the divorce and order Wylie to pay spousal support.

Lori Lincoln and Malcolm Morris are married with two children. They divorce and Malcolm is awarded custody and child support. Two years later, Lori receives a significant promotion at work. Malcolm's salary increases slightly over the same period. Malcolm seeks an increase in child support that Lori opposes because, she notes, the children's needs and desires are more than adequately met by the existing order.

132.   Will Lori's child support obligation be increased?

(A)   No, unless it can be shown that the needs of the children have changed, e.g., because of orthodontia or private schooling costs.

(B)   Yes, because Lori's salary has changed substantially and a child's station in life should not be tied to the station of life at the time of divorce.

(C)   No, because any other ruling would provide noncustodial parents a disincentive to working hard.

(D)   Yes, unless Lori has not been taking full advantage of her visitation rights.

Ordered to pay child support until her child, Able, has either reached age 18 or has been emancipated, Jill Johnson argues that Able is already emancipated and does not need her support.

133. Which of the following factors would not provide a basis for finding that Able should be declared emancipated?

  (A) Able has joined the Army.

  (B) Able has married his high school sweetheart.

  (C) Able is self-supporting and is living in his own apartment.

  (D) Able has impregnated his girlfriend.

Mickey Mooney and Rachel Runnington, each age 16, have married each other. This pleases Rachel's father, Thomas, who had been ordered to pay child support. However, Rachel's marriage to Mickey has been declared void by a court because neither Mickey nor Rachel, both minors, had secured the necessary parental permission before marrying. Rachel, who no longer likes Mickey, wants to go back to living with her mother, Wendy. Wendy seeks to have Thomas's child support obligation reinstated because the condition for Rachel's emancipation — marriage — has not taken place in the eyes of the law. Thomas would prefer not to start paying child support again and consults with an attorney to find out whether the support obligation can be reinstated.

134. What should the attorney tell Thomas?

  (A) Because the marriage between Mickey and Rachel was declared void by a court, that marriage will be viewed as never having existed and Thomas will not only be forced to start paying support again but will also be required to pay any missed payments during that time that the purported marriage existed.

  (B) Thomas should not worry. No state de-emancipates an emancipated child, so Thomas cannot be forced to resume payments.

  (C) Because the condition emancipating Rachel never existed in the eyes of the law, Thomas may well be forced to resume support payments, although he is unlikely to have to pay back support for payments suspended during the purported marriage.

  (D) Thomas will only be forced to resume payments if he made an independent agreement to do so in the event that the marriage was invalidated.

135. Under the Uniform Interstate Family Support Act, which of the following cannot serve as a basis for affording a state personal jurisdiction over the non-resident parent?

  (A) A letter was sent to the last known address of the non-resident parent telling him or her that a hearing would be taking place regarding a support obligation for a child of that parent.

  (B) The parent once resided with the child in the jurisdiction.

  (C) The parent conceived the child in the jurisdiction.

  (D) The parent was personally served while in the jurisdiction.

Carol and Cain Cartright are divorced and Carol is required to pay Cain spousal support until his death or remarriage. Cain has started living with Donna. Carol seeks to have her spousal support obligation ended, contending that she should not be forced to pay support if Cain is cohabiting with Donna. Carol consults an attorney.

136. What should the attorney say?

(A) If Carol had wanted spousal support to end upon Cain's cohabitation with someone else, she should have included that condition in the separation agreement incorporated into the final decree. Absent that condition having been explicitly made, no state would permit Carol to stop paying support on these facts.

(B) Because Cain and Donna are married for all intents and purposes, Cain will be treated as if he had remarried and Carol will no longer be required to pay spousal support.

(C) Jurisdictions differ with respect to whether spousal support will end upon cohabitation even where that condition was never stated explicitly, so the attorney will have to do some research (assuming that she does not know already) to find out how that issue is addressed in that particular jurisdiction.

(D) Because states do not wish to provide couples an incentive to cohabit rather than marry, courts as a general matter have interpreted the remarriage provision to include cohabitation.

Same facts as in Question 136 except that assume that Cain has started cohabiting with Donald rather than Donna.

137. What result?

(A) Even assuming that cohabitation with someone of a different sex could relieve an ex-spouse from a duty of support, only states recognizing same-sex marriage would say that cohabiting with someone of the same sex would similarly relieve a duty of support.

(B) Among those states treating cohabitation as a basis to end a spousal support obligation but refusing to recognize same-sex marriage, some will permit cohabitation with a member of either sex to relieve a duty of support while others will not.

(C) If Donald and Cain would marry if only their jurisdiction permitted them to do so, then Carol's support obligation would end. However, if Cain and Donald would not marry even if they were permitted to do so, then Carol's support obligation would not end.

(D) Whether the support obligation will end will depend upon whether Donald and Cain have registered with the state or with a private employer as domestic partners.

Rachel Roberts is a highly paid physician who has been ordered to pay child support to her ex-spouse Kim, who has custody of their child. Rachel decides that she is tired of her practice and wants to serve the poor at a much lower salary. She seeks a modification of support, which Kim opposes.

138. What result?

ANSWER:

Otto and Penelope are divorced. Otto has been ordered to pay Penelope spousal support of $2000/month until Penelope's death or remarriage. One year after the divorce is final, Otto receives a large salary increase. When Penelope learns of Otto's salary increase, she seeks to have the support increased.

139. What result?

ANSWER:

Same facts as in Question 139. However, assume that Penelope has been awarded custody of their child, Ulysses, and Penelope now seeks an increase in child support.

140. What result?

ANSWER:

Peter and Martha have lived together for a long time. They do not want to marry, but they expect to remain together for the rest of their lives. They have been trying for some time without success to have a child and they agree that Martha should undergo artificial insemination.

She undergoes insemination and eventually becomes pregnant. However, Peter suspects that Martha has been having an affair and that Martha's lover is the child's father, Martha's protestations to the contrary notwithstanding.

In part because of their continued fighting, Peter decides to leave Martha and refuses to help support or have any contact with the child born to Martha. Martha seeks to establish Peter's duty of support.

141. What result?

ANSWER:

Minnie and Melvin are divorced, with Melvin being awarded custody of their child, Nancy. Minnie has been ordered to pay support. Two years after their divorce is final, Melvin wins one million dollars in the lottery. Minnie seeks to have her support payments reduced in light of Melvin's good fortune.

142. Will Minnie's support payments be reduced?

ANSWER:

Oren and Penny live in Connivania. Oren requires medical treatment, which he approves and receives. However, Oren does not have enough money to pay the hospital, and the hospital sues Penny, Oren's wife. Penny says that she is not financially responsible, because she did not approve the procedure.

143. Will Penny be financially responsible for Oren's medical expenses?

   (A) Because Oren rather than Penny approved the procedure, only Oren can be held responsible for the medical debts owed.

(B) Assuming that Connivania still recognizes the doctrine of necessaries and applies it in a gender-neutral fashion, Penny may well be responsible for Oren's medical expenses.

(C) Because this case does not involve food, clothing or housing, the doctrine of necessaries is inapplicable and Penny will not be forced to pay anything.

(D) If it can be shown that Penny thought a less expensive procedure more suitable, then the doctrine of necessaries only makes her responsible for the lower costs associated with the treatment she preferred.

Nancy Newhouse and Ozzie Olson were married for several years. When they divorced, Nancy was ordered to pay permanent spousal support. Nancy wishes to retire, which would have a substantial impact on her income. She consults an attorney to find out whether her support obligation could be modified were she to retire.

144. What result?

ANSWER:

Barry and Linda have dated a few times but then Barry disappeared and never returned any of Linda's calls. Linda, who is pregnant, decides not to tell Barry about the pregnancy because she plans on putting the child up for adoption. When she gives birth, she claims not to know who the father is and places the child with a childless couple. One year after the adoption is finalized, Barry discovers that he has fathered a child and consults with an attorney to determine whether the adoption can be annulled.

145. What should the attorney say?

   (A) Barry can easily have the adoption annulled because his fundamental interest in parenting affords him the right to refuse to consent to an adoption.

   (B) Barry can have the adoption annulled as long as he, himself, wants to have custody of the child.

   (C) Barry can have the adoption annulled only if he and Linda would be raising the child together.

   (D) Absent some state statute or constitutional provision protecting the biological father in this kind of case, Barry will likely be unable to have the adoption annulled.

Wanda and Terry have been living together for years. Wanda announces that she is pregnant and their relationship begins to change. They argue more frequently and cannot seem to agree about anything. Eventually Wanda moves out to live with her sister. Terry is listed as the father on the birth certificate. However, he never contacts Wanda nor is contacted by her. The day after her daughter, Barbara, reaches her first birthday, Wanda meets Sam, whom she marries after a whirlwind courtship. After they have been married a year, Sam wants to adopt Barbara. Terry is notified and he objects to the adoption.

146. Will Sam be able to adopt Barbara?

   (A) No, because the acknowledged biological father objects to the adoption. However, Terry may now have to begin paying child support.

   (B) Yes, because the custodial parent agrees that it would be in Barbara's best interests to be adopted by her stepfather.

   (C) No, because as a general matter states do not allow a child to have three legal parents.

   (D) Yes, assuming that Wanda agrees and that the adoption would promote Barbara's best interests. Because Terry has neither paid child support nor established a relationship with Barbara, he is unlikely to be permitted to block the adoption.

Daniel and Eve are married and living in Famuvania. During a rocky part of their marriage, Eve has a brief affair with Frank, resulting in her becoming pregnant. During the pregnancy, Daniel and Eve see a marriage counselor. By the time that she gives birth to Connie, Daniel and Eve have worked out their differences. Famuvania law does not provide non-marital fathers with any rights over and above those guaranteed by the United States Constitution. Frank seeks either custody of or visitation with Connie.

147. Is Frank likely to be awarded custody of or visitation with Connie?

ANSWER:

Gregg and Gertrude are married and Gertrude has just found out that she is pregnant. However, she is not yet ready to have a child and wants to abort. Greg is quite ready to be a father and offers to be the primary caretaker if Gertrude will carry the child to term. Gertrude considers his offer but ultimately decides that the timing is all wrong. As the child's father, Greg seeks to enjoin Gertrude from obtaining an abortion.

148. Is the court likely to issue the injunction?

   (A) The court will issue the injunction because Gertrude has not offered a good reason to get an abortion, e.g., medical risks that would be assumed by carrying the fetus to term, and because Greg has promised to be the child's primary caretaker. In this kind of case, the state's interest in life will tip the scales in favor of the father.

   (B) The court will not issue the injunction. A woman's right to decide what happens to her own body is absolute and cannot be limited by the state or a spouse.

   (C) The court will issue the injunction. A mother cannot put a child up for adoption if that child has been born into a marriage, the husband has not consented, and the husband's parental rights have not been terminated. So, too, a mother cannot abort her child without her husband's consent unless his rights have been terminated. When the parents' fundamental rights are in equipoise, the child's best interests will determine the outcome, just as is true when parents compete for custody.

   (D) The court will not issue the injunction because the United States Constitution requires that the mother be allowed to make the ultimate decision in this kind of case.

Paula is sixteen years old and pregnant. She wishes to abort her pregnancy but state law requires that minors have parental consent before obtaining an abortion. Her parents refuse to consent to her getting an abortion and Paula challenges the law as a violation of her constitutional rights.

149. Will the constitutionality of the law be upheld?

   (A) Yes, the law is likely to be found constitutional. Just as states may require minors to obtain parental consent before marrying, states can require minors to obtain parental consent before obtaining an abortion.

   (B) No, because minors have constitutional rights just as adults do.

   (C) Yes, the law will likely be upheld, because parents have fundamental interests in the care of their children and because parents are presumed to know what is best for their own children.

(D) The law is likely to be struck down, because a statute requiring parental consent before minors can obtain abortions must include a judicial bypass option so that mature minors can obtain abortions in certain circumstances, parental objections notwithstanding.

Anne and Francisco have been married for several years and have been having difficulty conceiving, so they decide to try in vitro fertilization (IVF). They harvest several eggs from Anne and fertilize them with Francisco's sperm. A few embryos are implanted in Anne and the rest are frozen.

When learning the Anne was pregnant with twins, Anne and Francisco had very different reactions. Francisco was ecstatic but Anne had never envisioned carrying twins. Anne and Francisco began to argue incessantly and divorced shortly after the twins were born. They could agree about everything except what to do with the embryos. Anne wants them destroyed, whereas Francisco wants to keep them frozen for possible use later.

150. Assuming no prior agreement, to whom is the court likely to award the embryos?

   (A) The court will likely award to embryos to Anne. Just as a woman has the final decision with respect to whether to terminate a pregnancy, she should have the final decision about the appropriate disposition of embryos.

   (B) The court will likely award the embryos to Francisco, because his being awarded the embryos offers the only realistic chance that they might eventually be implanted and lead to live births.

   (C) The court is likely to award roughly half of the frozen embryos to Anne and the other half to Francisco, assuming that he agrees never to seek child support from Anne.

   (D) The court is likely to award the embryos to Anne, emphasizing the right not to be a parent against one's will, especially when there had been no prior agreement with respect to the disposition of the remaining embryos.

South Floraho has a law criminalizing exposure of a third-trimester fetus to illegal substances. Sarah Smith repeatedly uses cocaine during the third trimester of her pregnancy, for which she is prosecuted. Sarah challenges the law as a violation of the privacy rights guaranteed by the Fourteenth Amendment to the United States Constitution.

151. Is the South Floraho law likely to be struck down as a violation of constitutional guarantees?

   (A) Yes, because the right to privacy protects decisions regarding reproductive autonomy and this statute clearly impacts reproductive decision-making. This law will likely be considered a violation of privacy guarantees.

   (B) No, because the state has a compelling interest in preventing fetal harm, this statute will be subjected to strict scrutiny and will be held to pass muster in light of that standard.

   (C) Yes, because the state does not have a legitimate interest in paternalistically regulating what individuals do to or with their own bodies.

   (D) No, because the right to privacy does not prevent states from trying to promote the health of newborn children.

The West Nebrada Legislature has criminalized partial birth abortion within the state without incorporating an exception to preserve the life or health of the mother. The statute is challenged as a violation of constitutional guarantees.

152. Is the statute likely to be struck down as a violation of constitutional guarantees? Why or why not?
ANSWER:

Joseph Johnson and Karen Knudsen have been having an affair. When Karen and her husband, Carl, divorce, she receives no spousal support, specifically because of her adulterous behavior. Karen challenges the statutory prohibition of spousal support for those committing adultery as a violation of privacy guarantees.

153. Is the statute likely to be struck down?

(A) The statute is likely to be struck down as a violation of constitutional guarantees, because the Constitution must treat married and unmarried individuals alike.

(B) The challenge is unlikely to be successful because states have plenary power over marriage and divorce.

(C) The statute is likely to be struck down as a violation of constitutional guarantees, because the Constitution protects the right of both unmarried and married adults to engage in consensual sexual relations with another adult.

(D) The challenge is unlikely to be successful unless the state constitution provides more robust protection than does the federal constitution.

In part because of the added stress caused by moving to a new state, Quentin and Prunella decide to divorce shortly after moving to the state of Illiwa. However, the state has a one-year residency requirement, which means that Quentin and Prunella have a significant amount of time to wait before they can divorce within the state. They challenge the constitutionality of the residency requirement.

154. What result?

(A) The residency requirement is likely to be struck down because the right to marry is fundamental.

(B) The residency requirement is likely to be upheld. If the individuals had wanted to divorce, they should not have moved there in the first place.

(C) The residency requirement is likely to be upheld because states virtually have plenary power over marriage and divorce, as long as they do not impose limitation on who may marry whom that are barred by the federal or state constitutions.

(D) The residency requirement is likely to be upheld because in effect the statute merely delays rather than precludes the divorce and because the state has an important interest in preventing fraud.

The town of Famville has adopted a zoning ordinance that restricts occupancy of dwellings to single families, where a family is defined in the following way:

> One or more persons related by blood, adoption or marriage, living and cooking together as a single housekeeping unit. A number of persons, not exceeding two, living and cooking together as a housekeeping unit, though not related by blood, adoption, or marriage, shall be deemed to constitute a family.

John Jones and Sally Smith live together in a house with Sally's three minor children. They are told that John must move elsewhere because they do not constitute a family for purposes of the ordinance. John and Sally challenge the constitutionality of the ordinance.

155. Is the ordinance likely to be upheld?

    (A) The ordinance is clearly constitutional and in fact the Court has upheld a local zoning ordinance similar to the one at issue here.

    (B) The ordinance is clearly unconstitutional and in fact that Court has struck down the application of a similar ordinance to a family because it defined family too narrowly.

    (C) The local ordinance will be struck down because any ordinance defining family will violate rights of association protected by the First Amendment to the United States Constitution.

    (D) It is unclear whether this ordinance will be upheld. This family is not all related by blood, although it fits the traditional notion of family more closely than families that the Court has suggested may be regulated.

Gladys Gladstone is 39 weeks pregnant and in the hospital. She has been advised by several doctors that she should have a caesarian section both for her own sake and for the sake of the fetus. However, Gladys has religious objections to having the procedure performed. While no one questions her competency, the hospital nonetheless seeks a court order requiring her to have a caesarian.

156. Will Gladys be successful in avoiding the caesarian?

    (A) Gladys will be successful only if she can find some doctors who will testify that the fetus is not in any danger.

    (B) Gladys would have been successful if this had involved pitting her interests against those of the fetus, but because both would benefit from the caesarian, the hospital will win.

    (C) Gladys will be successful only because the procedure was so invasive. Had the procedure been less invasive, e.g., a blood transfusion, then her decision would have been overridden.

    (D) Gladys will likely be successful in avoiding a caesarian because she is competent and because this is a very invasive procedure.

Sharon and Steven Smith are deeply religious. One of the tenets of their faith is that medicine is to be avoided. Their daughter, Ruth, is ill. Normally, a child with this illness would be treated with antibiotics and everything would be fine. However, because Ruth receives no treatment, she eventually dies. The Smiths are charged with manslaughter and they claim that that United States Constitution protects them because they were merely practicing their religion.

157. Will the Smiths avoid prosecution for failing to have their daughter treated with

antibiotics?

(A)   The Smiths are protected by the United States Constitution against the state's punishing them for the exercise of their religion and cannot be prosecuted.

(B)   As long as Ruth is also a sincere believer, the Constitution will preclude the Smiths from being charged. However, if Ruth is not also a believer, then the Smiths can be charged.

(C)   While parents are entitled to believe as they wish, the state is always free to second-guess parenting practices because of the state's special interest in children.

(D)   The Smiths' claim will likely be rejected. While parents are free to believe as they wish, the Constitution does not afford them the right to sacrifice their children.

Norma is eighteen years old, although she has the mental age of a four-year-old and is very compliant. Her parents are fearful that someone will take advantage of her sexually. They have been told by several physicians that it would be devastating for Norma if she were to become pregnant. Norma's parents seek court permission to have her sterilized.

158.   What is the likely result?

(A)   She will not be sterilized. Because of the fundamental interest in procreation, Norma can only be sterilized if she herself consents.

(B)   She will likely be sterilized. Because Norma's becoming pregnant would be very burdensome for her parents, the sterilization may of course be performed.

(C)   She likely will be sterilized because both she and her child might well need state support were she to become pregnant.

(D)   Authorization is likely to be granted if it can be established that such a procedure would be in Norma's best interests and she, if competent for only a few minutes, would chose to have such a procedure performed for herself (given her own general incompetency).

Timothy Thompson, a mature seventeen year old, has a terrible disease. With invasive treatment, he has a twenty five per cent chance of recovery. Without treatment, he has no chance of recovery absent a miracle. The proposed treatment violates the religious beliefs of Timothy and his family. The state seeks to appoint a guardian to authorize treatment. Timothy and his parents oppose the appointment of the guardian.

159.   What is the likely result?

(A)   The guardian will not be appointed because both Timothy and his parents are in agreement about the treatment decision.

(B)   The guardian will be appointed because Timothy is losing a significant opportunity to overcome his disease by refusing treatment.

(C)   The guardian will likely not be appointed. However, had it been more likely than not that Timothy would have survived with treatment, then his and his parents' expressed wishes would have been overridden.

(D) It is unclear whether a guardian will be appointed. That will depend in part upon whether Timothy is viewed as sufficiently mature and informed to make such a decision for himself.

Jon and Gene Smith, a married same-sex couple, hire Lori Langenfeld to be a gestational surrogate. They use donated eggs and Gene's sperm to create the embryos. Eventually, Lori becomes pregnant. When she delivers, she is unwilling to relinquish the child, Carol. Jon and Gene sue to establish their parental rights.

160. What result?

(A) Because Lori would never have become pregnant but for her agreement to surrender the child, she will be forced to relinquish the child.

(B) Because Lori was a gestational rather than traditional surrogate, she will be forced to surrender the child. Had she been a traditional surrogate, custody would have been determined in light of the "best interests of the child" test.

(C) Jurisdictions vary greatly. While some would enforce such a gestational surrogacy agreement, others would not, instead determining custody in light of other factors, e.g., the best interests of the child.

(D) Because surrogacy contracts are void as a matter of public policy, the court will treat this custody dispute as if it were between members of a non-marital couple.

Mildred Monahan calls Mayville Department of Family Services to report possible mistreatment of a child, Agatha, in the next-door-neighbor's home. After three more calls on three separate occasions, a social worker appears, but is told that Agatha is sick with the flu. The social worker is again rebuffed on the next two attempts to see the child. Three weeks after the last unsuccessful attempt, Abigail is rushed to the emergency room where she dies from severe head injuries allegedly caused by Abigail's mother.

Arnold Adams, Abigail's father who has been away on business for the previous several months, sues Maryville Department of Family Services for having failed to protect his daughter.

161. What is the likely result of Arnold's suit?

ANSWER:

John and Mary have been married for two years. John has repeatedly expressed his dissatisfaction with the frequency with which they have sexual relations. One day in exasperation John forces himself on his wife. Mary presses charges. John claims that he cannot be charged because the United States Constitution protects marital privacy.

162. What result?

ANSWER:

Same facts as in question 162. Assume in addition that there was a criminal trial and during that trial John sought to prevent Mary from testifying against him, claiming that she cannot do so without his consent.

163. What result?

ANSWER:

The United States Supreme Court has frequently described the interest in marriage as fundamental.

164. What implications does such a designation have?

    (A) States cannot regulate marriage without offending constitutional guarantees.

    (B) While states can regulate marriage, the restrictions must promote sufficiently important interests and must be closely tailored to promote only those interests.

    (C) A marriage celebrated in accord with the law of one state must be recognized throughout the United States.

    (D) States must permit individuals to end their marriages whenever they wish to do so.

Sarah and Thomas Weingard have one child, Betty, who is in great need of a bone marrow transplant. Regrettably, neither Sarah nor Thomas is a suitable match. However, Thomas has a son, Howard, from a former marriage who might be a suitable donor. Ann, Thomas's ex-spouse and Howard's custodial parent, refuses to permit Howard to be tested to see if he would be a suitable donor. Believing that Ann's refusal is based on spite, Thomas seeks a court order requiring that Howard be tested for suitability as a donor.

165. What result?

ANSWER:

Mary Morningstar has strict religious beliefs prohibiting the use of animal by-products. For some reason, she is unable to breastfeed her newborn, Amy. Amy is allergic to soy, so soymilk is not an option. While Mary does her best to assure that Amy receives enough protein, Mary's efforts fall woefully short. Eventually, Child and Family Services removes Amy from the home. Mary challenges the removal as a denial of her constitutionally protected right to practice her religion.

166. What result?

ANSWER:

Samuel Smith, age 23, and Teresa Thomas, age 24, wish to marry in accordance with their religious beliefs. Teresa already has a husband, but the religion to which both Teresa and Samuel are adherents permits women to have more than one husband. The state in which they reside, New Mexarkana, does not allow any individual to have more than one spouse at a time, religious beliefs and customs to the contrary notwithstanding. Samuel and Teresa seek a declaratory judgment that the New Mexarkana law, as applied, violates federal constitutional guarantees.

167. The court hearing the challenge is likely to hold the following:

    (A) The marriage statute abridges the fundamental right to marry and hence is unconstitutional.

(B) The marriage statute is rationally related to a legitimate state interest and hence is constitutional.

(C) The marriage statute is unconstitutional as applied because it violates the Free Exercise Clause.

(D) The marriage statute is constitutional even under strict scrutiny.

The Wiskegan State Legislature holds hearings to reduce the deficit. There is testimony that the state pays out substantial sums to support children living in poor households and that an individual who is unable to meet current child support obligations is likely to be unable to support additional children. The Legislature decides that because money would be saved were there fewer Wiskegan children requiring state assistance, noncustodial parents behind in their child support payments will be prohibited from marrying absent a waiver. A waiver will be granted if an individual can establish that he or she can meet current support obligation and is likely to be able to meet those obligations in the future.

Mary Martin is the noncustodial parent of a child. However, Mary cannot meet her current support obligations. Wishing to marry Nigel Nathanson, she has applied for a waiver but has been unsuccessful. Mary challenges the Wiskegan law as a violation of her federal constitutional rights.

168. Will Mary's challenge be successful?

ANSWER:

Although unmarried, Alvin Adams and Barbara Birney have been living together for a long time in New Caledonia, which does not recognize de facto or psychological parents. They decide that they are finally ready to have a child together. Regrettably, Alvin is sterile so they agree that Barbara should be artificially inseminated with sperm from an anonymous donor. Eventually, Barbara gives birth to a child, Carole, whom Alvin and Barbara raise for the next six years. During this period, Barbara grows very close to a friend at work, John, until she discovers that her feelings for him are not merely platonic. Barbara leaves Alvin, and she and Carole move into John's house. Barbara refuses to let Alvin see Carole, and Alvin consults an attorney to explore whether he is likely to be awarded custody of or visitation with Carole.

169. What should the attorney tell Alvin?

   (A) A man cannot be recognized as a child's father if his partner was artificially inseminated with a different man's sperm.

   (B) Alvin may well not succeed. He would have been must more likely to have been awarded custody had he adopted Carole or had he married Barbara before Carole's birth.

   (C) As long as Carole views Alvin as her father, he will be awarded custody or visitation.

   (D) As long as the court finds that Carole's best interest would be promoted by her continuing to have contact with Alvin, he will be awarded visitation at the very least.

Gerald and Henrietta Isaacs have been married for several years and have been trying to have a child. Testing reveals that Gerald is sterile. He and Henrietta decide that she should be artificially inseminated and commit that understanding to writing. Eventually, she gives birth to a child, Peter. Regrettably, shortly after Peter's birth, the marriage falls apart. Gerald denies that he is Peter's father, because he can prove that he and Peter are not genetically related and because he and Peter do not have a strong emotional bond. Seeking child support, Henrietta argues that Gerald is Peter's father, lack of genetic or emotional connection notwithstanding.

170. What result?

   (A) To establish paternity, a man must show that he has a genetic connection to the child and, in addition, has a relationship with the child. Gerald will not be found to be Peter's father.

   (B) As long as Gerald challenges his paternity within the period specified by local law, he will be recognized as not being Peter's father. However, had Gerald sat on his rights, he likely would have been recognized as Peter's father.

   (C) Gerald is likely to be found to be Peter's father or, perhaps, estopped from denying paternity.

(D)   Because Gerald was married to Henrietta when she gave birth to Peter, he will be found to be Peter's father.

Susan is not currently seeing anyone but would like very much to raise a child. She contacts a law school friend, Byron, explaining that she would like him to provide the sperm with which she will be artificially inseminated. Byron agrees.

Although ecstatic after giving birth to Zelda, Susan is dismayed when Byron makes clear that he wants to play a parental role in Zelda's life. Susan refuses to allow Byron to see Zelda, and Byron seeks to establish his parental rights in court.

171.   What result?

(A)   It is unclear how this case will be decided. Much will depend upon the explicit or implicit agreement between Susan and Byron when he provided the sperm.

(B)   Because Susan became pregnant through artificial insemination rather than coital relations, Byron is unlikely to be found Zelda's legal parent.

(C)   Assuming that Byron can establish his genetic connection to Zelda, he will be held to be her father regardless of how conception occurred.

(D)   Because Susan will have custody of Zelda in any event, the determination of who will be allowed to have contact with Zelda must be left up to Susan's discretion.

Wally and Wendy Wallinger have been the foster parents of Bobby, age 3, for two years. They wish to adopt him, but Bobby's mother, Anita, retains her parental rights. In the same proceeding, Anita's parental rights are terminated and the Wallingers become Bobby's adoptive parents. On appeal, the trial court decision is reversed.

172.   Which of the following rationales might plausibly explain the appellate court's decision to reverse?

(A)   Because Bobby was too young to express a preference, the adoption had to be deferred until he could articulate a deliberate and informed choice about who should be parenting him.

(B)   Because Anita's rights were terminated in the very proceeding in which the adoption was granted, it would be too tempting for the court to compare Anita's parenting skills to those of the Wallingers when deciding whether her rights should be terminated.

(C)   Because the Wallingers had been doing the parenting over the past two years, they had an unfair advantage — if, indeed, Anita's parental rights should have been terminated, then Bobby should have been awarded to someone new.

(D)   Because Anita opposed Bobby's adoption by the Wallingers, the adoption should not have been granted.

Gladys and Herbert Stoningham desperately wish to adopt a child. They meet with Sonia Cunningham, who is pregnant and wishes to put her child up for adoption. Sonia will consent to the Stoninghams adopting the child if they will consent to an open adoption. The Stoninghams agree.

Sonia gives birth to a little girl, Wanda, who is adopted by the Stoninghams. Sonia gets to see Wanda every month. However, two months after the adoption is final, Sonia starts to criticize the Stoninghams for their parenting practices. The Stoninghams retaliate by refusing to let Sonia see Wanda. Sonia seeks to have the open adoption agreement enforced or, in the alternative, the adoption declared void.

173. What result?

(A) Because open adoptions are those adoptions that have not yet been finalized, the open adoption agreement is no longer in force once the adoption has been made final. Sonia's suit will be dismissed.

(B) Because open adoptions in effect permit the biological parent to retain her parental rights, the Stoninghams must try to implement Sonia's parenting suggestions in good faith or else be at risk of losing their own parental rights.

(C) Because states vary with respect to how and whether open adoptions are enforceable, the availability of a remedy for Sonia will depend upon local law.

(D) Because open adoptions are simply adoptions where the medical histories of an adoptees' biological parents are made available to facilitate disease detection and cure, Sonia did not acquire any enforceable rights by virtue of her having entered into an open adoption. Her suit will be dismissed.

Bill Billingsley, a widower, and Jill Johnson, a widow, have married. Each has children from a first marriage and each wants to take advantage of the stepparent exception permitted under local law.

174. What is each hoping to do?

(A) Each is hoping to help raise the other's children without thereby becoming financially responsible for those children should the marital relationship end.

(B) Each wants to adopt the other's children without forcing the other parent to give up parental rights as a condition of the adoption going forward.

(C) Each wants to be respected as a parent by the other's children.

(D) Each seeks to be treated as a de facto parent entitled to possible visitation with the other's children should the marriage end.

Yolanda Young has agreed to place her newborn child with the Zollingers, who have agreed to pay Yolanda whatever would be permissible under Wyoxico law, which is in accord with the majority of states on this issue.

175. How much if anything can the Zollingers give Yolanda in compensation?

(A) The Zollingers cannot offer Yolanda any money, because money changing hands would constitute baby-selling which all states prohibit.

(B) The Zollingers can pay whatever amount the parties can agree on as long as a court finds that the adoption would promote the bests interests of the child.

(C) The Zollingers can pay the reasonable expenses associated with the birth as well as reasonable attorney and, perhaps, counseling fees.

(D) The Zollingers cannot give anything to Yolanda directly but can pay whatever fees are determined to be appropriate by a licensed attorney.

176. What is an equitable adoption?

(A) An equitable adoption is an adoption that rewards functioning parents for their services to a child. The paradigmatic example involves permitting foster parents to legally adopt the child for whom they have been caring.

(B) An equitable adoption involves an adoptee who was not formally adopted but who nonetheless was treated as if she had been formally adopted. Where an equitable adoption is recognized, the individual can inherit from the adults raising her if they die intestate.

(C) An equitable adoption is one that treats all parties fairly, where, for example, the would-be adoptive parents are not asked to pay too much but also where the biological parent receives something for her expenses.

(D) An equitable adoption is one that considers the effects of an adoption on all of the interested parties so that, for example, a couple will not be able to split twins or triplets and only adopt one of the children.

Mary Mooney gives birth to Barbara Mooney in the state of South Floramba. Mary, who is quite poor, agrees to relinquish her parental rights if her neighbors, Walter and Tess Anderson, will adopt Barbara. Barbara lives with the Andersons, is treated by them as their daughter, and is held out to the community as their daughter. However, they never formally adopt her. When Barbara is sixteen, Walter dies, leaving everything to Tess. Tragically, when Barbara is eighteen years old, Tess dies intestate. Arguing that she is Tess's sole surviving relative, Tess's sister, Winona, claims the entire estate. Barbara consults an attorney to see if she has any options.

177. What should the attorney say?

ANSWER:

Assume the same facts as in Question 177. Assume further that Barbara is found to have been equitably adopted by the Andersons. Suppose that Barbara's biological mother, Mary, wins the lottery and upon being apprised of her good fortune, has a heart attack and dies intestate.

178. Would Barbara having been equitably adopted by the Andersons preclude her from inheriting her mother's estate? Why or why not?

ANSWER:

179. What does a second parent adoption involve?

(A) A process whereby a parent's new spouse establishes a legal relationship with the parent's child.

(B) A process whereby a child who had once been adopted by one family is now adopted by another family.

(C) A process by which an individual who has successfully adopted one child performs the same process again so that the child can have a new sibling.

(D) A process whereby a parent's non-marital partner establishes a legal relationship with the parent's child.

Ken and Jill, who have both sworn never to marry again, have been living together for three years with Jill's four-year-old son, Oscar, in the state of Famuvania. Jill's ex-husband's parental rights were terminated the previous year and Ken wishes to adopt Oscar. Ken consults an attorney to find out what he must do to adopt Oscar.

180. What should the attorney say?

ANSWER:

181. What is an adult adoption?

(A) An adoption that is not finalized until after the adopted individual reaches majority, notwithstanding that the process commenced while the individual was still a minor.

(B) An adoption of an adult by another adult.

(C) An adoption of an individual who is an adult chronologically but not mentally.

(D) An adoption that does not take place until the adopted individual is an adult, although the relationship between the adopter and the adoptee began while the latter was still a child.

John Jones and Karen Killingham had two children together, Penelope and Richard. John and Karen no longer live together. Over the past few years, Karen has only paid child support sporadically and has spoken to her children on the telephone about once or twice a year. John seeks to have Karen's parental rights terminated because he wants his current spouse to adopt the children. John argues that Karen has abandoned the children.

182. What result?

(A) Because Karen never left her children in an unknown place without appropriate supervision, she will not be found to have abandoned her children.

(B) Because Karen has only paid sporadic support and has only had occasional phone contact with the children, she may well be found to have abandoned them.

(C) Karen cannot be found to have abandoned her children as long as she cannot be shown to have had a settled intention not to see or support them ever again.

(D)   Because Karen has paid some support for and maintained some contact with the children, she cannot be found to have abandoned them.

Able and Bettina have been living together with Bettina's children, Wayne and Xerxes, for several years. Carl, Bettina's ex-spouse, has a good relationship with the children, although he does not get to see them very often. One day, Bettina is killed in a terrible auto accident. Carl and Able each seek custody of Wayne and Xerxes. The guardian ad litem suggests that Able has a better relationship with the children and so should be awarded custody.

183.   What result?

(A)   As the sole remaining legal parent, Carl must be awarded custody.

(B)   Assuming that the guardian ad litem's testimony is accepted as accurate with respect to whose having custody would better promote the children's interests, Able is likely to be awarded custody.

(C)   Carl is likely to be awarded custody because he has a good relationship with the children and there is no showing that he is an unfit parent.

(D)   Under these circumstances, the court is likely to order shared custody.

John has two children from a previous marriage, Adam and Bernice. John meets and marries Matilda, who develops a very good relationship with the children. Regrettably, after several years, the marriage falls apart. While Matilda does not dispute that John should have custody of the children, she challenges his request for child support.

184.   Will John be able to get child support for Adam and Bernice?

(A)   John is unlikely to be awarded child support. Because a stepparent does not have a duty of support during the marriage absent exceptional circumstances, the stepparent generally will not have a duty of support once the marital relationship ends.

(B)   John is unlikely to be awarded support. While a stepparent generally has a duty of support during the marriage, that duty of support generally does not survive the dissolution of the marriage.

(C)   John is likely to be awarded support. Because stepparents as a general matter have a duty of support during the marriage, they will also have such a duty if the marriage breaks down.

(D)   John is likely to be awarded support. Because John and Matilda remained together for several years and because Matilda developed a good relationship with the children, she will likely have a duty of support imposed.

Assume the facts of 184. Assume also that Matilda seeks court-ordered visitation but nonetheless challenges the request for child support.

185.   What is the likely result?

(A)   If Matilda is granted visitation, she will also be ordered to pay child support.

(B) Because Matilda is neither the children's biological nor adoptive parent, she cannot be awarded visitation or custody rights.

(C) Matilda might be awarded visitation rights if that would promote the best interests of the children while nonetheless not having a support obligation imposed.

(D) Matilda is unlikely to be awarded visitation rights. However, because imposing a duty of support would of course benefit the children, she will likely have that obligation imposed.

Nancy and Oscar have been married for several years. Recently, they have decided to divorce, in part because they cannot agree about the religious views that they should be imparting to their children. Nancy agrees that if she has custody, she will teach them about both Oscar's and her own religious views.

After the divorce, Nancy's religious views evolve. She now believes that exposing her children to Oscar's beliefs would put them at risk of eternal damnation and so she refuses to do what she had once agreed to do. Oscar seeks to have their prior agreement enforced or, in the alternative, a modification of custody.

186. What result?

(A) Nancy must abide by her agreement with Oscar or risk losing custody of the children.

(B) Nancy cannot be forced to teach Oscar's religious beliefs, although he can instruct the children about his beliefs should he wish to do so. Further, Nancy will not lose custody merely because she refuses to instruct the children as previously agreed.

(C) Because Nancy's beliefs have changed since the divorce, she cannot be held to the agreement she had made at the time of the divorce. However, if she now professed the same beliefs that she had professed at the time of the agreement, she would either have to abide by the agreement or risk losing the children.

(D) Nancy's refusal to instruct the children as agreed constitutes a material change in circumstances which would justify a modification in custody, especially if Oscar is willing to instruct the children about both his own and Nancy's beliefs.

Sarah and Thomas, who were of different faiths when they married, have two children, Able and Betty. Eventually, Sarah and Thomas divorce with Sarah being awarded custody and Thomas being awarded liberal visitation. It has recently come to Sarah's attention that Thomas has been telling the children that all people who do not believe as he does will burn in everlasting hell once they die. Sarah seeks to enjoin her ex-spouse from saying this to the children, especially because they do not share his religious beliefs.

187. Is Sarah's attempt to enjoin Thomas from making these comments likely to be successful?

(A) Because the custodial parent determines the children's religious upbringing, Sarah's request will likely be granted.

(B) The court is unlikely to grant Sarah's request because doing so would implicate constitutional guarantees of freedom of speech.

(C) The court is unlikely to grant Sarah's request because doing so would implicate constitutional guarantees regarding the free exercise of religion.

(D)   The court is likely to grant Sarah's request only if Thomas's comments are found to cause or likely to cause significant harm to the children.

Alexandra and Benjamin have been dating for several months. One day, they have a terrible fight. Three days later, Alexandra texts Benjamin announcing that she is pregnant. He immediately texts back that he is probably one of ten who might be the father, but that he is nonetheless willing to help her get an abortion.

Rather than get an abortion, Alexandra decides that she will put the child up for adoption. She eventually gives birth and places the child with a couple who had long wished to be parents. About three months after the adoption had been finalized, a friend mentions to Benjamin in passing that Alexandra had put a child up for adoption. Benjamin figures out that he is likely the father and seeks to establish his parental rights.

188.   What result?

ANSWER:

John and Karen have been dating sporadically, although each has a heavy workload and it is not uncommon for them to go several weeks without communicating to each other. Karen calls John, asking him to return her call. John is swamped at work and does not return the call for a few weeks, leaving a message. When Karen returns his call a few weeks later, he leaves a message. After awhile, neither calls to leave a message.

Karen never mentioned in her messages that she was pregnant. When she gave birth, she listed the father as "Unknown" on the birth certificate and put the child up for adoption. A few days after the child had been placed, John hears what had happened from a friend. John contacts Karen, who admits that he was the father. John consults an attorney so that he can establish his parental rights.

189.   What result?

ANSWER:

Zeke and Yolanda are married and live in Missabama, which recognizes actions for criminal conversation. Zeke and Wendy meet at a Parent-Teacher Conference night, and find that they have a lot in common while they wait to talk to the teacher. They eventually decide to empty the family checking accounts and move to Las Vegas to start a new life together.

Yolanda consults an attorney to find out whether the state affords any remedies to someone in her position.

190. What should the attorney say?

   (A) The attorney should say that Yolanda may well be able to have civil damages imposed if it can be established that Zeke and Wendy engaged in criminal conversation by having sexual relations while Zeke was still married to Yolanda.

   (B) The attorney should say that Yolanda may well be able to have civil damages imposed if it can be established that Zeke and Wendy engaged in criminal conversation by conspiring to steal family monies from the different checking accounts.

   (C) The attorney should say that Yolanda may well be able to have a criminal prosecution initiated if it can be established that Zeke and Wendy engaged in criminal conversation by having sexual relations while Zeke was still married to Yolanda.

   (D) The attorney should say that Yolanda may well be able to have a criminal prosecution initiated if it can be established that Zeke and Wendy engaged in criminal conversation by conspiring to steal family monies from the different checking accounts.

Assume the facts contained in Question 190. However, assume that the Missabama Legislature passes a statute precluding criminal conversation actions. Also assume that Missabama still permits alienation of affections claims to be brought.

191. What should the attorney say when Yolanda comes to find out whether the state affords any remedies to someone in her position?

   (A) The attorney should say that Yolanda will likely be able to recover civil damages if and only if it can be established that by having sexual relations with him, Wendy alienated Zeke's affections for his wife, Yolanda.

   (B) The attorney should say that Yolanda will likely be able to recover civil damages if it can be established that Wendy intentionally alienated Zeke's affections for his wife, Yolanda.

   (C) The attorney should say that Yolanda will likely be able to recover civil damages if it can be established that Zeke fell in love with Wendy, which caused him to fall out of love with Yolanda.

(D) The attorney should say that Yolanda will likely be able to have civil damages imposed if it can be established that Wendy through her actions caused Yolanda's children to hate their father, Zeke.

Donald, a widower, is stopped at a red light when Ned negligently rams into the car. Donald suffers severe injuries and his minor child, Abigail, sues Ned for loss of consortium.

192. What result?

(A) While loss of consortium is available for a spouse, it is not available for a child.

(B) Loss of consortium is an available cause of action whenever an individual has lost a loved one.

(C) Because loss of consortium refers to the loss of sexual relations, it can only be asserted by someone who was having sexual relations with the injured individual.

(D) While this is a matter of state law, many states permits children to bring a loss of consortium claim but do not permit any and all individuals who have a sexual relationship with the victim to bring a claim.

William and Terry plan to marry in a year and William has given Terry a beautiful engagement ring. A few months before the wedding is to take place, William realizes that he simply is not ready to marry anyone and so calls off the wedding and asks for the ring back. Terry refuses. William sues for its return.

193. What is the likely result?

(A) Terry may well be ordered to return the ring, although some jurisdictions will not require a ring to be returned if the individual giving the ring is at fault for the breakdown of the relationship.

(B) Because William is calling off the wedding, Terry will likely be permitted to keep the ring.

(C) Because the ring was given in anticipation of marriage, it should be treated as belonging to both. The ring must be sold and the proceeds distributed equitably.

(D) Because the ring was a gift, Terry can keep it regardless of why the wedding was called off or by whom.

Carol and Donald Everson each have a family history of having a particular dreadful disease. They each undergo genetic testing to find out the likelihood that their child would have the disease. They are assured that they are no more likely to have a child with the disease than is any other couple.

Carol and Donald have a child, Edward, who is diagnosed with the dread disease. They later discover that those doing the genetic testing had mislabeled the blood samples, so that the Eversons were wrongly told that they did not have an elevated risk of having a child with the disease and another couple was wrongly told that they did have an increased risk of having a child with the dread disease. The Eversons sue the genetic counselor for damages.

194. What result?

(A) The Eversons will likely be successful as long as they can establish that they would not have conceived had they been told about the increased risks, and that they suffered emotional and financial harm because of the negligence regarding their test results.

(B) The Eversons are unlikely to be successful because having a child cannot constitute a harm as a matter of law.

(C) The Eversons are unlikely to be successful because they knew from their family histories that there was a chance that their child would have the disease.

(D) The Eversons are unlikely to be successful because it is against public policy to promote parents saying that they wish that they had not had their child.

Assume the same facts as in Question 194. However assume that the Eversons sue for wrongful life.

195. Are the Eversons more likely to be successful because they sued for wrongful life?

(A) No, because very few jurisdictions recognize a cause of action for wrongful life and even in these a very high threshold must be met to be successful in the claim that the child would have been better off never having lived than having lived her life.

(B) Yes, because the harm associated with having the disease was not incurred by them but by their child.

(C) No, because no jurisdiction recognizes a cause of action which essentially claims that an individual would have been better off never having been born.

(D) Yes, because a wrongful birth claim might be time-barred under the state's statute of limitations, while the wrongful life claim on behalf of a child might not yet be time-barred.

Barbara and Billy Bassingham have three children and are having great difficulty in making ends meet. Barbara decides to have a tubal ligation so that the couple does not have any more children. Regrettably, the procedure is performed improperly and Barbara eventually becomes pregnant and gives birth to a healthy baby boy. The Bassinghams sue the doctor who negligently performed the procedure for wrongful conception.

196. What result?

(A) Because the birth of a healthy child is a boon rather than a harm, no jurisdiction would permit recovery under these facts.

(B) Because Barbara would have aborted the child, she will be found to have failed to mitigate the harm and thus will be precluded from recovery.

(C) Because Barbara and Billy clearly did not wish to have another child, most jurisdictions would permit the cause of action and award them the average costs associated with raising a child through majority.

(D) The Bassinghams may well be able to recover some of the expenses associated with the pregnancy, e.g., lost wages or pain and suffering, but most jurisdictions would not permit them to recover the costs of raising the child.

Melinda Mercury is a grade-school teacher living in New Jervania. She is pregnant and has just discovered that one of her pupils has been diagnosed with German Measles. Melinda calls her doctor, who assures her that her fetus would not be harmed by exposure to the disease. When she gives birth, Melinda discovers that her child has severe birth defects, likely caused by exposure to German Measles during the first trimester. Melinda sues her doctor for wrongful birth, a cause of action recognized in New Jervania.

197. What result?

   (A) Melinda will likely be successful if she can establish that she would have aborted her child had she been apprised of the severe risks presented.

   (B) Melinda will likely be unsuccessful because she assumed the risk by being a grade-school teacher.

   (C) Melinda will be successful only if she can establish that the doctor could have done something during the pregnancy to reduce the risk that her child would be harmed by the exposure.

   (D) Melinda is unlikely to be successful unless she can show that she was exposed to German Measles at the doctor's office.

Steve is the custodial parent of a beautiful and vivacious four-year-old daughter, Virginia, who loves to play with dogs. Steve has repeatedly warned her not to approach any dog that she does not know. One day, while Steve is watching Virginia play in her sandbox, Steve receives a call from an important client. Engrossed in the conversation, Steve does not notice that a pit bull has come into their yard.

The dog attacks Virginia. Fortunately, a neighbor was eventually able to rescue Virginia, but not before she suffered severe injuries. Steve's ex-wife, Dolly, sues Steve on behalf of their daughter for negligent supervision.

198. Will this suit on behalf of Virginia be successful?

   (A) No. No jurisdiction permits a child to sue her parent. Otherwise, parents would be subjected to a barrage of suits for perceived parenting errors of commission or omission.

   (B) Possibly, if the state has abolished parent-child immunity. The availability of insurance may mean that the suit would be the only way the family could avoid financial ruin from all of the expensive medical bills.

   (C) Yes, in all of the states. But for Steve's failure to adequately supervise his daughter, she would not have suffered these grievous injuries.

   (D) No, whether or not the state has abrogated parent-child immunity, the dog owner rather than Steve is liable for Virginia's injuries.

Winston and his son, Robert, live in North Alanoia, which recognizes parent-child immunity. Winston has a bad temper and frequently beats his young son. The physical abuse continues through Robert's teenage years. When Robert turns eighteen, he moves out of his father's house and sues him for the physical abuse that had been endured for years.

199. Is Robert's suit likely to be successful?

(A) Yes, many states that recognize parent-child immunity do not extend that immunity to intentional torts.

(B) No. Those states recognizing parent-child immunity preclude a child from suing his parent in tort.

(C) Yes, but only if Winston is successfully prosecuted.

(D) No, unless the Legislature has expressly limited parent-child immunity so that no protection is afforded for those parents who physically abuse their children.

Joan Johnson is driving Bonnie, her spouse, to the grocery store. They are having a spirited political discussion and Joan does not pay close enough attention to the traffic. Joan has to turn sharply to avoid an oncoming car, which hits their car anyway.

Joan and Bonnie live in Pennio, a comparative negligence state that has abrogated spousal immunity. The negligent driver, Sarah, is found by the jury to be 90% responsible for the serious injuries suffered by Bonnie in the crash, whereas Joan is found to be 10% responsible for those injuries. Bonnie sues Sarah, who seeks contribution from Joan.

200. What result?

(A) Because Bonnie would have sued Joan if Bonnie had wanted to do so, Sarah will be entirely responsible for the harms that she caused.

(B) Because Joan is partially responsible for Bonnie's injuries and because Joan and Bonnie are married, Bonnie's suit against Sarah will be barred.

(C) Because spousal immunity has been abrogated, Bonnie could have sued Joan and Sarah will likely to permitted to seek contribution from Joan.

(D) Because permitting Sarah to seek contribution from Joan would in effect reduce valuable and possibly needed family resources, Sarah will likely be barred from seeking contribution from Joan.

On the first day of the school year, Darla meets a little girl, Daniella, who has just moved into the district. Darla's mother, Francesca, hopes that this year her child will stop getting into trouble at school.

Three weeks after they first meet, Darla and Daniella have a playdate at a local playground. Darla pushes Daniella off a slide, causing Daniella severe injuries. Before too long, Francesca learns that she is being sued for the injuries that Darla caused. Francesca consults an attorney to find out whether she can be held liable for the injuries her daughter caused.

201. What should the attorney say?

(A) Francesca is strictly liable for any injuries caused by Darla.

(B) Francesca is strictly liable for any injuries intentionally or negligently caused by Darla.

(C) Because Francesca did not encourage Darla to cause the injury, Francesca cannot be liable for any injuries caused by Darla.

(D)   Depending upon the jurisdiction, Francesca may well be liable if she did not adequately supervise Darla and the injuries caused by Darla were reasonably foreseeable.

The Cunninghams wish to adopt a healthy boy of average intelligence with no known psychological or emotional difficulties. They are assured by Your Dreams Come True, a private agency that places children in adoptive homes, that Shawn is a healthy toddler in need of placement.

The Cunninghams are overjoyed. They notice that Shawn is somewhat quiet and withdrawn but figure that it may take some time before he comes comfortable with his new surroundings. Shawn continues to be quiet even after the adoption is made final. A few months later, Shawn starts to engage in very destructive behavior, including trying to set the house afire one night. Much to their consternation, the Cunninghams discover not only that Shawn has severe psychological difficulties, but that Your Dreams Come True had been aware of Shawn's diagnosis. The Cunninghams sue Your Dreams Come True for damages.

202.   What kinds of damages, if any, are the Cunninghams likely to recover?

   (A)   The Cunninghams are likely to recover the extraordinary costs associated with raising Shawn including, for example, counseling costs or, perhaps, the costs associated with institutionalizing him should that be deemed necessary.

   (B)   The Cunninghams are not likely to recover anything because adoption agencies cannot be thought to guarantee that adoptive parents will be happy with their children.

   (C)   The Cunninghams are likely to recover all of the costs associated with raising him through his reaching majority.

   (D)   Because Shawn may well not be able to support himself once he reaches adulthood and because the Cunninghams may well continue to be financially responsible for him even when he is an adult, the adoption agency will likely be responsible for the costs associated with providing for Shawn for the rest of his life.

Assume that same facts as in Question 202. However, also assume that the Cunninghams not only seek monetary damages but also seek to undo the adoption.

203.   Will the Cunninghams be successful in their attempt to have the adoption declared void?

   (A)   No. Once an adoption is final, the child is viewed by the law as if the child had been born into the family. Just as one cannot pretend that a birth had never occurred, one cannot pretend that a final adoption had never occurred.

   (B)   Yes. If one can return a defective product, then one of course can return a defective child.

   (C)   While jurisdictions vary, some will permit adoptions to be abrogated if an agency affirmatively misleads parents about important facts rather than merely negligently fails to discover or disclose such facts.

   (D)   While the adoption cannot be abrogated, the agency might not only be forced to pay the costs incurred in raising Shawn but they may also be required to afford the Cunninghams the first opportunity to adopt the next suitable child.

Rob and Sarah Wilson are divorced, with Sarah having custody of their six-year-old child, Chastity. One day, Rob calls Sarah to ask if it is O.K. if Chastity comes for the weekend because it will be Grandpa

Wilson's seventieth birthday celebration. Sarah calls Rob's father and is told that they are indeed having a weekend celebration and that they would very much like Chastity to come. Rob's father assures Sarah that everything will be fine.

Chastity goes to her grandfather's house. Sarah calls several times to check on Chastity but Chastity is always busy or asleep. The next Monday, Chastity does not come home. When Sarah calls, Rob's father claims that Rob had left early that morning to return her. After hearing nothing for a few more days, Sarah hires a private detective who eventually locates Rob and Chastity in Canada. Sarah discovers that there had been no party and that Rob's father had conspired with Rob to remove Chastity from the state.

204. What is the likelihood that Sarah will be successful when she sues Rob and his father for intentional interference with the parent's custodial relationship?

(A) While Rob is subject to criminal and civil penalties for taking his daughter out of the country, Rob's father cannot be sued on these facts.

(B) Both Rob and his father may be liable on these facts unless they have some legally valid justification or excuse.

(C) While Rob's father is potentially liable here, Rob cannot be sued because he is Chastity's legal parent.

(D) Because such a suit would make it difficult for Chastity to have good relations with her family members, the suit will be barred as a matter of public policy.

Harry and Icarus are divorced in the state of Libertania. Harry has custody of their three-year-old son, Daedalus, and Icarus is awarded overnight visitation with Daedalus every other weekend. The first time that Icarus goes to pick up Daedalus at Harry's home, no one is there. The second time, the same thing happens. While getting to see Daedalus occasionally, Icarus grows tired of Harry's transparently false excuses and sues Harry for intentional interference with a parental relationship.

205. What result?

(A) Icarus will likely be awarded money damages to compensate him for his many lost opportunities with his son.

(B) Even assuming that Harry has no legally valid justification or excuse, Icarus will be successful if and only if Libertania recognizes a cause of action for intentional interference with the parent's custodial relationship.

(C) Even if Libertania recognizes a cause of action for intentional interference with the parent's custodial relationship, it may well not recognize an analogous cause of action for the interference with the noncustodial parent's relationship. Icarus is unlikely to be successful at least in part because money damages awarded to Icarus might be viewed as monies that might otherwise be used to provide for Daedalus.

(D) Icarus will be awarded damages and may in addition be awarded custody unless Harry becomes more cooperative.

Wilhemina and Thomas Sullivan have been having marital difficulties and are separated in the state of Missamba. Wilhemina meets Stan and they start to date. Thomas learns of Wilhemina's relationship with Stan and sues for criminal conversation and alienation of affections.

206. What result?

ANSWER:

Penny and Peter Robinson live in Tortsylvania. They are home with their three-year-old child, Rollie, who has discovered the joys of playing with the neighbor's cat, Sadie. Penny believes that Peter is watching Rollie, while Peter believes that Penny is watching Rollie. Unbeknownst to his parents, Rollie goes out the front door to play with Sadie. For some reason, Sadie crosses the street. Rollie follows and does not notice the approaching car, which hits him. The Robinsons sue the negligent driver, who argues that the Robinsons were themselves negligent in their failure to properly supervise Rollie.

207. What result?

ANSWER:

Maurice and Nancy Osterbrook have been married for ten years in Texahoma. They have twins, Samantha and Roberta. One day, after Maurice has said something nasty to Nancy, Nancy responds, "Have you ever wondered why Samantha and Roberta look nothing like you? That is because Robert Smith is their father." She then marches out of the house to pick up Samantha and Roberta at school to take them to their grandmother's house.

208. Will Maurice be successful when he sues Nancy for intentional infliction of emotional distress in the divorce action?

ANSWER:

John and Jim have lived together for years. While they could enter into a civil union in Georgiana, their home state, they have decided not to do so. One day, John is walking several steps ahead of Jim in a parking lot when John is hit by a car whose driver is focused on texting. While John was never in any physical danger, he is devastated by seeing Jim run over by the car and John sues for negligent infliction of emotional distress.

209. What result?

ANSWER:

Alice and Bennett Campbell are having marital difficulties and they go to consult an attorney, Tom Thompson. Tom listens to them for awhile, believes that they can salvage their marriage, and urges them to reconcile. Tom charges them a small consulting fee. Eventually, Alice files for a divorce. Bennett comes to see Tom, explaining that Alice has filed and asking Tom to represent him. After making clear that paying Tom's fee will not pose any difficulty, Bennett admits that he has been having an affair. Tom explains that he refuses to represent anyone who has been having an affair. Tom immediately calls Alice, suggesting that she hire him. Alice fires her attorney and does quite well in the distribution of marital assets.

210. Tom would not be subject to professional discipline if only he:

(A) had not called Alice asking her if she wanted him to represent her.

(B) had refused to represent either of them after the initial consultation.

(C) had agreed to represent Bennett when asked to do so.

(D) had not done anything differently than described above, because he would not be subject to discipline for representing Alice on these facts.

Esther and Donna have decided to divorce. They consult Laura Lawyer about representing them both. Laura explains in writing that she would be representing both of them and that she would not be looking out for the interests of one to the detriment of the other. They agree, hire her and are both quite pleased by the result. Someone nonetheless reports Laura to the Office of Disciplinary Counsel and the issue at hand is whether Laura should be subject to discipline.

211. What result?

(A) As to whether dual representation is permissible in a divorce even with full disclosure, this is a matter of local law. Some states have a per se bar against such representation, whereas other states do not.

(B) Because the clients were satisfied, Laura cannot be sanctioned.

(C) Because Laura fully disclosed in writing and did exactly what she said that she would do, Laura cannot be sanctioned.

(D) Because there was a possibility that either Esther or Donna would be dissatisfied, Laura is subject to discipline.

Gary is a stay-at-home dad who wants to divorce his wife, Gladys, although he fears that he will be unable to afford an attorney because he is entirely dependent upon Gladys's income. Gary talks to Ann Attorney, who is willing to represent Gary on a contingency fee basis. Gary does very well in the distribution of property and in the amount of spousal and child support awarded. However, Gary now believes that the agreed upon one-third contingency fee arrangement is excessive.

212. What is the likely result when Ann sues Gary for her fee?

  (A) While some states prohibit contingency fee arrangements in divorce, others permit them, so this will be a question of local law.

  (B) States have long permitted contingency fee arrangements. Unless Gary can show why the contingency fee arrangement in these circumstances violated public policy because involving an exorbitant rate, Gary will be required to pay what he owes.

  (C) Contingency fee arrangements in the domestic relations context violate public policy because providing a disincentive to the attorney to encourage reconciliation. Gary will not be forced to pay anything.

  (D) While contingency fee arrangements in the domestic relations context violate public policy because providing an incentive to the attorney to encourage divorce, Gary will nonetheless be required to pay unless he can show that but for Ann's encouragement he would not have divorced.

Augustus Attorney has agreed to act as a scribe for Andrea and Terence, who are divorcing. Augustus has made clear in writing that he will neither advise them nor look out for their interests. It comes to Augustus's attention that Sandra is trying to defraud Terence.

213. What should Augustus do?

ANSWER:

214. The Supreme Court has recognized the domestic relations exception, which:

    (A) precludes federal courts from hearing any case involving family law matters.

    (B) divests federal courts of the power to issue divorce, spousal support, or child custody decrees.

    (C) relaxes the normal standing requirements in cases where the best interests of a child are at issue.

    (D) permits federal courts to issue an advisory opinion on the constitutionality of statutes restricting marriage.

According to Massecticut law, Kim and Robin are married. However, federal law does not recognize their marriage for federal purposes.

215. Under what conditions, if any, is it permissible for the federal government to displace state law in this way?

ANSWER:

PRACTICE FINAL EXAM: QUESTIONS

PRACTICE FINAL EXAM

(90 MINUTES)

Gerald and Don, both age 17 and living in New Hampticut, tell their respective parents that they are going skiing for the weekend in the neighboring state of Massmont. Both states recognize same-sex marriage. They neglect to mention that they plan to marry while they are there. They go to a Justice of the Peace, lie about their ages, and marry. They return home and live in their respective parents' homes, waiting for the right time to tell their parents the good news. By the time that they reach their eighteenth birthdays, they regret their impetuousness and wish that they had not married.

One night, Gerald does out with some friend to celebrate his having won the state lottery. Don was not invited. On the way home, Gerald dies in a terrible car accident. Don seeks his intestate share as Gerald's spouse.

216. What result?

   (A) Their marriage will be treated as void, because Don and Gerald never ratified the marriage after reaching majority. Don will not receive anything.

   (B) Don will be entitled to a share of Gerald's estate, as long as Massmont treats minor marriages as voidable.

   (C) The marriage will be treated as void and of no legal effect unless they lived together once they both had attained majority.

   (D) Don will be entitled to a share of Gerald's estate, because a marriage valid where celebrated is valid everywhere.

Assume the facts in Question 216 but also assume that while Massmont recognizes same-sex marriages, New Hampticut does not.

217. What result?

   (A) If New Hampticut has a very strong public policy against either same-sex marriages or minor marriages, then the marriage will not be recognized and Don will not receive a share of Gerald's estate.

   (B) Even if New Hampticut treats minor marriages as voidable, then marriage will nonetheless not be recognized because it could not have been celebrated locally. Don will not receive a share of the estate.

   (C) As long as New Hampticut does not have a strong public policy against recognizing same-sex marriage, Don will receive a share of the estate as a surviving spouse.

(D) Because New Hampticut does not recognize same-sex marriage, it would have been impossible for Don and Gerald to ratify the marriage within the state and thus Don is not entitled to any share of Gerald's estate.

Dorothy and Wally are seventeen-year-olds living in New Mexarkana. They lie about their age and are married by a Justice of the Peace. They live together in the basement of Dorothy's parents' house for about a year and a half, but they find that they have fallen out of love. They seek a declaratory judgment that their marriage is a nullity based on their having been incompetent to contract it in the first place.

218. What result?

ANSWER:

June and Norman live in Newviewington. They have heard a lot about each other ever since June was adopted by Norman's mother. But they have never met because June lives at Norman's mother's house and Norman lives with his father. They finally meet at a family funeral after each had already reached age 18. They fall in love at first sight, and, four years later, wish to marry. They consult an attorney.

219. What should the attorney say?

(A) As long as no one in the family objects, they will be permitted to marry.

(B) They will not be allowed to marry, assuming that their domicile like many jurisdictions treats marriages by adoptive siblings as void.

(C) They can of course marry, because they are of age and are not related by blood.

(D) They will not be allowed to marry unless they are unable to have a child through their union.

Veronica and Ollie, first cousins, are attending a wedding of their dearest friends, which will take place the following weekend in Freemarrizona. They are so overcome by the joy of the occasion with so many of their dearest friends in attendance that they decide to tie the knot as well. Their dearest friends were quite happy to do a double wedding, and Veronica and Ollie were married in accord with local law.

When Ollie and Veronica returned home, they consulted an attorney to find out whether their marriage would be recognized in Limitania, their domicile.

220. What should the attorney say?

ANSWER:

Wanda and William have a lot in common. They each lost spouses in plane crashes and they each have raised children as a single parent. Wanda and William are getting married in their domicile, Famvalington, over the objections of both sets of children. Wanda and William know that they are doing the right thing and they are so excited that they begin celebrating before the marriage takes place. When it was time to say, "I do," William's speech was so slurred that it was difficult to understand, and Wanda said something unintelligible. After a short silence, they were pronounced husband and wife. Wanda and William kissed each other and smiled broadly.

Although the hotel where they were staying was only one mile from the reception, they nonetheless were in a terrible collision with a truck. Wally died and Wanda was severely injured. To make a tragic situation even worse, Wally's children challenge the validity of the marriage, claiming that the parties had not been competent to give consent and that Wanda was not entitled to a share of the estate, given Wally's having died intestate.

221. What result?

    (A) Wanda will be entitled to a widow's share of the estate as long as she and Wally were not so drunk as not to know what they were doing. Even if they were not competent to contract the marriage, Wanda will still receive a widow's share as long as the state treats marriages contracted by temporarily incompetent parties as voidable rather than void.

    (B) Wanda will not receive anything. The two were too drunk to enter into a valid marriage contract and there was never an opportunity for them to ratify the marriage while sober.

    (C) Because Wanda and Wally never consummated the marriage, it will not be recognized and she will not receive any of the estate.

    (D) Because Wally and Wanda at least seemed to assent to the marriage, it must be treated as valid and Wanda will be entitled to her share.

Bob and Carol have been married for several years. All seems well. However, one day, to Bob's surprise, Carol comes home from work saying that she will seek a divorce unless Bob signs a postnuptial agreement making their vacation cabin her separate property. Bob agrees. One year later, Carol files for divorce. Bob challenges the validity of the postnuptial agreement, arguing coercion and lack of consideration.

222. What result?

    (A) Because Carl did not give Bob anything in return for the vacation cabin, the postnuptial agreement will be declared void for lack of consideration.

    (B) The postnuptial agreement will likely be upheld. Carol's remaining in the marriage is consideration and the threat to file for divorce does not constitute coercion in these circumstances.

    (C) Because Bob signed the agreement to avert a divorce, his signing was not voluntary and the agreement is unenforceable.

    (D) The postnuptial agreement will likely be held unenforceable. There was no consideration, because Bob received nothing for his share of the vacation cabin, and he signed the agreement under duress, because it was in response to a threat.

Donna and Edward have been having marital difficulties. Donna comes home and says that she is filing for divorce. Donna says she wants to reach an agreement with respect to the distribution of marital assets. She gives him a list of their holdings and they agree to a distribution. They divorce. Later, it becomes clear that Donna had inadvertently omitted some of their holdings. Edward challenges the separation agreement, arguing fraud, whereas Donna argues that because this was an honest mistake the agreement must stand.

223. What result?

ANSWER:

Nancy and Oscar are divorcing after seven years of marriage. Nancy challenges the prenuptial agreement as unenforceable based on unconscionability, whereas Oscar seeks to enforce it. At the time the agreement was made, both Nancy and Oscar were well-paid attorneys, so their agreeing to no spousal support made sense. However, now, Nancy is no longer able to work because she is undergoing aggressive cancer treatment.

224. What result?

(A) Because the agreement was not unconscionable at the time of signing, it cannot now be invalidated on the basis of unconscionability.

(B) Because it was foreseeable at the time the agreement was made that one of the parties might get sick and be unable to work, the agreement cannot now be held void on the basis of unconscionability.

(C) In some jurisdictions, prenuptial agreements are unenforceable if they are unconscionable either at the time they are made or at the time of enforcement. This agreement may well be unenforceable.

(D) No jurisdiction would enforce an agreement that would leave one of the parties in such a vulnerable position.

Wally and Teresa are divorcing after five years of marriage. Wally challenges the prenuptial agreement as unenforceable. Teresa had presented it to him two days before the wedding along with a list of all of the relevant assets. However, all of their guests had already arrived, and there was no time to consult an attorney and attend to all of the last-minute matters that needed to be addressed. Teresa argues that Wally could have seen an attorney if he had wanted to and that, in any event, he signed the agreement voluntarily.

225. What result?

(A) Because Wally had not had adequate time to consider the prenuptial agreement as a matter of law, it will be held unenforceable.

(B) Because Wally had time to consult an attorney and, in any event, could have delayed the wedding if he had wanted to do so, the agreement may well be held enforceable.

(C) The enforceability of the agreement will depend upon how many last-minute items had to be taken care of and whether Wally could have delegated the responsibility to someone else.

(D) Because Wally signed the agreement, it will be held enforceable.

Alice and Fred are deciding what to include in their prenuptial agreement. Alice is insistent that she should have custody of any children born during the marriage. Fred does not want custody anyway, and is quite willing to bargain away potential custody rights for an agreement that neither of them would provide spousal support in the event of divorce.

When Alice and Fred divorce ten years later, they have two minor children, Zeke and Zoe. Fred seeks to have the prenuptial agreement declared void, because he wants custody of the children and he seeks spousal support because he had been the stay-at-home parent for the past several years.

226. What result?

ANSWER:

Rhonda and William each run successful businesses. They are contemplating marriage and Rhonda insists that a prenuptial agreement be signed, because she wants to protect various assets for the sake of her children from a previous marriage. William is resentful, because he believes that signing a prenuptial agreement suggests that Rhonda does not believe that the marriage will be successful and also that Rhonda believes that William might need financial assistance should they divorce. When they divorce ten years later, William challenges the agreement, arguing duress because of Rhonda's threat that the marriage would not take place but for the agreement, and unconscionability because William is no longer in business and needs support.

227. What result?

(A) Assuming that William understood what he was signing, William will be unsuccessful because coercion, even if established, is not a basis to invalidate a prenuptial agreement, and the failure to his business is not enough to establish the unconscionability of enforcement.

(B) Assuming that William understood what he was signing, William is unlikely to be successful. A refusal to marry without a prenuptial agreement does not constitute coercion or duress, and the mere failure of one's business would not establish that enforcement of an agreement not to pay spousal support was unconscionable.

(C) The refusal to marry without a prenuptial agreement does not constitute coercion. However, it would be unconscionable to enforce an agreement providing that there would be no spousal support when William's business had failed.

(D) Even if William understood what he was signing, his being forced to sign the prenuptial agreement as a condition of marrying constitutes coercion. Further, it would be unconscionable not to pay him spousal support when his business had failed.

Colleen and Patrick marry. They already have two children when Colleen discovers both that Patrick had lied about never having married before and that his ex-spouse was still alive. Because Colleen has strong religious beliefs about not marrying anyone who has an ex-spouse still alive, Colleen seeks to have her marriage annulled.

228. What result?

(A) Because Colleen and Patrick had children together, the marriage cannot now be annulled.

(B) Because Patrick knew that it was important to Colleen not to marry someone with an ex-spouse still living and because he lied about his previous marriage to induce her to marry him, the marriage will be annulled.

(C)   The marriage will not be annulled if Patrick believed in good faith either that Colleen would never find out about his ex-spouse or that even if Colleen did find out she would nonetheless be willing to remain in the marriage.

(D)   The marriage may well be annulled if the court finds that this is a condition going to the essentials of marriage, notwithstanding their having had children together.

John and Jill are an unmarried couple living in New Arico, which does not afford more robust parental right protections than are afforded under the Federal Constitution. New Arico presumes that a child born into a marriage is a child of the marriage, and that presumption can only be rebutted if, within two years, the husband or wife challenges the marital partner's parental status.

Jill announces that she is pregnant and John urges her to get an abortion. Jill has no intention of getting an abortion and tries to convince John that their lives will be even more wonderful with a child. John is unconvinced. Eventually, Jill moves out to live with her sister. John is certain that Jill will come to her senses and come back to him, but she doesn't. After several months, John finds out that Jill married shortly before she gave birth and that she is now living with her infant son, Joshua, and her new husband, Kurt. John now decides that he wishes to establish his parental rights.

229.   What result?

(A)   Because there is no question that John is Joshua's biological father, John will not need to establish parental rights because he is already recognized as the father.

(B)   Because Jill's son was born into an existing marriage, he will likely be presumed a child of the marriage under local law. Assuming that both Jill and her new husband wish to bar John from establishing parental rights, John may well be unable to establish a legal relationship with his child.

(C)   Because the adoption of Joshua will not yet have been made final, John will still be able to establish his parental rights.

(D)   Because John did not support Jill during the pregnancy, his parental rights will be terminated due to parental unfitness.

Michael and Nancy are married and have been living together raising their child, Naomi. When Naomi is ten years old, Nancy announces that she wants a divorce and that Michael is not Naomi's father after all. Nancy seeks to bar Michael's establishing parental rights or responsibilities with respect to Naomi, while Michael seeks to establish his equitable parent status. The guardian ad litem has suggested that Naomi's best interests would be promoted were Michael's parental status recognized.

230.   What result?

(A)   An equitable parent is the individual who would have a parental relationship established in an equitable adoption proceeding. Since there was no equitable adoption claim implicated here, Michael will be unsuccessful.

(B)   Assuming that the jurisdiction recognizes equitable parent doctrine, Michael is likely to be protected on these facts.

(C) Even if the jurisdiction recognizes equitable parent doctrine, Michael is unlikely to be successful because that doctrine requires that the biological/adoptive parent wishes to have the other adult's parental rights recognized.

(D) Michael is likely to be recognized as the equitable parent because a necessary and sufficient condition for that status to be recognized is that the child's interests would thereby be promoted.

Ann has always wanted to be a parent, but she has never met anyone with whom she wanted to spend her life. Finally, she decides to ask Bill, her next-door-neighbor, if she could get sperm from him so that she could be artificially inseminated.

Bill agrees, and eventually a child, Carl, is born. To Ann's surprise and dismay, Bill wishes to establish a relationship with Carl. Ann refuses, and Bill seeks to establish his parental rights.

231. What result?

(A) Because Bill is Carl's biological father and because Bill seeks to establish his parent rights in a timely way, Bill will likely be recognized as Carl's father.

(B) Because Carl was born via artificial insemination, Bill will likely be viewed as a legal stranger to Carl.

(C) Because Ann wanted to raise Carl alone, Bill's parental rights will likely not be recognized.

(D) Whether Bill's parental rights are recognized will likely depend in part on the explicit or implicit agreement between Ann and Bill when he provided the sperm.

Patti and Robert have been seeing each other for two months when Patti announces that she is pregnant. Robert proposes marriage, Patti accepts and they are married one week later by a Justice of the Peace.

Five months later, Patti delivers full-term twins, Horace and June. All goes well until about three years later when Patti and Robert start to fight incessantly about Robert's parenting practices. Patti believes that Robert, who is the children's primary caretaker, is too attentive and is smothering the twins.

When Robert suggests that he may file for divorce and custody, Patti tells him that she welcomes ending the marriage and that he should forget about seeing Horace and June, because he is not their father.

232. What result?

ANSWER:

Wayne and Wanda have been fighting for so long that it is obvious to both of them that their marriage is over. They decide to formally end their marriage.

The day before they are going to their respective attorneys, Wayne decides that he is going to start out single life with a large amount of cash. He empties the joint savings account of $20,000 and goes to the local casino. By the time that he leaves that night, there is no money left in his wallet.

The only contested issue in the divorce is how to divide the marital property. Wanda argues that the $20,000 Wayne lost in the casino should be credited to him alone, whereas Wayne says that the remaining marital assets should be divided equally.

233. What result?

   (A) Because Wanda would have been entitled to a share of his winnings had he been more successful gambling, this expenditure of assets will not be viewed as waste or dissipation. The remaining assets will be divided equitably.

   (B) Because Wayne lost a large sum of money gambling after his marriage was over practically if not legally, Wayne's action will be viewed as a paradigmatic example of waste or dissipation of assets and Wanda will have the gambling debt treated as she suggests.

   (C) Because the gambling losses are not recoverable and because crediting those to Wayne might mean that he would get little or no marital property, the court will reject Wanda's suggestion about how the property should be treated.

   (D) As long as $20,000 of marital assets were used during the marriage for the benefit of Wanda, the expenditures will cancel each other out and the court will not attribute the gambling losses entirely to Wayne.

Agnes and Meredith are divorcing. They can agree about the appropriate characterization of all property except for a necklace that Agnes gave to Meredith for their third wedding anniversary, which Agnes paid for out of savings from her salary earned during the marriage. Meredith says that it is her separate property, while Agnes says that it should be treated as marital property and its value should be distributed equally.

234. What result?

   (A) The necklace is marital property because it was bought with marital funds.

   (B) The necklace is Agnes's separate property because it was bought with her separate funds, i.e., monies saved from her paycheck. The entire value of the necklace will have to be accounted for in the distribution of other property if Meredith is going to keep it.

   (C) The necklace may well be treated as Meredith's separate property if Agnes is viewed as having made an interspousal gift to Meredith.

   (D) The necklace will be viewed as marital property because it was received during the marriage.

John and Mary are divorcing. They can agree about everything except the appropriate characterization of their cars. John's car of which he is the sole driver is worth $75,000 and was purchased with monies earned during the marriage, whereas Mary's car of which she is the sole driver was purchased and maintained using monies she inherited during the marriage from her great aunt.

235. What result?

   (A) Because each is the sole driver of his/her respective car, each car will be treated as the separate property of the driver.

   (B) Because both cars were purchased with monies acquired during the marriage, both cars will be treated as marital property. While each car may well be awarded to the respective driver, there will be an offset because of the greater value of John's car.

(C) Because John's car was bought with marital funds and Mary's was bought with separate funds, his car is likely to be treated as marital and hers as separate. She will likely be credited with some of the value of his car if it is awarded to him.

(D) The characterization of the respective cars will depend entirely upon whether they are titled in this name, her name, or their names.

When Fred married Alice he moved into the house she inherited from her parents free and clear. While marital funds were used to pay for repairs to the house, no improvements were made to the house over the ten years that the couple lived there. During those ten years, the house appreciated in value by $100,000. Fred claims that the increase in value to the house during the marriage is marital property subject to distribution.

236. What result?

(A) Because Alice's home became the marital domicile, the house itself became marital property subject to distribution.

(B) Because the home increased in value during the marriage, that increase is marital property subject to distribution.

(C) Because Alice never put the house in Fred's name, it is separate property and, in addition, any increase in its value is separate property.

(D) Assuming that Alice did not make a gift of the house to Fred or the marital estate, it will be treated as separate and the increase in its value will likely be treated as separate as long as marital resources were not used to increase the house's value.

Larry and Karen are divorcing after ten years of marriage. Divorca employs a primary caretaker presumption when awarding custody. Pursuant to an agreement during the marriage made by Karen and Larry about how they would divide up family responsibilities, Larry has been a stay-at-home Dad to their six-year-old child, Lauren, while Karen has been the sole parent working outside the home. Both parents seek custody, and both parents are fit and loving.

237. Who is likely to be awarded custody?

(A) Larry, because he has been the parent who has attended to Lauren's daily needs.

(B) Karen, because a child of Lauren's tender age is presumably better off if her mother has custody of her.

(C) Because the division of responsibilities was a family decision based on what would be best for the family, neither parent is more likely to be awarded custody on these facts.

(D) Karen, because, as the primary wage-earner, she will be viewed as the primary caretaker.

Nadia Nottingham is 41 years old and has discovered that she is pregnant. She has an amniocentesis performed and is told that there is no reason to believe that her child will have Down's Syndrome.

When she gives birth, Nadia is very upset to discover that her child, Ophelia, has Down's Syndrome. She is even more upset when she later discovers that those performing the amniocentesis had mixed up the test results, and that she should have been told that her child would have the Syndromes. Nadia sues to recover for her financial and emotional damages.

238. Assuming that the jurisdiction recognizes the cause of action, what is the likely result?

    (A) Nadia will be successful in her wrongful birth action as long as she can establish that she would have had an abortion had she received the relevant information when she should have.

    (B) Nadia will be successful in her wrongful birth action if she can establish that her own emotional and financial harm was caused by the negligence at issue and that she would have aborted had she been properly informed.

    (C) Nadia will be successful in her wrongful birth action only if she can establish that her child would have been better off never having been born.

    (D) Nadia will be successful in her wrongful life action only if she can establish that her child would not have had Down's Syndrome but for the negligent communication of the test results.

Trinity and Tomaso have been unhappily married for years in New Caledonia. One day, Trinity decides that she has had enough. She packs some things and moves to her parent's home in West Calixico. Within a few months, she has found a job and apartment, and has met the residency requirement. She files for divorce in West Calixico, asking not only for a dissolution of the marriage but division of some of the property located in New Caledonia. Tomaso has never even visited much less lived in West Calixico.

239. What result?

ANSWER:

Darlene and Edward have been married for six years. They have three children. Darlene files for divorce, seeking custody. She is granted the divorce but denied custody, and is ordered to pay $2000 a month in child support.

Darlene decides that she is tired of working so hard, especially because she ends up paying so much in child support. She takes a less stressful position in the company, which means a reduction in hours and pay. She seeks to have her child support obligation reduced because of a significant change in circumstances.

240. What result?

ANSWER:

Miguel and Alfredo are married and living in New Meriana with their two children. After several years, they divorce with Alfredo being awarded custody. Miguel gets a wonderful job in Colozona. He continues to meet his child support obligation.

Because of an oil rig explosion in the Gulf of Mexico, Miguel's company loses many orders and is forced to lay off workers including Miguel. Miguel is unsuccessful in his attempts to find other work and files in Colozona to have his child support obligation reduced. Alfredo opposes such a reduction in support, making all of the appropriate arguments.

241. What result?

    (A)   Miguel is unlikely to be successful because he will likely be hired again once the economy improves.

    (B)   Miguel is unlikely to be successful because Colozona is unlikely to have jurisdiction under both states' versions of the Uniform Interstate Family Support Act (UIFSA).

    (C)   Miguel is likely to be successful but only if he can establish that he was not fired for cause.

    (D)   Miguel is likely to be successful but only because he was so responsible in making payments when he had the money to do so.

Karen is pregnant. She and John have been dating for a few months and she wants to be married before the birth of the child. They marry, even though John knows that he is not the child's father.

One year later, Karen seeks a divorce because John has been having an affair. John has never bonded with Karen's child, Zachary, and has never held him out as his son. Karen seeks child support. However, John argues that because he can prove that Zachary is not his son, no child support obligation should be imposed.

242. What result?

    (A)   Even assuming that John can show that he is not biologically related to Zachary, John will still likely be ordered to pay support, because a child born into a marriage is presumed to be the child of the parties.

    (B)   Assuming that John can show that he is not genetically related to Zachary, he may well not be found liable for support, because the presumption of paternity is rebuttable and because John never held the child out as his own.

    (C)   Even assuming that John can show that he is not genetically related to Zachary, John will likely still have a child support obligation imposed because he was not misled into believing that he was the child's father.

    (D)   Assuming that John can show that he is not genetically related to Zachary, he likely will not have a child support obligation imposed, because such obligations can only be imposed on biologically related fathers.

Rollie Ryder dies after his doctor commits medical malpractice during surgery. Rollie's adult son, Wendell, sues the doctor for loss of consortium.

243. What is the likely result?

    (A)   Because loss of consortium is a cause of action based on the loss of sexual relations with a loved one, this cause of action will not be permitted in this case.

    (B)   Wendell is likely to succeed as long as the jurisdiction permits actions by children for the loss of consortium with their parents.

    (C)   Even if the jurisdiction permits suits by minor children for loss of consortium with their parents, it may not recognize such a cause of action for an adult child. It is unclear on these facts whether the cause of action is likely to be successful.

(D) As long as Wendell can establish that he had a close relationship with his father and thus was harmed by his father's death, his cause of action is likely to be successful.

Mona and Michael marry. They decide to sell Mona's home and apply the proceeds to greatly improve Michael's home, where they both now live. When Mona and Michael divorce, the only issues in contention are whether to characterize the house as marital or separate property and, depending upon how that issue is resolved, how much of a credit, if any, Mona should receive for her contribution.

244. What result?

(A) As long as Michael kept the house in his own name it will remain separate property. Mona's contribution will likely be treated as a gift.

(B) Because Mona contributed separate property to the improvement of Michael's house, the house will be treated as marital and Mona is entitled to half of its value.

(C) Assuming that there is no evidence that Mona intended her contribution to be a gift, then either Mona will be entitled to a credit or the house will be treated as marital.

(D) Because Mona contributed separate rather than marital property to improve the house, the house must be treated as separate property. As to whether it will be viewed as Mona's or Michael's separate property, this will depend upon how sizable their respective contributions were.

Betty and Carl are first cousins living in East Pennio. They wish to marry but are precluded from doing so in their domicile. They move to a new state, Libertania, which permits them to marry. They celebrate their union there, where they settle.

A few years later, Betty's brother dies in an accident. Betty and Carl go back for the funeral. While there, they are in a terrible accident and Betty is severely hurt. Carl sues for loss of consortium and the negligent driver argues that Betty and Carl are not legally married so that Carl does not have standing to sue.

245. What result?

(A) Assuming that Betty and Carl are precluded from marrying in East Pennio, their Libertania marriage will not be considered valid and Carl will not have standing to sue.

(B) If first cousin marriages are voidable in East Pennio, then the marriage will be recognized. But if first cousin marriages are treated as void in East Pennio, then the marriage will not be recognized and Carl will be unable to bring this cause of action.

(C) Even if East Pennio treats first cousin marriages as void rather than voidable, the jurisdiction might nonetheless treat such marriages as valid if validly celebrated elsewhere, so Carl's suit may be permitted to proceed.

(D) Because Carl and Betty left East Pennio to evade local law, their marriage will not be recognized and the cause of action will not be allowed to proceed.

ANSWERS

1. **Answer (B) is the best answer.** Assuming that a will excluding children born outside of marriage does not violate public policy, *see Hood v. Todd*, 695 S.E.2d 31 (Ga. 2010) (honoring testator's intent to exclude non-marital children), the determinative issue will be whether the marriage is valid. If a minor marriage is merely voidable, it will be treated as valid and binding until declared void by a court. *See In re J.M.N.*, 2008 Tenn. App. LEXIS 346 (June 13, 2008). In that event, Cary will likely be recognized as a child born of the marriage. However if the marriage is treated as void by the state, it will not be considered as valid for any legal purpose. *See In re Estate of Everhart*, 783 N.W.2d 1, 7 (Neb. App. 2010). In that event, Cary will likely not be considered born of the marriage.

    Answer (A) is incorrect. Merely because Old Jersey domiciliaries married in accord with Old Hampshire law does not somehow force Old Jersey to recognize the marriage if such a marriage contravenes an important public policy of the domicile. *See Hesington v. Hesington's Estate*, 640 S.W.2d 824, 826 (Mo. Ct. App. 1982).

    Answer (C) is incorrect. If the marriage was void when contracted, then it never existed and cannot somehow be ratified. *See State ex rel. Dept. of Economic Sec. v. Demetz*, 130 P.3d 986, 989 (Ariz. Ct. App. 2006).

    Answer (D) is incorrect. If Old Jersey treats minor marriages as voidable, the marriage will be recognized as valid until declared void by a court. *See Campbell v. Thomas*, 897 N.Y.S.2d 460, 466 (App. Div. 2010) ("a voidable marriage may be treated as a nullity only if a court has made the requisite pronouncement").

2. **Answer (D) is the best answer.** Once a voidable minor marriage has been ratified by the parties by virtue of their living together once they have attained majority, the marriage is valid and the parties must seek a divorce or dissolution. *See Taylor v. Taylor*, 355 S.W.2d 383, 388 (Mo. Ct. App. 1962).

    Answer (A) is incorrect. Once a voidable minor marriage has been ratified by the parties, the marriage is valid and the parties must seek a divorce or dissolution. *See Taylor v. Taylor*, 355 S.W.2d 383, 388 (Mo. Ct. App. 1962) (once the parties have affirmed the marriage by continuing to live together once both are of age, they no longer have the option of contesting the validity of the marriage).

    Answer (B) is incorrect. A void marriage has no legal effect, *see In re Estate of Everhart*, 783 N.W.2d 1, 7 (Neb. App. 2010), and thus Alice will not have to seek a formal dissolution of the relationship even if she lived with Billy after she attained majority.

    Answer (C) is incorrect. If minor marriages are treated as void, then Alice and Billy will not have a legal marriage simply by virtue of their living together after they have reached majority. *Cf. State ex rel. Dept. of Economic Sec. v. Demetz*, 130 P.3d 986, 989 (Ariz Ct. App. 2006).

3.   **Answer (D) is the best answer.** In this case, because Teresa is so young, an exception for marriage would likely not apply, even though it might have been available had she been older. *See*, for example, N.C. Gen. Stat. Ann. § 14-27.7A (a) ("A defendant is guilty of a Class B1 felony if the defendant engages in vaginal intercourse or a sexual act with another person who is 13, 14, or 15 years old and the defendant is at least six years older than the person, except when the defendant is lawfully married to the person.").

      Answer (A) is incorrect. While the state might treat married and unmarried minors differently once the minor has reached a certain age, e.g., sixteen, *see State v. Pryes*, 2009 WI App 110, a state could and likely would prosecute someone who had had sexual relations with a twelve-year-old. *See* Wis. Stat. Ann. § 948.02 (e) ("Whoever has sexual contact with a person who has not attained the age of 13 years is guilty of a Class B felony."); Wis. Stat. Ann. 948.02 (4) ("A defendant shall not be presumed to be incapable of violating this section because of marriage to the complainant.").

      Answer (B) is incorrect. While consent might be a defense to a statutory rape charge in some cases involving a married minor, *see* 13 Vt. Stat. Ann. § 3252 (c) (1) ("No person shall engage in a sexual act with a child who is under the age of 16, except . . . where the persons are married to each other and the sexual act is consensual"), the ages are important to consider here. *See* 13 Vt. Stat. Ann. § 3253 (a) (8) ("A person commits the crime of aggravated sexual assault if the person commits sexual assault under any one of the following circumstances: . . . The victim is under the age of 13 and the actor is at least 18 years of age.").

      Answer (C) is incorrect. That Teresa and Wanda might suffer economically were Samuel prosecuted would not immunize Samuel from prosecution. *See* Texas Penal Code § 22.021 (a) (2) (b) (no defense to having intentional and voluntary sexual relations with a child under 14 years of age); *see also Fleming v. State*, 323 S.W.3d 540 (Tex. App. 2010) (upholding strict liability crime of statutory rape).

4.   **Answer (B) is the best answer.** Once one of the parties to a voidable marriage dies, the marriage can no longer be challenged. *See In re Estate of Randall*, 999 A.2d 51, 53 (D.C. 2010) (voidable marriage cannot be annulled after the death of one of the parties). Because Edward died intestate, it would be necessary to determine Frieda's share of the estate in light of local law. *See*, for example, Massachusetts Gen. Laws Ann. 190B § 2-102 (2) ("The intestate share of a decedent's surviving spouse is: . . . the first $200,000, plus 3/4 of any balance of the intestate estate, if no descendant of the decedent survives the decedent, but a parent of the decedent survives the decedent.").

      Answer (A) is incorrect. If Minihio treats minor marriages as voidable, then the marriage will be treated as valid until annulled by a court. The marriage has never been annulled and so will be treated as valid. *See In re J.M.N.*, 2008 Tenn. App. LEXIS 346 (June 13, 2008).

      Answer (C) is incorrect. Assuming that Minihio treats minor marriages as voidable, the marriage will be recognized as having been valid, regardless of anyone's views about the wisdom of the marriage. Once one of the parties to a voidable marriage dies, courts will no longer consider an action to annul it. *See Stuhr v. Oliver*, 2010 Ark. 189 ("a marriage can only be inquired into or dissolved by annulment during the lives of the parties").

      Answer (D) is incorrect. Assuming that Minihio treats minor marriages as merely voidable, the marriage could not be challenged even by a parent of a minor in the marriage, once one of the parties to the marriage had died. *See Greene v. Williams*, 9 Cal. App. 3d 559, 564 (1970) (nonconsenting parents cannot challenge the validity of the marriage of their deceased minor child).

5. The attorney should tell Harriet that she will be free to marry only after she gets her marriage to Gregory annulled. Legally, Harriet is married to Gregory. *See Greene v. Williams*, 9 Cal. App. 3d 559, 561 (1970) ("A marriage by an under-age child without parental consent is voidable only and remains in full force until dissolved."). Because Harriet is already a party to a voidable marriage, she would be committing bigamy by marrying without first having her marriage to Gregory annulled. *See Kleinfield v. Veruki*, 372 S.E.2d 407, 409 (Va. App. 1988) ("a party to a voidable marriage must obtain an annulment, or any subsequent marriage is bigamous").

6. Many states that do not permit minors to marry as a general matter have an exception permitting such marriages if the minor's parents consent. *See*, for example, La. Stat. Ann. — Children's Code art. 1545 (A)(1). Even if the parents do not consent, some states provide that a judge may issue a license to marry upon proof of the minor's pregnancy. *See* Fla. Stat. § 741.0405(3). Whether the state would permit John and Karen to marry would be a question of local law. If they would be unable to marry within the state, a separate question would be whether the state treated minor marriages as void or simply voidable. If the latter, then John and Karen might be able to go to another state to marry and have the marriage recognized locally. *See Greene v. Williams*, 9 Cal. App. 3d 559, 561 (1970) ("A marriage by an under-age child without parental consent is voidable only and remains in full force until dissolved."). However, the drawbacks of such an approach should also be explained, e.g., that the marriage might be annulled or that eloping might cause irreparable harm within the different families.

7.   **Answer (C) is the best answer.** Even if Mary entered the marriage in good faith, it was still bigamous and would likely be treated by the state as void ab initio. *See Lukich v. Lukich*, 627 S.E.2d 754, 758 (S.C. Ct. App. 2006) ("Wife's argument that she had a good-faith belief she was not married to Havron does not change the rule that the bigamous marriage was void. Even if Wife was acting under a good-faith belief, South Carolina will not recognize her bigamous second marriage because to do so would violate public policy."). A separate question would be whether the state would offer any protections for the spouse who had married in good faith. *See Eason v. Alexander Shipyards*, 47 So. 2d 114, 116 (La. Ct. App. 1950) ("We think, as the trial judge thought, that the evidence was proper and admissible, as it is the settled jurisprudence of this state that a woman, who was in good faith when she married, and remained so until her husband's death, is, as a putative wife, entitled to claim the benefits due a widow under the Workmen's Compensation Act.") *See also Estate of Hafner*, 184 Cal. App. 3d 1371 (1986) (splitting estate of bigamous husband between innocent putative spouse (and her children) and actual spouse (and her children).

Answer (A) is not the best answer. The marriage would likely not be recognized even if Mary had had a good faith belief that she was free to marry. *See Johns v. Johns*, 420 S.E.2d 856, 858–59 (S.C. Ct. App. 1992) ("The fact the appellant claims to have subjectively acted in 'good faith' does not change the rule that the bigamous marriage was void."); *Snyder v. Snyder*, 2009 WL 3184215, *2 (Ohio Ct. App. 2009) ("it is well established that a bigamous marriage is void ab initio and of no legal purpose. One who is already married has no capacity to enter into another marriage contract, either ceremonial or common law.").

Answer (B) is not the best answer. Merely because Mary had a good faith belief in the marriage would not make a void marriage voidable. While state law might classify a bigamous marriage as void or voidable depending on the circumstances, *see Estate of DePasse*, 97 Cal. App. 4th 92, 105–06 (2002) ("Section 2201 provides that bigamous and polygamous marriages are void or voidable, depending on the circumstances"), a state that classifies a bigamous marriage as void would not make a bigamous union immune to challenge merely because one of the parties to the marriage had died. *See Perlstein v. Perlstein*, 217 A.2d 481, 483 (Conn. Super. 1966) (rejecting that a bigamous marriage was merely voidable and hence could not be challenged after one of the parties to the marriage had died).

Answer (D) is not the best answer. While such a result could be achieved by statute, *see In re Estate of Banks*, 629 N.E.2d 1223, 1226 (Ill. App. 1994) ("Under section 212(b), therefore, prohibited bigamous marriages become valid marriages at the time the impediment to the marriage is removed."), absent such a statute the bigamous marriage would likely be treated as void ab initio and thus not validated merely by virtue of the removal of the impediment to the marriage. *See Byers v. Mount Vernon Mills, Inc.*, 231 S.E.2d 699, 700 (S.C. 1977) (to make their marriage valid, the couple could have participated in a ceremony after the impediment to their marriage had been removed).

8. **Answer (C) is the best answer.** If Sid had a wife who was living at the time that Sid and Roberta celebrated their marriage, then their bigamous marriage may well be treated as void. Nonetheless, some states prohibit the guilty party from asserting that a marriage was bigamous as a way of avoiding having to pay support or split "marital" property. *See Capo v. Estate of Borges*, 560 So. 2d 254, 255 (Fla. Dist. Ct. App. 1990) ("Florida has long recognized the principle that the invalidity of a bigamous marriage cannot be asserted against an innocent spouse."). *But see Guzman v. Alvares*, 205 S.W.3d 375, 380–81 (Tenn. 2006) ("When one of the parties to the purported marriage seeks to invoke the doctrine of marriage by estoppel in a case against the other party to the marriage, this Court has refused to apply the doctrine when the parties entered into a bigamous marriage, regardless of either party's knowledge of the impediment.").

    Answer (A) is incorrect. Many states will treat a bigamous marriage as void from the beginning, even if one of the parties did not know that it was bigamous and hence void. *See Johns v. Johns*, 420 S.E.2d 856, 858–59 (S.C. Ct. App. 1992) ("The fact the appellant claims to have subjectively acted in 'good faith' does not change the rule that the bigamous marriage was void.").

    Answer (B) is not the best answer. It is correct that to be married to him the impediment must be removed before they contract the marriage, *see Byers v. Mount Vernon Mills, Inc.*, 231 S.E.2d 699, 700 (S.C. 1977). However, it is unclear whether they have a valid marriage currently. If Sid's first wife had died before Sid and Roberta had married, then they would have a valid marriage. If Sid's first wife was still living when Sid and Roberta had celebrated their marriage, then Sid and Roberta's marriage would be void even without a court declaration of its validity. *See Clark v. Clark*, 719 S.W.2d 712, 713 (Ark. App. 1986) ("a bigamous marriage is void from its inception, and no decree of any court is required to declare it so"). Further, some states will allow an innocent spouse in a bigamous marriage to be treated as if the marriage had been valid. *See Taylor v. Taylor*, 362 S.E.2d 542, 547 (N.C. 1987) (approving use of "a quasi-estoppel doctrine to prevent one party from benefiting from his wrongful conduct by asserting the invalidity of the bigamous marriage").

    Answer (D) is not the best answer. Even if the marriage is bigamous and void, Mary still may receive some protection from the state because she married in good faith. *See Taylor v. Taylor*, 362 S.E.2d 542, 547 (N.C. 1987) (approving use of "a quasi-estoppel doctrine to prevent one party from benefiting from his wrongful conduct by asserting the invalidity of the bigamous marriage").

9. Terry has a few options even if it is true that Wally was legally married to someone else at the time that he and Terry celebrated their marriage. Once Wally's former wife died, then Wally and Terry might be able to establish a common law marriage, assuming that the state in which they live recognizes common law marriage. *See Rickard v. Trousdale*, 508 So. 2d 260 (Ala. 1987) (The court recognized a common law marriage of a couple whose ceremonial marriage was void because the husband had been married at the time of the ceremonial marriage. In this case, the husband had divorced his prior wife and then had continued to live with the woman with whom he had contracted a void because bigamous marriage.).

10. **Answer (C) is the best answer.** A marriage prohibited locally may nonetheless be recognized if validly celebrated elsewhere. *See Soley v. Soley*, 655 N.E.2d 1381 (Ohio App. 1995). As to whether an uncle-niece marriage validly celebrated elsewhere will be recognized within the domicile, this is a matter of state law. *Compare In re Stiles Estate*, 391 N.E.2d 1026 (Ohio 1979) (refusing to recognize a marriage between uncle and niece) with *In re May's Estate*, 114 N.E.2d 4 (N.Y. 1953) (upholding marriage between uncle and niece validly celebrated elsewhere).

Answer (A) is incorrect. *See In re Stiles Estate*, 391 N.E.2d 1026 (Ohio 1979) (refusing to recognize a marriage between uncle and niece).

Answer (B) is incorrect. A marriage that could not be celebrated locally might nonetheless be recognized if validly celebrated elsewhere. *See Soley v. Soley*, 655 N.E.2d 1381 (Ohio App. 1995) (upholding marriage, validly celebrated elsewhere, that could not be celebrated locally).

Answer (D) is incorrect. Traditionally, the law of the domicile at the time of the marriage determines the validity of the marriage, not the law of the state of celebration, in that a marriage that violates an important public policy of the domicile will not be recognized even if valid in the state of celebration. *See Ramsey County v. Yee Lee*, 770 N.W.2d 572, 577 (Minn. Ct. App. 2009).

11. **Answer (D) is the best answer.** Even if a state treats first-cousin marriages, like uncle-niece marriages, as void when celebrated within the state, the former marriage might nonetheless be recognized if validly celebrated elsewhere. *See Mason v. Mason*, 775 N.E.2d 706 (Ind. Ct. App. 2002) (recognizing first-cousin marriage, validly celebrated elsewhere, that would have been considered void if celebrated locally).

Answer (A) is incorrect. Even if a marriage is valid in the state of celebration, it will not be recognized if violating an important public policy in the domicile. *See Ramsey County v. Yee Lee*, 770 N.W.2d 572, 577 (Minn. Ct. App. 2009).

Answer (B) is incorrect. Even if both uncle-niece and first-cousin marriages are treated as incestuous and void if celebrated in the state, a state might nonetheless be willing to recognize one and not the other if validly celebrated elsewhere. *See Ghassemi v. Ghassemi*, 998 So. 2d 731 (La. Ct. App. 2008) (recognizing first-cousin marriage validly celebrated elsewhere, even though, like an uncle-niece marriage, such a marriage would have been considered void if celebrated within the state).

Answer (C) is incorrect. Even if expressly prohibited by state law, a first-cousin marriage might nonetheless be recognized if validly celebrated elsewhere. *See Ghassemi v. Ghassemi*, 998 So. 2d 731 (La. Ct. App. 2008).

12. Yolanda would be precluded from marrying her biological or adoptive son. *Cf. U.S. v.*

Dedman, 527 F.3d 577, 585 (6th Cir. 2008) (discussing how Arkansas incest laws apply even when the individual has been adopted). Here, however, she is neither the biological nor adoptive mother of Wade. Further, she is not his stepmother because she never married Zeke, and so she could not be precluded from marrying him on that account. *Cf.* Conn. Gen. Stat. Ann. § 46b-21 ("No person may marry such person's parent, grandparent, child, grandchild, sibling, parent's sibling, sibling's child, stepparent or stepchild. Any marriage within these degrees is void."). A separate question is whether local law bars an individual from marrying someone with whom she has a parent-child relationship. It should be noted, however, that their sexual relationship began after they were no longer in the same household and that they were both of age. Absent local law barring marriages between individuals who had had a parent-child type of relationship or, perhaps, where one of the parties had had an in loco parentis relationship, there would seem to be no bar to the relationship. A separate issue might arise if Yolanda wished to remain in contact with minor children who were Wade's siblings. *Cf. Allen v. Farrow*, 626 N.Y.S.2d 125 (App. Div. 1995) (upholding visitation limitations on father who had married his former cohabiting partner's adopted child).

13.   **Answer (B) is the best answer.** Even where nonconsummation is a ground for annulment, it may not be the basis for annulment where the parties knew ahead of time that the marriage would not be consummated. *See,* for example, 750 Ill. Comp. Stat. 5/301(2) ("The court shall enter its judgment declaring the invalidity of a marriage (formerly known as annulment) entered into under the following circumstances: . . . a party lacks the physical capacity to consummate the marriage by sexual intercourse and at the time the marriage was solemnized the other party did not know of the incapacity").

      Answer (A) is not the best answer. Some jurisdictions require that the complaining party not know at the time of the marriage that there would be no consummation. *See,* for example, 13 Delaware Code § 1506 (a) (2) ("The Court shall enter a decree of annulment of a marriage entered into under any of the following circumstances: . . . A party lacked the physical capacity to consummate the marriage by sexual intercourse and the other party did not, at the time the marriage was solemnized, know of the incapacity.").

      Answer (C) is incorrect. There is no requirement that no other ground be applicable in order for an annulment based on nonconsummation to be granted. *See Lang v. Reetz-Lang,* 488 N.E.2d 929, 932 (Ohio App. 1985) (granting annulment based on nonconsummation).

      Answer (D) is not the best answer. Because Beverly knew that Alvin was paralyzed before they married, some states would not permit her to seek an annulment either. *See,* for example, 13 Delaware Code § 1506 (a)(2).

14.   **Answer (C) is the best answer.** Many states define impotency in terms of the inability to have sexual relations rather than the ability to have children. *See Dolan v. Dolan,* 259 A.2d 32, 37 (Me. 1969) ("As a ground for divorce or annulment of marriage it [impotence] means an inability to engage in, or a lack of capacity for, normal and complete sexual intercourse.").

      Answer (A) is not the best answer. The basis for annulment in many states is the ability to have sexual relations rather than the ability to have a child. *See T v. M,* 242 A.2d 670, 673 (N.J. Super. Ch. Div. 1968) ("Impotency is the inability to have sexual intercourse; impotence is not sterility.").

      Answer B is not the best answer. David is more likely to succeed, assuming that incompatibility is a recognized ground for divorce, *see,* for example, N.M. Stat. Ann. § 40-4-2 ("Incompatibility exists when, because of discord or conflict of personalities, the legitimate ends of the marriage relationship are destroyed preventing any reasonable expectation of reconciliation."), and that the specified conditions are satisfied, e.g., that there is no reasonable possibility of reconciliation. *See id.* However, the focus is on whether the marriage can no longer be saved rather than on who is right or wrong. *See Cedrins v. Shrestha,* 2009 U.S. Dist. LEXIS 50251 (D.N.M. Mar. 31, 2009) ("When determining whether a divorce should be granted on grounds of incompatibility, fault is not relevant to the determination.").

Answer (D) is incorrect. The question is not who is fertile but whether the parties can have sexual relations. *See Dolan v. Dolan*, 259 A.2d 32, 37 (Me. 1969); *T v. M*, 242 A.2d 670, 673 (N.J. Super. Ch. Div. 1968).

15.   As to whether this ground was lost after Fred and Georgina consummated their marriage on their wedding night, this will depend upon why the relations were dissatisfying. If the relations were dissatisfying because the relations were "painful" or "incomplete," then the ground may still exist. *See Stepanek v. Stepanek*, 193 Cal. App. 2d 760, 762 (1961) ("The inability need be only for normal copulation, not partial, imperfect, unnatural or painful copulation.") However, if indeed the marriage was consummated, then this ground for an annulment no longer exists. *See Dolan v. Dolan*, 259 A.2d 32, 37 (Me. 1969) ("The incapacity must have existed at the time of the marriage.") That said, there would still be other ways to end the marriage, e.g., by claiming cruelty. *See Broussard v. Broussard*, 462 So. 2d 1386, 1389 (La. Ct. App. 1985). Or, the parties might divorce based on incompatibility or irretrievable breakdown of the marriage. *See Jones v. Jones*, 2007 Conn. Super. LEXIS 404 (Feb. 8, 2007) (granting divorce based on irretrievable breakdown of the marriage, which seems to have been caused in large part by the sexual incompatibility of the parties).

16.   **Answer (B) is the best answer.** While a merely voidable marriage cannot be challenged after the death of one of the parties to the marriage, *see In re Estate of Randall*, 999 A.2d 51, 54 (D.C. 2010), a void marriage can be challenged even after one of the parties to the marriage has died. *See In re Estate of Santolino*, 895 A.2d 506, 510 (N.J. Super. Ch. Div. 2005) ("the prevailing rule continues to provide that a void marriage may be annulled after the death of one of the parties"). Further, the post-death challenge may be made by a third party. *See id.* at 508 (permitting sister of decedent to challenge the validity of his allegedly void marriage).

     Answer (A) is incorrect. Some states treat marriages involving those who are not sane as void, *see Harris v. Harris*, 506 N.W.2d 3, 4 (Mich. App. 1993) ("all marriages solemnized when either of the parties was insane or an idiot, shall, if solemnized within this state, be absolutely void"), whereas others treat them as voidable. *See Brown v. Brown*, 29 S.W.3d 491, 495 (Tenn. Ct. App. 2000) ("A marriage is voidable from the beginning (1) when either party was insane.") If the state treats the marriage as void, however, even those who are not parties to the marriage may challenge its validity. *See In re Davis' Estate*, 640 P.2d 692, 693 (Or. App. 1982) ("A void marriage, on the other hand, is invalid from the outset and may be challenged by third parties.").

     Answer (C) is incorrect. A marriage performed by a justice of the peace may be challenged if the marriage at issue was void or voidable. *See*, for example, *Peters v. Peters*, 214 N.W.2d 151, 154 (Iowa 1974) (discussing the annulment of a marriage performed by a justice of the peace).

     Answer (D) is incorrect. Those states treating a marriage involving someone who is not sane as voidable will treat the marriage as valid until it has been annulled by a court. *See In re J.M.N.*, 2008 Tenn. App. LEXIS 346 (June 13, 2008) ("A voidable marriage differs from a void marriage in that the former is treated as valid and binding until its nullity is ascertained and declared by a competent court.") Further, such a marriage can be ratified once the party is competent. *See In re Romano's Estate*, 246 P.2d 501, 505 (Wash. 1952) ("A marriage tainted with insanity or fraud, on the other hand, is not classified as 'absolutely void.' Instead, it is only void 'from the time its nullity shall be declared by a court of competent authority'. Moreover, such a marriage can, under certain circumstances, be ratified or affirmed at the option of the parties.").

17.   **Answer (B) is the best answer.** Yves does not seem to have been so drunk as to not know what he was doing, so he will likely be found to have been competent to consent to the marriage. *See Christoph v. Sims*, 234 S.W.2d 901, 904 (Tex. Civ. App. 1950) ("A party claiming he was intoxicated at the time of marriage cannot escape liability unless he was incapable at the time of understanding his acts; he must be so drunk that he did not understand what he was doing and the nature of the transaction.") Even if he had been so drunk as to not have understood what he was doing, his having subsequently lived with his

wife while sober would have constituted a ratification of the marriage. *See Abel v. Waters*, 373 So. 2d 1125, 1128 (Ala. Civ. App. 1979) ("If the mental impairment preventing such assent is only temporary, as where intoxication renders a person incapable of knowing what he or she has done, the marriage may be ratified upon removal of the disability."). *See also Christoph v. Sims*, 234 S.W.2d 901, 904 (Tex. Civ. App. 1950) ("Living together in the same house after marriage, contributing financial support to the wife when sober, raise the inescapable presumption of cohabitation and must be held to show condonation; thus preventing annulment of a marriage superinduced by a state of intoxication.").

Answer (A) is incorrect. The relevant issue is not merely whether Yves was noticeably drunk but whether he was so drunk that he did not know what he was doing. *See Christoph v. Sims*, 234 S.W.2d 901, 904 (Tex. Civ. App. 1950) ("A party claiming he was intoxicated at the time of marriage cannot escape liability unless he was incapable at the time of understanding his acts; he must be so drunk that he did not understand what he was doing and the nature of the transaction.").

Answer (C) is incorrect. The focus should not be on whether it was reasonable to believe that Yves was inebriated after a few drinks, but whether he was so inebriated that he did not know what he was doing, *see Christoph v. Sims*, 234 S.W.2d 901, 904 (Tex. Civ. App. 1950), and whether he ratified the marriage once he became sober. *See Abel v. Waters*, 373 So. 2d 1125, 1128 (Ala. Civ. App. 1979).

Answer (D) is not the best answer. The question is not the ability of Yves to walk but his understanding of what was taking place. If, for example, what he said during the ceremony made clear that he was unable to understand what was taking place, then his having been able to walk would not establish that he was competent. *See Christoph v. Sims*, 234 S.W.2d 901, 904 (Tex. Civ. App. 1950) (discussing the criterion for competency).

18.   **Answer (D) is the best answer.** Yves not having been competent to give consent will likely be viewed as making the marriage voidable rather than void. *Abel v. Waters*, 373 So. 2d 1125, 1128 (Ala. Civ. App. 1979) ("Such a marriage (i.e., one that is contracted while one of the parties is intoxicated) is voidable as opposed to void.") Because he remained with his wife after he had sobered up, he will likely be viewed as having ratified the marriage. *See id.* ("If the mental impairment preventing such assent is only temporary, as where intoxication renders a person incapable of knowing what he or she has done, the marriage may be ratified upon removal of the disability."). If he had never sobered up and thus had never become competent to ratify the marriage, that would have been a different matter. *See id.* ("Here, the administratrix has alleged the intoxication of her mother so greatly impaired her mental abilities as to render her incapable of assenting to the marriage. She claims this enfeebled condition remained constant until the mother's death, making ratification impossible. In essence, she claims her mother was insane prior to the marriage, remaining so until her death.").

Answer (A) is incorrect. If Yves was so drunk that he did not understand where he was or what he was doing, then he will not be viewed as having consented to the marriage. *See Christoph v. Sims*, 234 S.W.2d 901, 904 (Tex. Civ. App. 1950).

Answer (B) is incorrect. Because the individual and societal interests implicated in marriage are so important, the marriage will likely be considered voidable rather than void. *See Abel v. Waters*, 373 So. 2d 1125, 1128 (Ala. Civ. App. 1979) ("If the mental impairment preventing such assent is only temporary, as where intoxication renders a person incapable of knowing what he or she has done, the marriage may be ratified upon removal of the disability. . . . Such a marriage is voidable as opposed to void.").

Answer (C) is incorrect. Yves not having been competent will likely make the marriage voidable rather than void. *See Abel v. Waters*, 373 So. 2d 1125, 1128 (Ala. Civ. App. 1979).

19.   In order for Ben to be successful, he will have to show that the consent to marry was not valid, for example, by establishing that he was so drunk that he did not know where he was or what he was doing. Merely feeling tipsy or overoptimistic will not suffice to show that he was not competent. *See Christoph v. Sims*, 234 S.W.2d 901, 904 (Tex. Civ. App. 1950). Even if Ben were successful in establishing that he was not competent to give consent, this would likely merely make the marriage voidable rather than void. *See Abel v. Waters*, 373 So. 2d 1125, 1128 (Ala. Civ. App. 1979). But if the marriage were voidable, then he would likely be held to have ratified the marriage by living together with Alice after the marriage unless he could somehow show that he had not been competent to ratify the marriage during the period that they lived together. *See id.* If they wish to end the marriage on no-fault grounds within Nevarado, then they may well have to live separate and apart for a year to make use of that no-fault ground.

20.   **Answer (C) is the best answer.** Contracts based on nonmeretricious consideration may well be enforceable as long as the agreement was informed and voluntary and not based on fraud, duress, etc. *See,* for example, *Estate of Reaves v. Owen*, 744 So. 2d 799, 802 (Miss. Ct. App. 1999). However, even if such an agreement between nonmarital parties might be enforced within a state, the agreement in this case would likely not be enforced, because it was between nonmarital parties when one of the parties was married to someone else. *See Norton v. Hoyt*, 278 F. Supp. 2d 214, 227 (D.R.I. 2003) (noting that a "palimony cause of action will not prosper in Rhode Island especially when the relationship was adulterous").

        Answer (A) is incorrect. While Oscar did sign the agreement because he feared that Penelope would otherwise leave him, this would not constitute the kind of duress that would invalidate the agreement. For example, had they been married and had Penelope threatened to leave the marriage unless Oscar agreed to some very favorable concessions, such a threat would likely not be held to constitute duress. *See Aubrey v. Aubrey*, 2010 Ky. App. Unpub. LEXIS 879 (Nov. 19, 2010) ("Indeed, it seems logical to assume that any antenuptial or postnuptial agreement is the product of an express or implied threat that the marriage will not take place, or endure, unless the party requested to sign it does so. We decline to hold that such a threat constitutes duress *per se.*").

        Answer (B) is incorrect. While it is true that agreements solely based on meretricious considerations will not be enforced, *see Kozlowski v. Kozlowski*, 403 A.2d 902, 907 (N.J. 1979), it is false that they will be enforced as long as they are nonmeretricious. For example, the agreement might have been obtained through fraud, duress, or misrepresentation. *See Mallen v. Mallen*, 622 S.E.2d 812, 814 (Ga. 2005).

        Answer (D) is incorrect. Some cohabitation agreements will be enforceable. *See Byrne v. Laura*, 60 Cal. Rptr. 2d 908, 914 (Cal. App. 1997) ("Support agreements between cohabitants are enforceable."); *Boland v. Catalano*, 521 A.2d 142, 146 (Conn. 1987) ("our public policy does not prevent the enforcement of agreements regarding property rights between unmarried cohabitants in a sexual relationship"). Further, an agreement between cohabitants may be enforceable even if not officially recognized as a cohabitation agreement. *See Doe v. Burkland*, 808 A.2d 1090, 1094 (R.I. 2002) ("as long as the alleged consideration for the parties' putative agreement was not illegal, a suit for enforcement of that contract can proceed, subject to whatever other defenses may exist").

21.   **Answer (C) is the best answer.** Many states will not enforce a prenuptial agreement specifying the religious education of children not yet born. *See In re Marriage of Wolfert*, 598 P.2d 524, 526 (Colo. Ct. App. 1979) ("premarital agreements concerning the religious training of unborn children are unenforceable in the courts"). Prenuptial agreements are enforceable as a general matter as long as they are informed and voluntary and do not involve fraud, duress, overreaching, etc. *See Fletcher v. Fletcher*, 628 N.E.2d 1343, 1346 (Ohio 1994).

        Answer (A) is incorrect. Prenuptial agreements tend to be enforceable as long as they are informed and voluntary and do not involve duress, coercion, and overreaching. *See Copley v. Copley*, 2010 Ky. App. Unpub. LEXIS 694 (Sept. 3, 2010) ("To be enforceable, an antenuptial agreement must not have been obtained through fraud, duress or mistake, misrepresentation, or non-disclosure of material facts.").

Answer (B) is incorrect. Even if Sarah knew that this condition was important to Thomas and that he was relying on their agreement with respect to the religious education of any children that they might have, this would not make such a provision enforceable if its enforcement would violate public policy. *See Winchester v. McCue*, 882 A.2d 143, 146 (Conn. App. 2005) (such an agreement not enforceable if its terms violate public policy).

Answer (D) is incorrect. Merely because Sarah was willing to agree to such a condition when the agreement was made does not make it enforceable now. *See Stanton v. Stanton*, 100 S.E.2d 289, 293–94 (Ga. 1957) (upholding refusal to enforce provision of prenuptial contract specifying religious education of children).

22.   **Answer (D) is the best answer.** The guiding principle determining who should have custody involves consideration of who would best promote the interests of the children. *See Riley v. Doerner*, 677 So. 2d 740, 743 (Miss. 1996) ("In all child custody cases, the polestar consideration is the best interest of the child.") An agreement that runs counter to the interests of the children is unenforceable. *See McKee v. Flynt*, 630 So. 2d 44, 51 (Miss. 1993) ("With regard to child custody, the paramount issue is that of the best interest and welfare of the child. . . . Parents of minor children cannot, by entering into private contracts, subordinate the authority of the chancery court."). One of the relevant considerations is that splitting the children might run counter to their interests, *see Lukaszewicz v. Lukaszewicz*, 682 N.Y.S.2d 696, 698 (App. Div. 1998) ("It is well settled that the splitting of siblings is generally discouraged"); *Noland-Vance v. Vance*, 321 S.W.3d 398, 418 (Mo. Ct. App. 2010) ("absent exceptional or unusual circumstances, Missouri courts do not support the separation of siblings or split custody"), although splitting custody might be warranted in a particular case. *See Brocato v. Brocato*, 731 So. 2d 1138, 1143–44 (Miss. 1999) ("In conclusion, this Court finds that the chancellor did not err in splitting custody of the minor children between the parents based upon the best interests of the children and the unusual aspects of this particular situation.").

Answer (A) is not the best answer. A provision of an antenuptial agreement specifying child custody will not be enforced if contrary to the best interests of the child. *See Osborne v. Osborne*, 428 N.E.2d 810, 816 (Mass. 1981) (explaining that provisions can be modified when running counter to the child's best interests).

Answer (B) is not the best answer. It is unclear whether Gregory wants custody of both children but feels constrained by the premarital agreement or whether, instead, he would prefer only to have custody of his son. In any event, assuming that shared custody is not an option, custody will be awarded to the parent who will promote the best interests of the children. *See Riley v. Doerner*, 677 So. 2d 740, 743 (Miss. 1996) ("In all child custody cases, the polestar consideration is the best interest of the child.").

Answer (C) is not the best answer. While it is true that individuals should not be able to profit by wrongdoing, *see Barker v. Kallash*, 459 N.Y.S.2d 296, 299 (App. Div. 1983) (discussing the public policy that an individual "not be allowed to profit from his wrongdoing"), the question here is which parent would best promote the interests of the children. If indeed Hilary's having custody would best promote the interests of the children, then they should be placed with her whether or not she had made an agreement that was in any event unenforceable because contrary to public policy.

23. **Answer (B) is the best answer.** The court may well find that the wife's staying in the marriage was itself consideration, *see Gilley v. Gilley*, 778 S.W.2d 862, 864 (Tenn. Ct. App. 1989) ("We find no merit to the assertion that the agreement was without consideration. Wife had several grounds upon which to prosecute a divorce, which she did not do at the husband's request, receiving promises of faithfulness secured by a property distribution, in the event of divorce, satisfactory to wife.") Had the facts been different, a promise to continue the marriage might not have been viewed as consideration. For example, a promise to remain in a marriage where there is no evidence of marital discord might well not be viewed as consideration. *See Bratton v. Bratton*, 136 S.W.3d 595, 603 (Tenn. 2004) ("Ms. Bratton's promise not to leave her husband is clearly not consideration for the agreement. Both parties' admitted that they were not having marital difficulties at the time the agreement was signed.").

Answer (A) is incorrect. While a postnuptial agreement that promotes divorce will be viewed as unenforceable, *see In re Cooper's Estate*, 403 P.2d 984, 989 (Kan. 1965), postnuptial agreements are not unenforceable as a general matter. *See Rauso v. Rauso*, 902 N.Y.S.2d 573, 574 (App. Div. 2010) ("A postnuptial agreement which is fair on its face will be enforced according to its terms unless there is proof of fraud, duress, overreaching, or unconscionability.").

Answer (C) is not the best answer. It is not likely that the threat of a divorce, alone, would be held to constitute duress. *See Aubrey v. Aubrey*, 2010 Ky. App. Unpub. LEXIS 879 (Nov. 19, 2010) ("Absent any evidence or claim that Elizabeth or anyone acting on her behalf did more than threaten Joel with a divorce action and demand that he move out of the house unless he signed the postnuptial agreement, Elizabeth's conduct and that of anyone acting on her behalf falls far short of duress as defined by Kentucky law.").

Answer (D) is incorrect. There are other bases upon which a postnuptial agreement might be held invalid, for example, that the agreement was unfair. *See Boyer v. Boyer*, 925 P.2d 82, 85 (Okla. Civ. App. 1996) or that there was fraud or misrepresentation. *See Casto v. Casto*, 508 So. 2d 330, 333 (Fla. 1987) ("a spouse may set aside or modify an agreement by establishing that it was reached under fraud, deceit, duress, coercion, misrepresentation, or overreaching").

24. **Answer (D) is the best answer.** Because Carole never had any intention of giving the marriage another chance, the postnuptial agreement was based on a fraudulent promise. *See Fogg v. Fogg*, 567 N.E.2d 921, 923 (Mass. 1991) ("The agreement before us was signed as a result of the wife's implied fraudulent promise that she would attempt to preserve the marriage. Thus, it is invalid.") However, the agreement might otherwise have been upheld. *See Rauso v. Rauso*, 902 N.Y.S.2d 573, 574 (App. Div. 2010) ("A postnuptial agreement which is fair on its face will be enforced according to its terms unless there is proof of fraud, duress, overreaching, or unconscionability.")

Answer (A) is not the best answer. While the agreement was clear, voluntary, and not unconscionable, the agreement must also be made in good faith. Else, the agreement might well be viewed as void because fraudulent. *See Fogg v. Fogg*, 567 N.E.2d 921, 923 (Mass. 1991) ("The agreement before us was signed as a result of the wife's implied fraudulent promise that she would attempt to preserve the marriage. Thus, it is invalid.").

Answer (B) is not the best answer. As long as the bargained-for result was not unfair and did not involve overreaching, the fact that there was valuable consideration to induce her to give the marriage another chance would not require the agreement's invalidation. *See Rauso v. Rauso*, 902 N.Y.S.2d 573, 574 (App. Div. 2010).

Answer (C) is not the best answer. While there of course was no guarantee that the marriage would be saved, Carole was at least promising to give the marriage another chance. Because she did not even intend to try to save the relationship and was merely trying to secure more property, the agreement will likely be viewed as having been fraudulently secured. *See Fogg v. Fogg*, 567 N.E.2d 921, 923 (Mass. 1991).

25.   **Answer (B) is the best answer.** While her insisting that the agreement be signed before the wedding would not constitute duress, especially because it had been presented to him early enough for his lawyer to review it, a separate question would be whether assets had been hidden. *See Porreco v. Porreco*, 811 A.2d 566, 570 (Pa. 2002) (discussing "two alternate bases for invalidating a prenuptial agreement: (1) any ground for voiding a contract under the common law (such as fraud); and (2) where a party fails to make 'full and fair' disclosure of his or her own assets prior to entering the agreement").

Answer (A) is not the best answer. Many courts will not treat the shortness of time given to sign a prenuptial agreement as alone enough to establish duress, *see Lebeck v. Lebeck*, 881 P.2d 727, 734 (N.M. Ct. App. 1994) ("A lawful demand or a threat to do that which the demanding party has a right to demand is not sufficient to support a claim of duress."). *See also In re Marriage of Miller*, 2002 WL 31312840, *2 (Iowa App. 2002) (suggesting that postponement or cancellation of the wedding would be a reasonable option if one wished to have more time to consider the prenuptial agreement).

Answer (C) is not the best answer. The agreement was approved by Frank's attorney, so it would be difficult to establish that the agreement was unfair, especially since a high burden must be met before unfairness can be established. *See Darrin v. Darrin*, 838 N.Y.S.2d 678, 680–681 (App. Div. 2007) ("Considering all the provisions of the prenuptial agreement, we cannot say that it was so unfair as to shock the conscience and confound the judgment of any [person] of common sense.").

Answer (D) is not the best answer. While Frank cannot plausibly claim duress under these facts, he still could have the agreement declared unenforceable if Ellen had hidden her assets so that neither Frank nor Frank's attorney would have had an accurate understanding of Ellen's wealth. *See Wilson v. Moore*, 929 S.W.2d 367, 371 (Tenn. Ct. App. 1996) ("The disclosure will be deemed adequate if it imparts an accurate understanding of the nature and extent of a person's property interests.").

26.   **Answer (D) is the best answer.** Many states require that the agreement not be unconscionable at the time the agreement would be effectuated. *See Reed v. Reed*, 693 N.W.2d 825, 834 (Mich. App. 2005) (suggesting that a prenuptial agreement may be treated as void "when the facts and circumstances are so changed since the agreement was executed that its enforcement would be unfair and unreasonable"). However, the unconscionability standard sets a pretty high threshold. *See Colon v. Colon*, 2006 N.J. Super. Unpub. LEXIS 1795 (Aug. 11, 2006) ("an unconscionable agreement as one which would leave a spouse a public charge or close to it, or which would provide a standard of living far below that which

was enjoyed both before and during the marriage").

Answer (A) is incorrect. Even if all of these conditions are met, the agreement still would not be enforceable. If, for example, the agreement were unconscionable at the time it was signed, then it would not be enforceable. *See Reed v. Reed*, 693 N.W.2d 825, 834 (Mich. App. 2005) (prenuptial agreement unenforceable if unconscionable at the time it was signed).

Answer (B) is not the best answer. The knowledge requirement for making prenuptial agreements enforceable is that each of the parties has a general understanding of the other's financial position. *See Friezo v. Friezo*, 914 A.2d 533, 550 (Conn. 2007) (suggesting that "a fair and reasonable financial disclosure requires each contracting party to provide the other with a general approximation of their income, assets and liabilities").

Answer (C) is not the best answer. In addition to the listed considerations, many states require that the agreement not be unconscionable at the time of enforcement. *See Edwardson v. Edwardson*, 798 S.W.2d 941, 945 (Ky. 1990) ("the agreement must not be unconscionable at the time enforcement is sought").

27. **Answer (D) is the best answer.** Individuals cannot by contract nullify existing law. *See Lester v. Lester*, 87 N.Y.S.2d 517, 522 (Dom. Rel. Ct. 1949) ("Private individuals may not by agreement set aside the law of the land. They may not declare that which is valid in law null and void."). Because the law does not permit an individual to remain single merely because that party secretly wishes to remain single, *see Crosson v. Crosson*, 668 So. 2d 868, 870 (Ala. Civ. App. 1995) ("The husband's subjective intent, i.e., any unexpressed intent he may have had not to be married, must yield to the reasonable conclusion to be drawn from his objective acts such as his failure to dispute what appeared to be a marital relationship."), the parties' secret writing will not invalidate the marriage. It might be noted that this agreement would not be treated as a prenuptial agreement because a prenuptial agreement is entered into in contemplation and consideration of a future marriage. *See Fox v. Fox*, 2002-Ohio-6877 (Ohio Ct. App. 2002) ("A prenuptial agreement is a contract entered into between a man and a woman in contemplation, and in consideration, of their future marriage.").

Answer (A) is not the best answer. While the agreement was voluntary and it was made for the benefit of Peter, some kinds of voluntary agreement will be treated as void because violations of public policy. *See Lester v. Lester*, 87 N.Y.S.2d 517, 520 (N.Y. Dom. Rel. Ct. 1949) (holding unenforceable a private agreement between the parties to go through the motions of marrying but not really be married).

Answer (B) is not the best answer. As a general matter, as long as a prenuptial agreement is made voluntarily with the relevant knowledge and would not be unconscionable, *see Blue v. Blue*, 60 S.W.3d 585, 589 (Ky. Ct. App. 2001), it will be enforceable if, for example, it only involves the distribution of property. *See Edwardson v. Edwardson*, 798 S.W.2d 941, 946 (Ky. 1990). Prenuptial agreements may alter the property distribution that might otherwise have been ordered, but such a modification is an option afforded by existing law.

Answer (C) is incorrect. Even if those criteria are met, some agreements will be struck as void because violating public policy, for example, those mandating that the children be raised in a particular religion. *See Stanton v. Stanton*, 100 S.E.2d 289, 293–94 (Ga. 1957) (upholding refusal to enforce provision of prenuptial contract specifying religious education of children).

28. **Answer (A) is the best answer.** Many states permit spousal support to be waived in a prenuptial agreement. *See*, for example, *In re Marriage of Bridge*, 998 P.2d 780, 784 (Or.

App. 2000) (upholding waiver of spousal support), although some states treat such waivers as unenforceable); *see Sanford v. Sanford*, 694 N.W.2d 283, 293 (S.D. 2005) ("Provisions in a prenuptial agreement purporting to limit or waive spousal support are void and unenforceable as they are contrary to public policy."). However, states as a general matter will not enforce waivers of child support in a prenuptial agreement. *See Edwardson v. Edwardson*, 798 S.W.2d 941, 946 (Ky. 1990) ("Questions of child support, child custody and visitation are not subject to such agreements.").

Answer (B) is incorrect. Many states treat waivers of spousal support as enforceable. *See Hardee v. Hardee*, 585 S.E.2d 501, 503 (S.C. 2003) (noting that the "majority rule allows parties to prospectively contract to limit or eliminate spousal support").

Answer (C) is incorrect. States as a general matter will not enforce a prenuptial agreement to waive child support. *See Werther v. Werther*, 9 Misc. 3d 1114A (N.Y. Sup. Ct. 2005) ("Without question, a provision in an agreement eliminating a party's child support obligation is void as against public policy.").

Answer (D) is incorrect. States will not enforce a provision waiving child support. *See Werther v. Werther*, 9 Misc. 3d 1114A (N.Y. Sup. Ct. 2005). It might be noted that the other benefits listed might be achieved in other ways. *See*, for example, *Hartog v. Hartog*, 535 N.E.2d 239, 240 (Mass. App. Ct. 1989) (increasing time that the children were allowed to remain in the marital home because that would promote their interests).

29. An agreement that specifies who will have custody that runs counter to the interests of the child will be held unenforceable. *See McKee v. Flynt*, 630 So. 2d 44, 51 (Miss. 1993) ("With regard to child custody, the paramount issue is that of the best interest and welfare of the child. . . . Parents of minor children cannot, by entering into private contracts, subordinate the authority of the chancery court.") Thus, the agreement that Rachel have custody will only be enforced if her having custody would promote the best interests of the children, which means that the agreement would not be held to have any independent weight on this issue. An agreement specifying the religious training of the children will not be held enforceable against the custodial parent. *See*, for example, *Abbo v. Briskin*, 660 So. 2d 1157, 1159 (Fla. Dist. Ct. App. 1995) ("We have grave doubts, however, that the law could or should enforce an unwritten premarriage agreement to raise a child in one faith or the other. These doubts are intensified when the parent to be compelled later suffers, as here, a genuine, good faith change of religious conscience."). Many but not all states will enforce a premarital agreement waiving spousal support. *See Hardee v. Hardee*, 585 S.E.2d 501, 503 (S.C. 2003) (noting that the "majority rule allows parties to prospectively contract to limit or eliminate spousal support"). Thus, the only provision that is likely to be enforced would be the provision waiving spousal support.

30. **Answer (D) is the best answer.** Assuming that paramour services are viewed as essentially involving sexual services, the contract will be struck down as unenforceable. *See Jones v. Daly*, 122 Cal. App. 3d 500, 508 (1981) ("Viewed in the context of the complaint as a whole, the words 'cohabiting' and 'lover' do not have the innocuous meanings which plaintiff ascribes to them. These terms can pertain only to plaintiff's rendition of sexual services to Daly."). Further, if any additional services provided by Bertram are viewed as inextricably connected to his providing sexual services, then the agreement will still be viewed as unenforceable. *See id.* at 509 ("The latter [sexual] service forms an inseparable part of the consideration for

the agreement and renders it unenforceable in its entirety.").

Answer (A) is not the best answer. Although the parties agreeing about what would constitute reasonable support would remove one of the difficulties, a separate question would be whether this agreement would be viewed as primarily an agreement for sexual services and thus a violation of public policy. *See Liles v. Still*, 335 S.E.2d 168, 169 (Ga. App. 1985) ("A contract founded upon a promise to live in the future in a meretricious state is void.").

Answer (B) is not the best answer. The consideration would have been Bertrand having provided various paramour services. However, if those services are construed as simply being meretricious, then the agreement will be viewed as unenforceable. *See Alderson v. Alderson*, 225 Cal. Rptr. 610, 616–17 (Cal. App. 1986) (nonmarital contract unenforceable if "found to explicitly rest upon a consideration of meretricious sexual services and even then the contract will fail 'only to the extent' that it does so.").

Answer (C) is not the best answer. While these are the considerations for determining the validity of a prenuptial agreement, *see Casto v. Casto*, 508 So. 2d 330, 333 (Fla. 1987), this involves a cohabitation agreement, which of course is not in consideration or contemplation of marriage. *See Fox v. Fox*, 2002-Ohio-6877 (Ohio App. Ct. 2002) ("A prenuptial agreement is a contract entered into between a man and a woman in contemplation, and in consideration, of their future marriage."). Further, if indeed this agreement is construed as meretricious, then it will be held unenforceable, even if informed, consensual, and not unconscionable. *See Liles v. Still*, 335 S.E.2d 168, 169 (Ga. App. 1985).

31. Many states will enforce cohabitation agreements. *See Posik v. Layton*, 695 So. 2d 759, 761 (Fla. Dist. Ct. App. 1997) ("[T]he State has not denied these individuals their right to either will their property as they see fit nor to privately commit by contract to spend their money as they choose. The State is not thusly condoning the lifestyles of homosexuals or unmarried live-ins; it is merely recognizing their constitutional private property and contract rights."). While contracts for meretricious services are unenforceable, *see Jones v. Daly*, 122 Cal. App. 3d 500, 508 (1981), the agreement at issue here involved non-meretricious services including primary responsibility for childcare.

32. **Answer (B) is the best answer.** Absent fraud, coercion, or material nondisclosure, *see D'Aston v. D'Aston*, 808 P.2d 111, 113 (Utah Ct. App. 1990), parties may pick out a particular condition (e.g., the commission of adultery) that will trigger particular consequences. Here, Colleen is doing something (forgiving him and remaining in the marriage) in exchange for Carl's doing something (giving her valuable property should he stray in the future). *See Gilley v. Gilley*, 778 S.W.2d 862, 864 (Tenn. Ct. App. 1989) ("Wife had several grounds upon which to prosecute a divorce, which she did not do at the husband's request, receiving promises of faithfulness secured by a property distribution, in the event of divorce, satisfactory to wife.").

Answer (A) is not the best answer. There is no requirement that there be a like exchange as long as each party to a prenuptial is offering valuable consideration. *See* Indiana Code § 31-15-2-17 (a) (2) ("To promote the amicable settlements of disputes that have arisen or may arise between the parties to a marriage attendant upon the dissolution of their marriage, the parties may agree in writing to provisions for: . . . the disposition of any property owned by either or both of the parties.").

Answer (C) is incorrect. The consideration provided by Colleen was her remaining in the marriage rather than seeking a divorce. *See Gilley v. Gilley*, 778 S.W.2d 862, 864 (Tenn. Ct. App. 1989).

Answer (D) is incorrect. Such a provision might well be enforced against the adulterous party. *See Hall v. Hall*, 2005 Va. App. LEXIS 401 (Oct. 11, 2005) (suggesting that an agreement specifying that commission of adultery would bar receipt of support upon divorce is enforceable); *Laudig v. Laudig*, 624 A.2d 651, 652 (Pa. Super. Ct. 1993) (upholding postnuptial agreement that barred equitable distribution if wife committed adultery).

33.   **Answer (C) is the best answer.** Lack of wealth is unlikely to be held the kind of fraud that goes to the essence of marriage. *See In re Marriage of Meagher and Maleki*, 31 Cal. Rptr. 3d 663, 668 (Cal. App. 2005) ("In the absence of fraud involving the party's intentions or abilities with respect to the sexual or procreative aspect of marriage, the long-standing rule is that neither party may question the validity of the marriage upon the ground of reliance upon the express or implied representations of the other with respect to such matters as character, habits, chastity, *business or social standing, financial worth or prospects*, or matters of similar nature.") (italics added).

        Answer (A) is incorrect. As a general matter, states will not void a marriage merely because one of the parties explicitly or impliedly misrepresented his or her wealth. *See Chudnow v. Chudnow*, 2001 Mich. App. LEXIS 808 (Apr. 27, 2001) ("Fraudulent representations of wealth, or connections, or health, or temper and disposition, may in many cases be the chief inducements to matrimonial alliances, but no one has ever supposed that a marriage could be avoided for such frauds.").

        Answer (B) is incorrect. Henry will not be able to annul the marriage even if can establish that he relied on Heidi's false representations regarding her own prospects. *See Stepp v. Stepp*, 2004-Ohio-1617 (Ohio Ct. App. 2004) ("Husband states that he believed Wife's financial status to be other than what it was. Assuming arguendo that Husband stated the truth, it is still a general rule that false representation as to . . . wealth and external conditions do not constitute such fraud as will annul a marriage contract.").

        Answer (D) is incorrect. Even if Heidi correctly calculated that this fraudulent claim would be relied upon by Henry, this simply is not the type of fraud that will be the basis for an annulment. *See Tuchsher v. Tuchsher*, 184 N.Y.S.2d 131, 132 (Sup. Ct. 1959) ("It is basic principle of law that the fraud alleged as grounds for the dissolution of a marriage must relate to a vital representation; that it must consist of more than a puffing of financial worth and should be so weighty and material as to influence a person of average prudence and intelligence.").

34.   **Answer (D) is the best answer.** The basic issue is whether this misrepresentation goes to the essence of marriage. In many states, chastity does not and so could not support an annulment on the basis of fraud. *See Anonymous v. Anonymous*, 85 A.2d 706, 717–18 (Del. 1951) ("antenuptial chastity is not an essential element of the marriage relation, and . . . , in the absence of statute, concealment of premarital unchastity does not amount to fraud affording ground for annulment of the marriage."); *Lindquist v. Lindquist*, 20 A.2d 325, 328–29 (N.J. Err. & App. 1941) ("Fraudulent concealment of mere premarital unchastity has never been deemed a sufficient ground for nullification of the marriage. Antenuptial chastity is not an essential element of the contract of marriage.").

        Answer (A) is incorrect. While Joseph has reason to believe that chastity is important to Karen, that will not suffice to establish that the marriage should be annulled. Many qualities are subjectively important to individuals. Nonetheless, merely because someone falsely claims to have those important qualities does not establish that the marriage can be annulled on the basis of fraud. *See In re Marriage of Meagher and Maleki*, 31 Cal. Rptr. 3d 663, 668 (Cal. App. 2005) ("In the absence of fraud involving the party's intentions or abilities with respect to the sexual or procreative aspect of marriage, the long-standing rule is that neither party may question the validity of the marriage upon the ground of reliance upon the express or implied representations of the other with respect to such matters as . . . chastity.").

Answer (B) is incorrect. The difficulty here is in the content of the fraud and not in whether the fraud was express or merely implied. *See Williams v. Witt*, 235 A.2d 902, 903 (N.J. App. Div. 1967) (an undisclosed refusal to do something deemed an essential of the marriage can be the basis for an annulment action).

Answer (C) is incorrect. While Joseph may have destroyed the basis for trust, that might be true of any fraudulent misrepresentation regarding an issue subjectively important to one of the parties. The dispositive issue in this case is that the misrepresentation involves something that would not be deemed in most states to go to the essence of the marriage. *See Anonymous v. Anonymous*, 85 A.2d 706, 717–18 (Del. Super. 1951); *Lindquist v. Lindquist*, 20 A.2d 325, 328–29 (N.J. Err. & App.1941).

35. **Answer (D) is the best answer.** In order to be the basis of an annulment, Ned's hidden aversion to having children would have to have existed at the time of the marriage. *See Williams v. Witt*, 235 A.2d 902, 903 (N.J. App. Div. 1967) ("The annulment, in such a case, is granted on the theory that since procreation is considered to be an essential element of the marriage, there exists an implied promise at the time of the marriage to raise a family. An undisclosed contrary intention, therefore, constitutes a fraud going to an essential of the marriage. . . . The intention never to have children must antedate the marriage, for it is the implied promise to have children, coupled with the intent not to fulfill it, that constitutes the fraud.").

Answer (A) is incorrect. While it is true that many happily married couples do not have children, many states nonetheless view the unwillingness to have children as going to the essence of marriage. *See*, for example, *Chudnow v. Chudnow*, 2001 Mich. App. LEXIS 808 (Apr. 27, 2001) ("Grounds which have in the past supported an annulment decree include: . . . a misrepresentation that a party will consent to intercourse or to produce children.").

Answer (B) is incorrect. The refusal to have children goes to the essence of marriage. However, merely because Ned does not want children now does not establish that he did not want children at the time of the marriage. Only if he had not wanted them then would he have fraudulently induced Mary to marry him. *See In re Marriage of Ramirez*, 81 Cal. Rptr. 3d 180, 184 (Cal. App. 2008) ("to void a marriage, the fraud alleged must show an intention not to perform a duty vital to the marriage, which exists in the mind of the offending spouse at the time of marriage").

Answer (C) is incorrect. That the marriage was acceptable prior to the revelation of the fraud would not mean that the marriage would continue to be acceptable once the fraud had been revealed. The relevant questions are whether the fraud goes to the essence of marriage and whether no marriage would have taken place had the information been revealed in a timely manner. *See Di Pillo v. Di Pillo*, 184 N.Y.S.2d 892, 894 (Sup. Ct. 1959) ("Where the ground relied upon for dissolution is fraud, the fraud contemplated by the statute must be of a nature and import so serious that it destroys the essence of the marriage contract and of a magnitude that the person asserting the fraud as a ground for dissolution would not have entered the marriage contract, if, in advance thereof, the misrepresentations had been revealed.").

36. If, indeed, John is an innocent defrauded spouse who neither knew nor should have known that Joanna was already married to someone else, then he might well have remedies depending upon local law. Various states afford protection to such a spouse. *See Estate of Hafner*, 229 Cal. Rptr. 676 (Cal. App. 1986) (splitting estate of deceased between spouse and her children on the one hand and the innocent putative spouse and her children on the other). If John had known or had had reason to know that his marriage was bigamous, however, he likely would not have been afforded those protections. *See Capo v. Estate of Borges*, 560 So. 2d 254 (Fla. Dist. Ct. App. 1990) (individual on notice that his marriage was bigamous and thus would not have the protections accorded to an innocent spouse).

37. Traditionally, the refusal to have a child can be the basis of an annulment, because it goes to the essence of marriage. *See Zoglio v. Zoglio*, 157 A.2d 627, 628 (D.C. 1960) (suggesting that an annulment should be granted where the defendant had "refused to have marital relations unless some means were used to prevent conception"). An additional complication here is that Carol is willing to adopt, although courts in past have suggested that the unwillingness or inability to have a child though marital relations may be the basis for an annulment action. *See Stegienko v. Stegienko*, 295 N.W. 252, 254 (Mich. 1940) (annulment granted as a result of defendant's repeated refused to have unprotected sexual relations because she did not want to bear a child); *Vileta v. Vileta*, 128 P.2d 376, 377 (Cal. App. 1942) ("A woman who accepts the hand of her suitor thereby impliedly assures him of her ability, so far as lies within her knowledge, to bear children. Her concealment of her sterility is a fraud that vitiates the marriage contract . . . and justifies annulment.") While Bob and Carol could adopt, Bob will also likely be afforded the option of getting an annulment as long as he acts promptly once becoming aware of the fraud. *See id.*

38. **Answer (D) is the best answer.** For those states recognizing common law marriage, the elements tend to involve (1) capacity, (2) agreement to enter into such a relationship and be viewed by others as being married, and (3) cohabitation. *See Ram v. Ramharack*, 571 N.Y.S.2d 190, 191 (Sup. Ct. 1991); *Parks v. Martinson*, 694 So. 2d 1386, 1389 (Ala. Civ. App. 1997). Assuming that Oklanagon follows the general rule, then Pam and Quentin should be able to establish that they have met the relevant criteria for having contracted a common law marriage.

Answer (A) is incorrect. Even if the ceremonial marriage is not recognized by the state, the parties may be able to prove that they had a common law marriage. *See Wright v. Goss*, 494 S.E.2d 23, 25 (Ga. App. 1997) ("When the alleged marriage is unlicensed and nonceremonial, the burden is on the proponent to prove that a common law marriage existed.").

Answer (B) is incorrect. While states might choose to recognize a marriage entered into in good faith by the parties, *see Johnson v. Baker*, 20 P.2d 407 (Or. 1933) (upholding marriage entered into in good faith), the state need not recognize the validity of a marriage that does not meet the statutory requirements. *See Harlow v. Reliance National*, 91 S.W.3d 243 (Tenn. 2002) (refusing to recognize marriage that did not meet statutory requirements).

Answer (C) is incorrect. Even if they had had time to go through another ceremony before the required surgery and nonetheless did not do so, the question would still remain whether they had already contracted a common law marriage. *See Wright v. Goss*, 494 S.E.2d 23, 25 (Ga. App. 1997).

39. **Answer (D) is the best answer.** Once the impediment to the common law marriage was removed, the parties were free to establish a common law marriage. Some jurisdictions require an affirmative action by the parties once the impediment has been removed. *See Wilbert v. Commonwealth of Pa. Second Injury Reserve Account*, 17 A.2d 732, 736 (Pa. Super. Ct. 1941) ("to validate the relation it would require affirmative action after the death of her husband, Kearney, either in the way of a ceremonial wedding or a new agreement of common law marriage"); *Callen v. Callen*, 620 S.E.2d 59, 62 (S.C. 2005) ("after the impediment is removed, the relationship is not automatically transformed into a common-law marriage. Instead, it is presumed that relationship remains non-marital.") Here, that affirmative act would be represented by the exchange of rings, so Alice and Carl established a valid common law marriage upon the death of her former spouse.

Answer (A) is incorrect. The issue is not whether they had a common law marriage when they began living together, but whether they ever established a common law marriage in light of the relevant criteria: capacity, treating each other as husband and wife and being viewed by the community as husband and wife, and cohabitation. *See Parks v. Martinson*, 694 So. 2d 1386, 1389 (Ala. Civ. App. 1997).

Answer (B) is incorrect. While they may have treated each other as husband and wife and have been viewed in the community as husband and wife, they cannot contract a common law marriage while one of the parties is still legally married to someone else. *See Wilbert v. Commonwealth of Pa. Second Injury Reserve Account*, 17 A.2d 732, 736 (Pa. Super. Ct. 1941) ("with a husband living, from whom she had not been divorced, the claimant could not lawfully marry Wilbert either by a ceremonial wedding or a common law marriage").

Answer (C) is incorrect. Once Alvin had died, Alice was free to establish a common law marriage with Carl. *See Burdine v. Burdine*, 242 P.2d 148, 150 (Okla. 1952) (once impediment to common law marriage removed by former marriage having come to an end, the parties were free to establish a common law marriage).

40.   **Answer (C) is the best answer.** Even assuming that the parties have the capacity, treat each other as husband and wife and are known in the community as husband and wife, and cohabit, there are still other issues to be addressed. West Tenntucky law must accord recognition of common law marriages not only to those domiciled in the state but also to those with significant contacts to the state. *In re Willard's Estate*, 600 P.2d 298, 300 (N.M. Ct. App. 1979) (recognizing that individuals had enough contacts with state in which they were not domiciled to establish a common law marriage there). Further, South Florina must be willing to recognize a common law marriages validly celebrated elsewhere even if the parties are domiciled in South Florina at the time the marriage is contracted. *See In re McKanna's Estate*, 234 P.2d 673, 677 (Cal. App. 1951) (holding that a common law marriage can be established in a state recognizing such marriages even if the parties are not domiciled in that state).

Answer (A) is not the best answer. The question at hand is not merely whether Greg and Hannah met the requirements in some of the states that recognize common law marriage. Rather, the focus in particular is whether Greg and Hannah met the requirements imposed by West Tenntucky. Further, even if they did meet those requirements, the next issue to be determined is whether South Florina will recognize a common law marriage of its own domiciliaries that was contracted while they were visiting a state that recognizes such marriages. *Compare In re Binger's Estate*, 63 N.W.2d 784 (Neb. 1954) (refusing to recognize validity of common law marriage when domiciliaries of a state not recognizing common law marriage met the requirements of such a marriage while visiting a state recognizing common law marriages) *with In re McKanna's Estate*, 234 P.2d 673, 677 (Cal. App. 1951) (holding that a common law marriage can be established in a state recognizing such marriages even if the parties are not domiciled in that state).

Answer (B) is not the best answer. South Florina will recognize a common law marriage validly celebrated elsewhere, so the issue is whether the state requires that the parties have been domiciled elsewhere when contracting the marriage in order for the relationship to be recognized in South Florina. *See In re McKanna's Estate*, 234 P.2d 673, 677 (Cal. App. 1951) (holding that a common law marriage can be established in a state recognizing such marriages even if the parties are not domiciled in that state).

Answer (D) is incorrect. Some domiciles will recognize a common law marriage validly celebrated in another state as long as the parties had sufficient contacts with the non-domicile. *See Matter of Willard's Estate*, 600 P.2d 298, 300 (N.M. Ct. App. 1979); *In re McKanna's Estate*, 234 P.2d 673, 677 (Cal. App. 1951).

41.   **Answer (B) is the best answer.** A common law marriage validly contracted must be formally ended. Parties to a common law marriage may not enter into a ceremonial marriage

with someone else until first ending the common law marriage. *Crosson v. Crosson*, 668 So. 2d 868, 872–73 (Ala. Civ. App. 1995) ("Because we must take it as undisputed that the parties intended to become husband and wife in August 1993, and because they immediately began public assumption of marital duties and cohabitation, we must conclude that a common-law marriage was formed and that the husband's marriage to another, a year later, could not 'untie the knot.' ").

Answer (A) is incorrect. A common law marriage validly contracted must be formally ended. Parties to a common law marriage may not enter into a ceremonial marriage with someone else until first ending the common law marriage. *See Texas Emp. Ins. Ass'n v. Elder*, 274 S.W.2d 144, 147 (Tex. Civ. App. 1954) ("While the law does not favor, but merely tolerates, common-law marriages, yet when the facts establish such a marriage, it is as valid and binding as a ceremonial marriage and the law applicable to parties wed under a ceremonial marriage is applicable to parties to a common-law marriage.").

Answer (C) is incorrect. Once a common law marriage has been validly contracted, it must be ended formally and cannot be ended by even mutual agreement. *See Thomas v. Thomas*, 565 P.2d 722, 724 (Okla. Civ. App. 1976) (noting that if the couple entered into a common law marriage, then "nothing either party did or did not do thereafter could dissolve it. Only a court of law could do that.").

Answer (D) is incorrect. Even third parties can challenge a marriage that allegedly is void. *See Werden v. Thorpe*, 867 P.2d 557, 559 (Or. App. 1994) ("A *void* marriage . . . is invalid from the outset and may be challenged by third parties.").

42. If indeed their common law marriage is recognized, Zachary will likely not have to testify. *See People v. Schmidt*, 579 N.W.2d 431, 435 (Mich. App. 1998) ("the circuit court properly determined that Craven may not testify regarding the confidential communications made by defendant during their common-law marriage"). A separate question is whether that marriage will be recognized. While they meet the elements of common law marriage now — capacity, treat each other as spouses and are known in the community as spouses, and cohabitation, *see Parks v. Martinson*, 694 So. 2d 1386, 1389 (Ala. Civ. App. 1997), some jurisdictions require that something special be done once an impediment to the marriage has been removed, *see Callen v. Callen*, 620 S.E.2d 59, 62 (S.C. 2005) ("after the impediment is removed, the relationship is not automatically transformed into a common-law marriage. Instead, it is presumed that relationship remains non-marital."), whereas other jurisdictions may recognize the marriage as long as the parties continue to cohabit once the impediment to the marriage has been removed. *See Margulies v. Margulies*, 157 A. 676, 677 (N.J. Ch. Div. 1931) ("Where parties to an agreement and relationship which, but for the existence of an impediment, would have constituted a valid marriage, continue in the relationship in good faith, upon the removal of the impediment the law will establish between them a valid common-law marriage."). The important issue is whether Alalina requires that something special be done once the impediment has been removed. If so, then it is unlikely that the marriage will be recognized, because there is no evidence of something special having been done and Zachary did not even know about the impediment until during the trial. If the marriage will be recognized once the impediment has been removed, then it is likely that their marriage will be recognized and Zachary will not be forced to testify.

43.   **Answer (C) is the best answer.** Because Jim's civil union with Hank was never formally ended, his civil union with Matthew will likely be declared null and void and of no legal effect. *See* N.J. Stat. Ann. § 2A:34-1(2)(a) ("Judgments of nullity of a civil union may be rendered in all cases, when . . . Either of the parties has another wife, husband, partner in a civil union couple or domestic partner living at the time of establishing the new civil union.").

      Answer (A) is incorrect. Parties to civil unions have the benefits of marriage including the ability to sue for loss of consortium. *See* N.J. Stat. Ann. § 37:1-32(b) ("The following list of legal benefits, protections and responsibilities of spouses shall apply in like manner to civil union couples, but shall not be construed to be an exclusive list of such benefits, protections and responsibilities: . . . causes of action related to or dependent upon spousal status, including an action for wrongful death, emotional distress, loss of consortium, or other torts or actions under contracts reciting, related to, or dependent upon spousal status").

      Answer (B) is incorrect. A public disavowal of a civil union will not suffice to end it. *See* N.J. Stat. Ann. § 37:1-31(b) ("The dissolution of civil unions shall follow the same procedures and be subject to the same substantive rights and obligations that are involved in the dissolution of marriage.").

      Answer (D) is incorrect. A civil union must be formally dissolved before an individual enters into another civil union, just as would be true had the individuals married. *See* N.J. Stat. Ann. § 37:1-31(b) ("The dissolution of civil unions shall follow the same procedures and be subject to the same substantive rights and obligations that are involved in the dissolution of marriage.").

44.   Civil union status is a creature of state law and thus need not be recognized by other states. *See In re Marriage of J.B. and H.B.*, 2010 WL 3399074, *5 (Tex. App. 2010) (state will not give effect to civil union contracted in another state). However, such unions can be recognized by other states. *See*, for example, N.J. Stat. Ann. § 37:1-34 ("A civil union relationship entered into outside of this State, which is valid under the laws of the jurisdiction under which the civil union relationship was created, shall be valid in this State.") The question then will involve the law of Connachusetts in particular. Even if the state does not recognize civil unions, a separate question would be whether Joanne's employer would afford domestic partnership benefits. *See Leskovar v. Nickels*, 166 P.3d 1251, 1256 (Wash. App. 2007) (upholding decision by city of Seattle to afford domestic partner benefits).

45.   **Answer (D) is the best answer.** Bernard has made the home so dangerous that Bobbi Sue would be risking life and limb to remain. *See Edwards v. Edwards*, 356 A.2d 633, 637 (D.C. 1976) ("For the desertion to be 'constructive' in character, one spouse must show misconduct by the other spouse forcing the former to abandon the marital abode. If such misconduct is shown the spouse remaining in the marital abode is treated, in the eyes of the law, as the deserter."). By the same token, Bernard might be thought to have constructively abandoned Bobbi Sue. *See Blair v. Blair*, 121 N.Y.S.2d 30, 36 (N.Y. Dom. Rel. Ct. 1953) ("To entitle a wife who has left her husband to support on ground of 'constructive abandonment,' court must find as a matter of fact that it is impossible or unsafe for the wife to continue to live with her husband").

       Answer (A) is incorrect. An individual will be found guilty of desertion only if she left without just cause. *See Edwards v. Edwards*, 356 A.2d 633, 637 (D.C. 1976) ("Desertion contemplates a voluntary separation of one party from the other, without justification, an intention not to return, and the absence of consent or connivance of the other party.").

       Answer (B) is incorrect. Here, the question is whether Bobbi Sue was justified in leaving. *See Edwards v. Edwards*, 356 A.2d 633, 637 (D.C. 1976). A more plausible account of her packed bags is that this had happened before and she wanted to be prepared.

       Answer (C) is not the best answer. Constructive desertion might refer to an unjustified refusal to engage in marital relations. *See Handshoe v. Handshoe*, 560 So. 2d 182 (Miss. 1990) (finding that wife had constructively deserted husband by refusing to have any marital relations with the husband for a very long period without his consent and without just cause or excuse). The same might be said about constructive abandonment. *See Davis v. Davis*, 889 N.Y.S.2d 611, 613 (N.Y. App. Div. 2009) (defining constructive abandonment as "the refusal by a defendant spouse to engage in sexual relations with the plaintiff spouse for one or more years prior to the commencement of the action, when such refusal is unjustified, willful, and continual, and despite repeated requests for the resumption of sexual relations"). However constructive desertion or abandonment might also refer to one spouse's having made the home unsafe for the other spouse. *See Edwards v. Edwards*, 356 A.2d 633, 637 (D.C. 1976); *Blair v. Blair*, 121 N.Y.S.2d 30, 36 (N.Y. Dom. Rel. Ct. 1953).

46.   **Answer (D) is the best answer.** Adultery is taken seriously, *see Hokin v. Hokin*, 243 N.E.2d 579, 583 (Ill. App. 1968) (discussing "the more serious charge of adultery"), and both disposition and opportunity must be established. *See Roach v. Roach*, 487 A.2d 27, 28 (Pa. Super. Ct. 1985) ("Under this doctrine adultery will be presumed where three elements are shown: (1) the adulterous disposition or inclination of the defendant; (2) the adulterous disposition, or inclination, of the co-respondent; and (3) the opportunity created to satisfy their mutual adulterous inclination.") Mere suspicion will not suffice. Instead, the facts and circumstances must lead to the conclusion that the adultery took place. *See Renner v. Renner*, 12 A.2d 195, 198–99 (Md. 1940) ("The conduct of her husband may have aroused her

suspicion, but a divorce cannot be granted on suspicion, unless accompanied by facts which by fair inference must lead to the necessary conclusion that adultery has been committed."); *Boldon v. Boldon*, 354 So. 2d 275, 276 (Ala. Civ. App. 1978) ("There must be evidence presented which would lead to a necessary inference of adultery.").

Answer (A) is incorrect. While adultery is a serious charge, *see Hubbard v. Hubbard*, 317 So. 2d 489, 492 (Ala. Civ. App. 1975) (discussing "the very serious charge of adultery"), most states do not require direct and positive evidence, *see Harris v. Harris*, 81 So. 2d 705, 707 (La. 1955) ("the offense can seldom be established by direct or positive evidence"), much less that the spouse witness the act.

Answer (B) is incorrect. While adultery charges are taken seriously, *see Gray v. Hoover*, 381 S.E.2d 472, 475 (N.C. App. 1989) (discussing the seriousness of such a charge), there is no requirement that the spouse admit to having committed adultery in order for such a charge to be sustained. *See Husband v. Wife*, 253 A.2d 63 (Del. 1968) (finding that wife had committed adultery, her denial notwithstanding).

Answer (C) is incorrect. There is no requirement that third parties witness the adulterous act. For example, an admission by one of the parties plus some corroborating evidence might suffice. *See McLaurin v. McLaurin*, 363 S.E.2d 110 (S.C. Ct. App. 1987).

47.   **Answer (C) is the best answer.** Jurisdictions are split on whether the individuals must live in different households in order to establish that they live separate and apart. Compare *McCoy v. McCoy*, 888 A.2d 906 (Pa. Super. Ct. 2005) (noting that separate and apart ground does not require that the members of the couple live in different households) with *Mallard v. Mallard*, 68 S.E. 2d 247 (N.C. 1951) (requiring physical separation).

Answer (A) is not the best answer. States that have a separate-and-apart ground for dissolution of a marriage may require not only that the couple not have sexual relations but also that they live in separate abodes. *See In re Marriage of Norviel*, 126 Cal. Rptr. 2d 148, 157 (Cal. App. 2002) ("The plain language of the statute and the weight of persuasive authority thus support the view that spouses are not 'living separate and apart' within the meaning of the statute unless they reside in different places.").

Answer (B) is not the best answer. Some states with a separate-and-apart ground require physical separation and no matrimonial relations. *See Mallard v. Mallard*, 68 S.E.2d 247, 248 (N.C. 1951) ("A husband and wife live separate and apart for the prescribed period . . . when, and only when, these two conditions concur: (1) They live separate and apart physically for an uninterrupted period of two years; and (2) their physical separation is accompanied by at least an intention on the part of one of them to cease their matrimonial cohabitation.") However, not all states require the couple to live apart physically if their separation can be established in other ways. *See In re Marriage of Uhls*, 549 S.W.2d 107, 112 (Mo. Ct. App. 1977) (finding that "petitioner and respondent have been living separate and apart for over two years immediately prior to the filing of the petition, that there remains no reasonable likelihood that the marriage can be preserved, that the marriage is irretrievably broken, and that petitioner is entitled to a decree of dissolution of her marriage with the respondent").

Answer (D) is not the best answer. That the couple can cooperate so that they can have minimal contact with each other in the same household does not establish that their marriage is salvageable. *See In re Marriage of Uhls*, 549 S.W.2d 107, 112 (Mo. Ct. App. 1977) (finding marriage irretrievably broken notwithstanding that the couple had been living in the same household for the past two years).

48. **Answer (D) is the best answer.** *See In re Marriage of von der Nuell*, 28 Cal. Rptr. 2d 447, 450 (Cal. App. 1994) ("legal separation requires not only a parting of the ways with no present intention of resuming marital relations, but also, more importantly, *conduct* evidencing a *complete and final break* in the marital relationship"). *See also In re Marriage of Marsden*, 181 Cal. Rptr. 910, 914 (Cal. App. 1982) ("the parties' conduct would appear to be an attempt to effect a reconciliation . . . and certainly does not reflect a complete and final break in the marital relationship").

Answer (A) is not the best answer. The separate and apart ground requires that they not have frequent sexual relations during the relevant period. *See Reilly v. Reilly*, 190 A. 476, 478 (R.I. 1937) (couple had not been living separate and apart when they had had sexual relations during the relevant period).

Answer (B) is not the best answer. While it is likely that the dissolution will not be granted in this case, some states would not treat an isolated instance of sexual relations as requiring the clock to begin again. *See* N.C. Gen. Stat. Ann. § 50-6 ("Isolated incidents of sexual intercourse between the parties shall not toll the statutory period required for divorce predicated on separation of one year."); *Millon v. Millon*, 352 So. 2d 325, 327 (La. Ct. App. 1977) (isolated acts of intercourse do not preclude divorce).

Answer (C) is not the best answer. Although they are not sharing the same roof, their frequently having sexual relations will likely preclude them from getting a dissolution on this ground. *See In re Marriage of von der Nuell*, 28 Cal. Rptr. 2d 447, 450 (Cal. App. 1994) ("legal separation requires not only a parting of the ways with no present intention of resuming marital relations, but also, more importantly, *conduct* evidencing a *complete and final break* in the marital relationship").

49. **Answer (A) is the best answer.** Merely because fault is not required does not mean that the couple can end their marriage immediately. *See*, for example, *Thomas v. Thomas*, 483 A.2d 945, 948 (Pa. Super. Ct. 1984) ("Under New Jersey's 'no-fault' divorce statute, a unilateral divorce may be granted if the parties have lived separate and apart in different habitations for an eighteen month period and there is no reasonable prospect of reconciliation.").

Answer (B) is incorrect. In a no-fault divorce, neither of the parties is charged with having committed a marital fault. *See Pennings v. Pennings*, 786 A.2d 622, 625 n.3 (Me. 2002) (" 'No-fault divorce' is a term frequently used in the literature as a short-hand way to describe a ground for divorce that does not require as a predicate some culpable act of wrongdoing by a party."). It need not be true that both parties are entirely above reproach.

Answer (C) is incorrect. While spousal support may not be required when there is a no-fault divorce, *see McElroy v. McElroy*, 249 S.E.2d 538, 538 (Ga. 1978) ("It is not required that alimony be awarded in no-fault divorce cases."), such an award is not precluded.

Answer (D) is incorrect. A no-fault divorce can be obtained when a child is born of a marriage. *See*, for example, *Rude v. Rude*, 246 S.E.2d 311, 312 (Ga. 1978) (upholding award of custody of child to mother in no-fault divorce).

50. **Answer (D) is the best answer.** Post-separation adultery may affect a spousal support award, *see Roberts v. Roberts*, 519 So. 2d 229 (La. Ct. App. 1988) (upholding denial of spousal support because of post-separation adultery) or the distribution of marital assets), see *Legat*

v. Legat, 1999 Va. App. LEXIS 497 (Aug. 10, 1999) (upholding trial court's considering post-separation adultery when distributing marital assets). However, if it can be established that the adultery played no role in the breakdown of the marriage, then the adultery may not affect spousal support or the distribution of assets. *See Perlberger v. Perlberger*, 626 A.2d 1186 (Pa. Super. Ct. 1993) (post-separation adultery not a factor in distribution of marital assets); *Wallace v. Wallace*, 416 A.2d 1317 (Md. App. 1980) (refusing to preclude wife from receiving support for her post-separation adultery when the break-up of the marriage had been husband's fault).

Answer (A) is not the best answer. Post-separation adultery can affect spousal support in some jurisdictions. *See*, for example, *Helms v. Helms*, 534 So. 2d 502 (La. Ct. App. 1988) (upholding divorce based on post-separation adultery and permitting that finding to affect spousal support award).

Answer (B) is incorrect. If the post-separation adultery did not contribute to the irretrievable breakdown of the marriage, then it need not affect the distribution of marital assets. *See Perlberger v. Perlberger*, 626 A.2d 1186 (Pa. Super. Ct. 1993).

Answer (C) is not the best answer. While the attorney would be correct that, for example, there would be no need to wait for the statutorily required period of living separate and apart if the divorce were granted because of adultery, he is incorrect that she should be pleased. The finding of adultery might be the basis for refusing to award spousal support. *See Roberts v. Roberts*, 519 So. 2d 229 (La. Ct. App. 1988) (upholding denial of spousal support because of post-separation adultery).

51.   **Answer (D) is the best answer.** As long as the court has personal jurisdiction over at least one of the parties and subject matter jurisdiction based on the domicile of one of the parties, and at least one of the parties has resided there for the requisite period, *see Abernathy v. Abernathy*, 482 S.E.2d 265, 267 (Ga. 1997) ("party seeking a divorce need show only that the trial court has jurisdiction over the res of the marriage which results from his or her domicile in this state for the six-month period preceding the filing of the action") and West Virginia Code § 48-5-105 (2) (A-B) (discussing residency requirement), then the court will apply local law to determine if the requisite conditions have been met. *See Sinha v. Sinha*, 834 A.2d 600, 605 (Pa. Super. Ct. 2003) ("In the context of marriages and divorces, it is generally accepted that the local law of the domiciliary state in which the action is brought will be applied to determine the right to divorce.").

Answer (A) is incorrect. Alice may well be able to file in Pennio, because Bob has met the relevant residency and domiciliary requirement. *See*, for example, West Virginia Code § 48-5-105 (2) (A-B) ("If the marriage was not entered into within this state, an action for divorce is maintainable if: . . . One of the parties was an actual bona fide resident of this state at the time the cause of action arose, or has become a resident since that time; and . . . The residency has continued uninterrupted through the one-year period immediately preceding the filing of the action.").

Answer (B) is incorrect. The divorce can be based on the Pennigan statute. *See Sinha v. Sinha*, 834 A.2d 600, 605 (Pa. Super. Ct. 2003) ("In the context of marriages and divorces, it is generally accepted that "[t]he local law of the domiciliary state in which the action is brought will be applied to determine the right to divorce.").

Answer (C) is incorrect. There must not only be personal jurisdiction over at least one of the parties but the court must also have jurisdiction over the marriage itself. *See Abernathy v. Abernathy*, 482 S.E.2d 265, 267 (Ga. 1997) (party must show that "the trial court has jurisdiction over the res of the marriage").

52. **Answer (D) is the best answer.** Because Zelda could easily have given Yevgeny actual notice, the notice requirement will not have been met and Yevgeny will be considered her widower. *See In re Roedell's Estate*, 112 N.W.2d 842 (Iowa 1962) (failure to give actual notice when address was known made divorce decree invalid).

Answer (A) in incorrect. Merely because a divorce decree has become final would not preclude a court from later declaring it void. *See*, for example, *DeGroot v. DeGroot*, 260 S.W.3d 658, 665 (Tex. App. 2008).

Answer (B) is incorrect. Constructive notice will not suffice when actual notice could easily have been given. *See Golson v. Golson*, 351 So. 2d 100 (La. 1977).

Answer (C) is incorrect. The difficulty was the lack of notice. *See Golson v. Golson*, 351 So. 2d 100 (La. 1977). The court was correct in applying local law to determine the length of time that the parties had to live separate and apart. *See Sinha v. Sinha*, 834 A.2d 600, 605 (Pa. Super. Ct. 2003) ("In the context of marriages and divorces, it is generally accepted that "[t]he local law of the domiciliary state in which the action is brought will be applied to determine the right to divorce.").

53. **Answer (C) is the best answer.** While only giving constructive notice may defeat the validity of a divorce if it would have been easy to have given actual notice, *see In re Roedell's Estate*, 112 N.W.2d 842 (Iowa 1962) (failure to give actual notice when address was known made divorce decree invalid), this does not mean that Ida as an innocent (but not legally married) spouse will be unprotected. *See Estate of Hafner*, 229 Cal. Rptr. 676, 679 (Cal. App. 1986) (splitting estate between spouse and innocent putative spouse); *Seizer v. Sessions*, 940 P.2d 261, 269 (Wash. 1997) (discussing ways in which both Texas and Washington protect innocent putative spouse).

Answer (A) is incorrect. While only giving constructive notice may defeat the validity of a divorce if it would have been easy to have given actual notice, *see In re Roedell's Estate*, 112 N.W.2d 842 (Iowa 1962) (failure to give actual notice when address was known made divorce decree invalid), this does not mean that Ida as an innocent (but not legally married) spouse will be unprotected. *See In re Marriage of Ramirez*, 81 Cal. Rptr. 3d 180, 183 (Cal. App. 2008) ("An innocent party to an invalid marriage may obtain relief as a putative spouse if the party believed in good faith that the marriage was valid.").

Answer (B) is incorrect. Because there was inadequate notice, the first marriage never ended. *See Crenshaw v. Crenshaw*, 471 S.E.2d 845, 846 (Ga. 1996) (inadequate notice meant divorce decree had to be set aside).

Answer (D) is incorrect. Here, Georgina asserted her claim within a reasonable amount of time and thus could not be barred by laches. *See Sullivan v. Mandigo*, 332 N.Y.S.2d 200, 201 (N.Y. App. Div. 1972) (action challenging validity of divorce six years later not barred by laches).

54. **Answer (D) is the best answer.** Depending upon the jurisdiction, marital fault may be considered when determining which parent should have custody. *See Etheridge v. Etheridge*, 375 So. 2d 474, 475 (Ala. Civ. App. 1979) ("such conduct is a matter to be considered in

determining whose custody will secure and protect the best interest of the child at this time"). It also may be considered when determining spousal support, *see King v. King*, 681 S.E.2d 609, 613 (S.C. Ct. App. 2009), or a division of property. *See Paulson v. Paulson*, 783 N.W.2d 262, 270 (N.D. 2010) (the trial court may consider fault when distributing property).

Answer (A) is not the best answer. Were a court to find that her having an affair was the ultimate cause of the couple's divorce, it could affect, for example, the distribution of marital property. *See Paulson v. Paulson*, 783 N.W.2d 262, 270 (N.D. 2010) (the trial court may consider fault when distributing property).

Answer (B) is not the best answer, because marital fault might affect spousal support. *See Bodkin v. Bodkin*, 694 S.E.2d 230, 237 (S.C. Ct. App. 2010) (trial court should consider marital misconduct or fault when determining spousal support).

Answer (C) is not the best answer. Depending upon the jurisdiction, adultery may be considered when determining which parent's having custody would promote the best interests of the child. *See Etheridge v. Etheridge*, 375 So. 2d 474, 475 (Ala. Civ. App. 1979) ("such conduct is a matter to be considered in determining whose custody will secure and protect the best interest of the child at this time"). Misconduct during the marriage can be considered as one factor in determining spousal support. *See Elliott v. Elliott*, 11 So. 3d 784, 786 (Miss. Ct. App. 2009).

55.   **Answer (C) is the best answer.** *See M.T. v. J.T.*, 355 A.2d 204 (N.J. App. Div. 1976) (recognizing marriage between man and post-operative male-to-female transsexual where he was well aware of her transgender status).

Answer (A) is incorrect. A state might refuse to recognize a marriage even if no fraud was involved and both parties were well aware that one of the parties was transgendered. *See In re Estate of Gardiner*, 42 P.3d 120, 124 (Kan. 2002) (refusing to recognize marriage between man and male-to-female transsexual even though husband was well aware of his wife's transgender status).

Answer (B) is incorrect. A state that does not recognize same-sex marriage might nonetheless recognize a marriage between a man and a male-to-female transsexual. *See M.T. v. J.T.*, 355 A.2d 204 (N.J. App. Div. 1976).

Answer (D) is incorrect. The transgendered are not precluded from marrying. *See M.T. v. J.T.*, 355 A.2d 204 (N.J. App. Div. 1976).

56.   **Answer (B) is the best answer.** *See In re Estate of Gardiner*, 42 P.3d 120, 137 (Kan. 2002) (suggesting that the sex of a post-operative transsexual is defined in terms of that person's chromosomes for purposes of the marriage statute).

Answer (A) is incorrect. The transgendered are not precluded from marrying. *See M.T. v. J.T.*, 355 A.2d 204 (N.J. App. Div. 1976) (recognizing marriage between man and post-operative male-to-female transsexual).

Answer (C) is not the best answer. A state that defines the sex of an individual in terms of his or her chromosomes, *see Kantaras v. Kantaras*, 884 So. 2d 155 (Fla. Dist. Ct. App. 2004) (suggesting that Florida defines sex that way), might permit such a marriage. Separate issues might arise when Kim has the relevant surgical procedure. *See*, for example, La. Stat. Ann. § 40:62(B) (discussing requirements when an individual with a spouse seeks to have a birth certificate changed because of sex reassignment surgery).

Answer (D) is not the best answer. That a Justice of the Peace had married them would not guarantee the validity of the marriage. *See Estate of Goldwater v. Commissioner of Internal Revenue*, 64 T.C. 540, 551 (Tax Court 1975) (discussing marriage performed by a Justice of the Peace that was subsequently declared void and of no legal effect).

57. **Answer (D) is the best answer.** The question would be whether these complaints would make life in the marriage intolerable. *See McGehee v. McGehee*, 448 S.W.2d 300, 302 (Mo. Ct. App. 1969) ("to constitute indignities sufficient to warrant the granting of a divorce, the episodes complained of must amount to an intolerable continuous course of conduct that connotes settled hatred and a plain manifestation of alienation and estrangement equaling a species of mental cruelty, and must evidence a course of action whereby the other's condition is rendered intolerable").

Answer (A) is incorrect. While the marriage is not thriving, that does not establish that the conduct complained of meets the relevant test. Traditionally, this criterion is met when one of the parties endangers the health or safety of the other or acts in a way that would make it unreasonable to expect the other party to continue living in the household. *See Gazzillo v. Gazzillo*, 379 A.2d 288, 291 (N.J. Ch. Div. 1977) (defining mental cruelty as "including any physical or mental cruelty which endangers the safety or health of the plaintiff or makes it improper or unreasonable to expect the plaintiff to continue to cohabit with the defendant").

Answer (B) is incorrect. Merely because each is doing something that the other does not like does not mean that the two are acting equally objectionably. *Cf. Maranto v. Maranto*, 297 So. 2d 704, 706 (La. Ct. App. 1974) ("Having found mutual fault, the question for resolution is whether or not the fault on the part of either one is more grievous than that of the other so as to entitle the party 'lesser' at fault to a judgment of separation."). For example, one may have committed domestic violence. *See Peters-Riemers v. Riemers*, 644 N.W.2d 197 (N.D. 2002) (granting divorce based in part on husband's domestic violence).

Answer (C) is not correct. The point is not that the ability to perform a core function was questioned but the degree to which the alleged mental cruelty made life in the marriage unbearable. *See McGehee v. McGehee*, 448 S.W.2d 300, 302 (Mo. Ct. App. 1969).

58. **Answer (D) is the best answer.** Many states will permit a couple to divorce even if they had relations once during the relevant period. *See*, for example, N.C. Stat. § 50-6 ("Isolated incidents of sexual intercourse between the parties shall not toll the statutory period required for divorce predicated on separation of one year."). Any other rule might deter couples from attempting to reconcile.

Answer (A) is incorrect. Not all jurisdictions would say that a couple's having marital relations a couple of times during the period of living separate and apart would require the clock to begin anew. *See McVicker v. McVicker*, 1998 Pa. Dist. & Cnty. Dec. LEXIS 14 (Nov. 9, 1998) (suggesting that a few "instances of sexual relations during a separation period do not, without more, defeat a claim that the parties have lived separate and apart").

Answer (B) is incorrect. The couple having repeatedly and consistently had marital relations during the period might well preclude them from asserting this ground until they had lived separately for the requisite period without continuing to have marital relations. *See Wellner v. Wellner*, 699 A.2d 1278, 1282 (Pa. Super. Ct. 1997) ("Wife then further explained that the parties resumed their marital relations after she moved to their daughter's home and did not finally separate until August of 1992. Accordingly, we find no error in the court's determination that neither party revealed an intent to dissolve the marital union apart from mere physical separation until August of 1992.").

Answer (C) is incorrect. The requirement is that the couple live apart and not have a sexual relationship during the proscribed period. *See Smith v. Smith*, 564 S.E.2d 591, 592 (N.C. App. 2002) ("Marriages may be dissolved and the parties thereto divorced from the bonds of matrimony on the application of either party, *if and when the husband and wife have lived separate and apart for one year*.") There is no further requirement that the members of the couple dislike one another.

59.   Penny is correct that the requirements of residence and domicile are two separate requirements. Domicile can be established when a person moves to a state and has the intention to remain there permanently. *See Sasse v. Sasse*, 249 P.2d 380, 381–82 (Wash. 1952) ("A legally competent person may choose his domicile. To acquire a domicile of choice, he must establish a dwelling place with the intention of making it his home."). Residence is measured in terms of whether the person has been living in the state for the required period of time. *See*, for example, Minn. Stat. § 518.07 ("No dissolution shall be granted unless (1) one of the parties has resided in this state, or has been a member of the armed services stationed in this state, for not less than 180 days immediately preceding the commencement of the proceeding; or (2) one of the parties has been a domiciliary of this state for not less than 180 days immediately preceding commencement of the proceeding.").

60.   Stewart will be barred from challenging the divorce in Marryvania when he had been personally served in the state in which the divorce was granted. *See Lofton v. Lofton*, 924 So. 2d 596, 601 (Miss. Ct. App. 2006) ("a party to a divorce may not collaterally attack a foreign divorce decree if . . . the defendant spouse was personally served in the state where the divorce action was filed.") If he had wanted to challenge the jurisdiction of the Divorca court, he could have done so in the Divorca proceeding. He has now lost his opportunity to challenge the divorce.

61.   **Answer (C) is the best answer.** In this case, Jack reached an agreement with Jill that she would commit adultery. *See* Miss. Code Ann. § 93-5-1 ("Divorces from the bonds of matrimony may be decreed to the injured party for . . . [a]dultery, unless it should appear that it was committed by collusion of the parties for the purpose of procuring a divorce.").

    Answer (A) is incorrect. Recrimination is a defense which basically asserts that the other party to the marriage has also committed a marital fault. *See Jenkins v. Jenkins*, 55 So. 3d 1094 (Miss. Ct. App. 2010) ("Under the common-law doctrine of recrimination, if each party to a marriage proved a fault-based ground for divorce, then neither party was entitled to a divorce.").

    Answer (B) is incorrect. Condonation should be understood to involve one party's forgiving the other party for having committed a marital fault. *See Moore v. Moore*, 375 A.2d 37, 39 (Md. Ct. Spec. App. 1977) ("Condonation is a conditional forgiveness of a marital offense. The resumption of marital relations is evidence of condonation.").

    Answer (D) is incorrect. This is not ingenuity but the perpetration of a fraud on the court. *See Billington v. Billington*, 595 A.2d 1377, 1383 (Conn. 1991) ("the concept of fraud on the court in the marital litigation context is properly confined to situations where both parties join to conceal material information from the court"). *Cf. Garza v. Garza*, 183 N.W.2d 880, 885 (Mich. App. 1970) ("plaintiff did practice fraud on the court in concealing the fact that he and defendant had resumed marital relations").

62.   Gertrude can plead recrimination, which basically asserts that each party has committed a marital fault. Traditionally, a plea of recrimination would preclude the parties from divorcing, because only innocent parties were entitled to divorce. *See Jenkins v. Jenkins*, 55 So. 3d 1094 (Miss. Ct. App. 2010) ("Under the common-law doctrine of recrimination, if each party to a marriage proved a fault-based ground for divorce, then neither party was entitled to a divorce.") However, recrimination is no longer a bar to divorce in many states. For example, recrimination might be used to preclude a party from seeking a fault-based divorce, but permit the parties to end the marriage on a no-fault ground. *See*, for example, *Krause v. Krause*, 1990 WL 751283, *3 (Va. Cir. Ct. 1990) ("[B]ecause the doctrine of recrimination bars Mr. Krause from obtaining a divorce based on fault, his obligation to pay spousal support continues. The right to spousal support is not affected by an award of no-fault divorce.") That way, Gertrude would not receive a less favorable distribution of assets.

63.   Norman's attorney should explain that condonation of an adulterous act precludes the use of that act to establish the existence of that ground for divorce. *See Vinson v. Vinson*, 880 So. 2d 469, 475 (Ala. Civ. App. 2003) (" 'Condonation' in the context of a divorce case means forgiveness by the offended spouse. Where there has been a condonation of adultery, a divorce may not be granted on the ground of adultery.") However, not all jurisdictions would treat the couple having marital relations after revelation of the marital fault as necessarily

constituting forgiveness. *See Rush v. Rush*, 551 So. 2d 1075, 1077 (Ala. Civ. App. 1989) ("Our courts have held that something more than a mere temporary cohabitive relationship must occur to act as a condonation in a divorce proceeding."). Any contrary rule might deter innocent parties from trying to save their marriages, for fear that they would thereby be precluded from making use of the marital fault that in fact destroyed the marriage. Thus, the attorney will have to explore whether Forgivahoma treats a single instance of marital relations after admission of a marital fault as condoning that fault. In any event, Norman having marital relations with Mary would not be treated as condoning a marital fault of which he had no knowledge, i.e., her having had relations with Oscar when she and Oscar broke up. Further, Norman condoning the first act of adultery would not thereby immunize other acts of adultery. *See Bourlon v. Bourlon*, 670 P.2d 1004, 1005 (Okla. Civ. App. 1983) ("It is possible that the husband did know of one of his wife's sexual acts and did condone it. However, condonation is conditional upon future good behavior and on not repeating the offense.") Once Norman becomes aware of Mary's having comforted Oscar, Norman will have the basis for a fault-based divorce whether or not he is viewed as having condoned the earlier adultery.

64.   **Answer (D) is the best answer.** Laches involves a failure to assert one's rights resulting in someone else's detrimentally relying on the status quo. *See Adam v. Adam*, 624 A.2d 1093, 1096 (R.I. 1993) ("Laches is an equitable defense that involves not only delay but also a party's detrimental reliance on the status quo."). This might especially be applicable if parties married in reliance on the validity of a divorce and then had a child. *See Fairclough v. St. Amand*, 114 So. 472, 474 (Ala. 1927) ("[I]t has been declared that when a child has been born to one of the parties to a divorce by a marriage succeeding such divorce, the decree of divorce will not be set aside at the instance of one who by his laches has acquiesced in such decree.") Here, Sandra waited twenty years, and her ex-husband had long since remarried and had a child with his second wife.

Answer (A) is not the best answer. Condonation implies forgiveness and Sandra having done nothing is unlikely to be construed as implicit forgiveness. *See Nemeth v. Nemeth*, 481 S.E.2d 181, 185 (S.C. Ct. App. 1997) ("To establish condonation, there generally must be proof of reconciliation, which implies normal cohabitation of the husband and wife in the family home.").

Answer (B) is not the best answer. Connivance is usually thought to involve one spouse's consent to the other spouse's commission of a marital fault. *See Greene v. Greene*, 190 S.E.2d 258, 260 (N.C. App. 1972) ("Connivance in the law of divorce is the plaintiff's consent, express or implied, to the misconduct alleged as a ground for divorce.") What is at issue here is Thomas's failure to accord Sandra due process.

Answer (C) is not the best answer. Recrimination is the assertion that the allegedly innocent party also committed a marital fault. *See Bakala v. Bakala*, 576 S.E.2d 156, 167–68 (S.C. 2003) ("Recrimination is a defense to an action for divorce if the acts of recrimination charged constitute in themselves a ground for divorce.").

65.   **Answer (C) is the best answer.** Able has acted to promote his wife's infidelity and so might be accused of connivance. *See Santoro v. Santoro*, 55 N.Y.S.2d 294, 295 (Sup. Ct. 1945) ("Connivance, which is a defense most available in cases of adultery although applying in other instances, may be defined as the corrupt consenting of a married party to that offense

of the spouse for which that party afterward seeks a divorce.").

Answer (A) is incorrect. Condonation involves forgiving a spouse for having committed a marital fault. *See Moore v. Moore*, 375 A.2d 37, 39 (Md. Ct. Spec. App. 1977) ("Condonation is a conditional forgiveness of a marital offense. The resumption of marital relations is evidence of condonation.").

Answer (B) is incorrect. Recrimination involves the allegedly innocent party also having committed a marital fault. *See Bakala v. Bakala*, 576 S.E.2d 156, 167–68 (S.C. 2003) ("Recrimination is a defense to an action for divorce if the acts of recrimination charged constitute in themselves a ground for divorce.").

Answer (D) is incorrect. Collusion involves an agreement between the husband and wife to bring about the divorce. *See Maimone v. Maimone*, 90 N.E.2d 383, 386 (Ohio App. 1949). Here, Brianna was not a party to the agreement.

66. **Answer (B) is the best answer.** Because Michael was domiciled in Divorca and because Michaela had actual notice of the proceeding, the divorcee granted there was valid and subject to full faith and credit. *See Gage v. Gage*, 89 F. Supp. 987, 990 (D.D.C. 1950) ("A divorce decree based on a bona fide domicil and procedural due process is valid and entitled to recognition in other states.").

Answer (A) is incorrect. Divorca does not need to have personal jurisdiction over both parties to grant a divorce. *See De Marigny v. De Marigny*, 92 N.Y.S.2d 217, 220 (Sup. Ct. 1949).

Answer (C) is incorrect. Because Divorca had jurisdiction to grant the divorce, the court could of course apply local substantive law to the matter before it. *See Sinha v. Sinha*, 834 A.2d 600, 605 (Pa. Super. Ct. 2003) (noting that the "local law of the domiciliary state in which the action is brought will be applied to determine the right to divorce").

Answer (D) is incorrect. If Divorca had not had jurisdiction to grant the divorce, for example, because Michael was not domiciled there, Michaela would have been able to challenge the divorce collaterally in Connsylvania, her ability to have flown to Divorca notwithstanding. *See Gentry v. Gentry*, 924 S.W.2d 678, 680 (Tenn. 1996) ("a divorce decree is void and subject to collateral attack . . . where the trial court lacks general jurisdiction of the subject matter, . . . or lacks jurisdiction over the party complaining").

67. **Answer (D) is the best answer.** In order for West Texicana to have jurisdiction to grant the divorce, Sam would have to have been domiciled there. *See Melillo v. Melillo*, 18 Conn. Supp. 397 (1953) ("judicial power to grant a divorce — jurisdiction, strictly speaking — is founded on domicil").

Answer (A) is incorrect. The issue is whether the West Texicana court had jurisdiction to grant the divorce, not whether the laws of West Texicana and West Mexico were comparable. For West Texicana to have jurisdiction to grant a divorce, Sam would have to have been domiciled there. To be domiciled there, Sam would had to have had the intention to remain there permanently. *See Das v. Das*, 603 A.2d 139, 140 (N.J. Ch. Div. 1992) (suggesting that the two requirements to establish domicile are "(1) physical presence; and (2) a concomitant unqualified intention to remain permanently and indefinitely").

Answer (B) is incorrect. If West Texicana had jurisdiction to grant the divorce, local law would have been appropriate to apply. *See Sinha v. Sinha*, 834 A.2d 600, 605 (Pa. Super. Ct. 2003) (noting that the "local law of the domiciliary state in which the action is brought will be applied to determine the right to divorce").

Answer (C) is incorrect. A divorce decree can be attacked collaterally for lack of jurisdiction. *See Gentry v. Gentry*, 924 S.W.2d 678, 680 (Tenn. 1996) ("a divorce decree is void and subject to collateral attack . . . where the trial court lacks general jurisdiction of the subject matter").

68. **Answer (D) is the best answer.** Because Winston already contested the jurisdictional of the Nevodu court, he will not be offered an opportunity to relitigate that same issue. *See Cummiskey v. Cummiskey*, 107 N.W.2d 864, 865 (Minn. 1961) ("Where, however, the jurisdictional facts as to residence were litigated in the court in which the decree of divorce was rendered, the decree may not be attacked collaterally in another jurisdiction with respect to such facts. The jurisdictional fact of domicile in the divorce-granting forum, having been litigated and determined by judgment of the court, becomes res judicata, and by force of the full faith and credit clause it may not be questioned collaterally in another jurisdiction.").

Answer (A) is incorrect. While it seems likely that Violet did not change her domicile, that issue has already been litigated and will not be subject to collateral attack. *See Cummiskey v. Cummiskey*, 107 N.W.2d 864, 865 (Minn. 1961).

Answer (B) is incorrect. While the decree is likely to be given full faith and credit, that is not because the court applied local law correctly but, instead, because the jurisdictional issue had already been litigated. *See Cummiskey v. Cummiskey*, 107 N.W.2d 864, 865 (Minn. 1961). Had Winston not challenged the court's jurisdiction in Nevodu, he could have made a collateral challenge in New Caledonia, correct application of local law by the Nevodu court notwithstanding. *See Gentry v. Gentry*, 924 S.W.2d 678, 680 (Tenn. 1996) ("a divorce decree is void and subject to collateral attack . . . where the trial court lacks general jurisdiction of the subject matter").

Answer (C) is incorrect. Violet could have changed her domicile to take advantage of the less stringent divorce requirements and the decree would have been given full faith and credit. *See Gage v. Gage*, 89 F. Supp. 987, 990 (D.D.C. 1950) ("A divorce decree based on a bona fide domicil and procedural due process is valid and entitled to recognition in other states.").

69. **Answer (D) is the best answer.** While the jurisdiction might treat the divorce as void for lack of jurisdiction, *see Rappel v. Rappel*, 240 N.Y.S.2d 692, 696 (Sup. Ct. 1963) (holding divorce void because decree-granting state lacked jurisdiction to grant the divorce), the jurisdiction might not allow someone who has benefited from a divorce to later challenge its validity. *See In re Marriage of Gryka*, 413 N.E.2d 153, 155 (Ill. App. 1980) ("one who accepts the benefits of a divorce decree may be estopped from subsequently challenging the validity of that decree").

Answer A is incorrect. Absent a treaty or statute to the contrary, *see Van Kooten Holding B.V. v. Dumarco Corp.*, 670 F. Supp. 227, 229 (N.D. Ill. 1987) ("the UFMJR specifically incorporates the standards of the Constitution's full faith and credit clause and applies those standards to judgments of foreign countries"), full faith and credit need not be given to the judgments of other countries. *See id.* ("the full faith and credit clause of Article IV, § 1 of the Constitution does not, of its own force, require the states to enforce the judgments of foreign countries").

Answer (B) is incorrect. While courts may recognize a foreign judgment out of comity, they are not required to do so out of comity. *See Aleem v. Aleem*, 947 A.2d 489, 499 (Md. 2008) (while foreign divorce judgments are entitled to deference and respect, they need not be recognized if they would violate an important public policy of the forum).

Answer (C) is not the best answer. Depending upon the jurisdiction, Anthony might be estopped from challenging the validity of the divorce, given his having relied on its validity so that he could marry his paramour. *See In re Marriage of Gryka*, 413 N.E.2d 153, 155 (Ill. App. 1980) (stopping man who had remarried from asserting invalidity of prior divorce).

70.   **Answer (D) is the best answer.** The validity of the marriage will depend upon the degree to which such a marriage violates an important public policy of the state. The fact that it is prohibited locally will not be dispositive, however. *See In re Loughmiller's Estate*, 629 P.2d 156, 161 (Kan. 1981) ("Although our statutes prohibit first cousin marriages and impose criminal penalties where such marriages are contracted in Kansas, we cannot find that a first cousin marriage validly contracted elsewhere is odious to the public policy of this state.").

        Answer (A) is incorrect. Some but not all marriages that could not be celebrated locally may nonetheless be recognized if validly celebrated elsewhere. *See In re Loughmiller's Estate*, 629 P.2d 156, 158 (Kan. 1981) (upholding validity of marriage of first cousins, valid where celebrated, although it could not be celebrated locally).

        Answer (B) is incorrect. Some marriages that cannot be celebrated locally will not be recognized even if validly celebrated elsewhere if they are thought to violate an important policy of the state. *See In re Mortenson's Estate*, 316 P.2d 1106 (Ariz. 1957) (refusing to recognize first cousin marriage, validly celebrated elsewhere, because such marriages were thought to violate an important public policy of the state).

        Answer (C) is incorrect. Even marriages that are prohibited locally because thought to involve individuals too closely related by blood may nonetheless be recognized if validly celebrated elsewhere and not thought to violate an important public policy of the state. *See Mazzolini v. Mazzolini*, 155 N.E.2d 206 (Ohio 1958) (recognizing first cousin marriage validly celebrated elsewhere, even though such a marriage could not be celebrated within the state).

71.   **Answer (D) is the best answer.** A state may be more deferential to marriages validly celebrated in another domicile than it would be to marriages celebrated elsewhere by its own domiciliaries. *See*, for example, *In re Estate of Toutant*, 633 N.W.2d 692, 696 (Wis. Ct. App. 2001) (refusing to recognize a marriage of a Wisconsin domiciliary who had married her husband only 3 months after he had divorced). However, Wisconsin may recognize a marriage validly contracted in another domicile, even if it could not be contracted by Wisconsin domiciliaries. *See Xiong ex rel. Edmondson v. Xiong*, 648 N.W.2d 900, 906 (Wis. Ct. App. 2002) (recognizing common law marriage of couple domiciled in Pennsylvania); *In re Estate of Boyd*, 2000 WI App 31 ("common law marriages are not recognized in this state").

        Answer (A) is incorrect. Traditionally, marriages are not subject to full faith and credit guarantees. *See Brinson v. Brinson*, 96 So. 2d 653, 659 (La. 1957) ("It is a well established rule of conflict of laws that the spirit of comity between states does not require a state to recognize a marriage which is contrary to its own public policy.").

        Answer (B) is incorrect. Merely because a marriage cannot be celebrated locally does not establish that it will not be recognized if validly celebrated elsewhere. *See In re Loughmiller's Estate*, 629 P.2d 156, 158 (Kan. 1981) (upholding validity of marriage of first cousins, valid where celebrated, although it could not be celebrated locally).

Answer (C) is incorrect. A state may recognize a marriage validly contracted by domiciliaries living elsewhere that would not be recognized were it contracted by its own domiciliaries temporarily living elsewhere. *Compare Xiong ex rel. Edmondson v. Xiong*, 648 N.W.2d 900, 906 (Wis. Ct. App. 2002) (recognizing common law marriage of couple domiciled in Pennsylvania) *with In re Estate of Boyd*, 2000 WI App 31 ("common law marriages are not recognized in this state").

72. Two distinct issues must be addressed. One issue is whether the divorce is valid. Because Bob was not a domiciliary of Dakatacut, the divorce secured there will likely be treated as void and not entitled to full faith and credit by the Bismarkania court. *See In re Gibson's Estate*, 96 N.W.2d 859, 861 (Wis. 1959) ("A divorce granted by a court of a state in which neither party to the marriage has a bona fide domicile is void and such divorce decree is not entitled to full faith and credit.") A different issue is the effect of Bob's affair with Aurelia. Adultery notwithstanding, some jurisdictions would not require that Bob receive an unfavorable distribution of the assets if he could show that the marriage was already irretrievably broken. *See*, for example, *Redden v. Redden*, 44 So. 3d 508, 514 (Ala. Civ. App. 2009) (remanding a case "to the trial court for it to reconsider its award without regard to the husband's post-separation infidelity"). On the other hand, some jurisdictions treat even post-separation adultery as the basis for denying support, *see Kirtley v. Kirtley*, 1997 Va. Cir. LEXIS 662 (Dec. 15, 1997) ("Post-separation adultery is a bar to spousal support"), or for adversely affecting the distribution of marital assets. *See Legat v. Legat*, 1999 Va. App. LEXIS 497 (Aug. 10, 1999).

73. A marriage of domiciliaries, prohibited locally, will be recognized if validly celebrated elsewhere as long as the marriage does not violate an important public policy of the domicile. The question at hand will be whether Texarkana treats a marriage between adoptive siblings as it would a marriage between a brother and sister related by blood. If so, *see* Minn. Stat. § 517.03(a)(2) (discussing prohibited marriage "between a brother and a sister, whether the relationship is by the half or the whole blood or by adoption"), then the marriage would likely not be recognized even if validly celebrated elsewhere, because marriages between siblings are generally viewed as violating an important public policy. That said, a court could distinguish between adoptive siblings and other kinds of siblings and suggest that a marriage between adoptive siblings would not violate an important public policy. *See Israel v. Allen*, 577 P.2d 762 (Colo. 1978) (upholding marriage between adoptive siblings).

74.   **Answer (D) is the best answer.** Walter is wasting marital assets solely for his own benefit at a time when the marriage has broken down. *See In re Marriage of Hagshenas*, 600 N.E.2d 437, 450 (Ill. App. Ct. 1992) (defining dissipation as "the use of marital property for the sole benefit of one of the spouses for a purpose unrelated to the marriage at a time when the marriage is undergoing an irreconcilable breakdown").

Answer (A) is incorrect. While this might well be viewed as a waste, this would not meet qualify as dissipation, because there was no evidence here that the marriage was breaking down. *See Williams v. Williams*, 2005 WL 2205913, *9 (Tenn. Ct. App. 2005) ("Dissipation of marital property occurs . . . at a time when the marriage is breaking down.").

Answer (B) is incorrect. While this would not be a good investment of money, there is no suggestion that the painting was bought for Roberta's benefit rather than for her husband's benefit, misunderstanding of what he would like notwithstanding. *See Kothari v. Kothari*, 605 A.2d 750, 753 (N.J. Super. Ct. App. Div. 1992) (suggesting that dissipation involves one of the spouses spending extravagantly solely for his or her own benefit).

Answer (C) is incorrect. Here, there is no suggestion that Zelda is wasting the monies on herself. *See Kothari v. Kothari*, 605 A.2d 750, 753 (N.J. Super. Ct. App. Div. 1992). *See also Grathwohl v. Garrity*, 871 N.E.2d 297, 303 (Ind. Ct. App. 2007) ("The fact that Steven ultimately made a poor decision in purchasing the stock does not render such purchase frivolous. ") Nor is there any suggestion that the marriage is failing. *See Nelson v. Nelson*, 2005 Neb. App. LEXIS 181 (Aug. 16, 2005) (reversing trial court finding of dissipation of assets because of a lack of evidence that the marriage was failing at the time).

75.   **Answer (D) is the best answer.** Absent a showing of need by Myrna or a showing of financial misconduct on Myron's part, the court would be unlikely to require Myron to sell the cabin and distribute the proceeds. *See Murray v. Murray*, 636 So. 2d 536, 538 (Fla. Dist. Ct. App. 1994) ("Misconduct of a party, however, will not justify an unequal distribution of assets absent evidence demonstrating a sufficient relationship between the misconduct and the dissipation of assets."); *Smith v. Smith*, 938 N.E.2d 857, 861 (Ind. Ct. App. 2010) ("Absent a finding of dissipation of assets, a property division cannot exceed the value of the marital assets without being considered an improper form of maintenance and an abuse of discretion."). *See also Reeves v. Reeves*, 575 N.W.2d 1, 3 (Mich. Ct. App. 1997) ("this statute permits invasion of the separate estates if after division of the marital assets the estate and effects awarded to either party are insufficient for the suitable support and maintenance of either party").

Answer (A) is incorrect. Because Myron alone inherited the cabin, it is his separate property. *See Robert M. v. Christina M.*, 29 Misc. 3d 1209A (N.Y. Sup. Ct. 2010) ("Separate property is: 'Property acquired before marriage or property acquired by bequest, devise, or descent, or gift from a party other than the spouse.' ") Many jurisdictions would prohibit the distribution of separate property in these circumstances. *See, for example, Tannen v.*

Tannen, 3 A.3d 1229, 1248 (N.J. Super. Ct. App. Div. 2010) ("property owned by a husband or wife at the time of marriage will remain the separate property of such spouse in the event of divorce and will not qualify as an asset eligible for distribution"); *Mugno v. Mugno*, 695 S.E.2d 495, 498 (N.C. Ct. App. 2010) (trial court precluded from distributing separate property).

Answer (B) is incorrect. Some jurisdictions will distribute separate property where needed or where equity so requires. *See Wilson v. Wilson-Michelakis*, 2010-Ohio-370, 2010 Ohio App. LEXIS 296.

Answer (C) is incorrect. Merely because the property was acquired during the marriage would not make it marital property. Property acquired by bequest by one of the parties to the marriage is separate property. *See Linville v. Linville*, 2010-Ohio-5736, 2010 Ohio App. LEXIS 4826, at ¶ 7 (noting that separate property would include an "inheritance by one spouse by bequest, devise, or descent during the course of the marriage").

76.   Brad has dissipated the marital assets. *See In re Marriage of Hagshenas*, 600 N.E.2d 437, 450–451 (Ill. App. Ct. 1992) ("the use of marital property for the sole benefit of one of the spouses for a purpose unrelated to the marriage at a time when the marriage is undergoing an irreconcilable breakdown"). The court is likely to try to help rectify the situation by attributing the lost monies to the one who dissipated them and thus give the innocent spouse a larger share of the remaining assets. *See Rodriguez v. Rodriguez*, 994 So. 2d 1157, 1161 (Fla. Dist. Ct. App. 2008) ("The unequal distribution of marital assets or debts is allowed when one party's conduct has caused the dissipation of assets or has otherwise adversely affected the financial status of the other party at a time when the marriage is undergoing an irreconcilable breakdown.") *See also Strang v. Strang*, 635 N.Y.S.2d 786, 789 (App. Div. 1995) ("Where the wasteful dissipation of assets can be traced to a party's poor judgment, unwillingness or inability to manage, that portion of the amount dissipated must be charged against said party's equitable share.").

77.   **Answer (C) is the best answer.** While the court could not transfer title to property located outside the jurisdiction, *see In re Demis*, 191 B.R. 851, 860 (Bankr. D. Mont. 1996) ("a divorce court cannot by its order effect title to real property in a foreign jurisdiction"), the court could nonetheless order Brad to transfer the property or perhaps sell it and split the proceeds. *See Phillips v. Phillips*, 272 S.W.2d 433, 434 (Ark. 1954) (noting that a court "has power to compel a conveyance of lands situated in another country or state, where the persons of the parties interested are within the jurisdiction of the court. . . . The decree acts only on the person, and obedience is compelled by proceedings in the nature of contempt, attachment, or sequestration.") *See also In re Marriage of Campbell and Burnett*, 240 P.3d 986 (Kan. Ct. App. 2010) ("when dividing real property in a divorce action, the court may . . . order a sale of the property and then divide the proceeds.").

Answer (A) is incorrect. The court might order Brad to sell the property. *See In re Marriage of Campbell and Burnett*, 240 P.3d 986 (Kan. Ct. App. 2010).

Answer (B) is incorrect. While a court might be able to transfer ownership of property owned within the jurisdiction, *see Bell v. Bingham*, 484 N.E.2d 624, 627 (Ind. Ct. App. 1985) ("the trial court has the power to transfer real property between the parties"), the court cannot transfer title to property located outside the jurisdiction. *See In re Demis*, 191 B.R. 851, 860 (Bankr. D. Mont. 1996) ("a divorce court cannot by its order effect title to real property in a foreign jurisdiction").

Answer (D) is incorrect. While the court could punish Brad for refusing to comply with its orders, *see Phillips v. Phillips*, 272 S.W.2d 433, 434 (Ark. 1954) (noting that holding a party in contempt is one option), a court would not be permitted to undermine the interests of the children as a way of punishing Brad. *See Verity v. Verity*, 486 N.Y.S.2d 505, 507 (App. Div. 1985) ("an award of custody must be based on the best interests of the children and not a desire to punish a recalcitrant parent").

78. **Answer (A) is the best answer.** The court may well find that the winnings are marital property, *see Campbell v. Campbell*, 624 N.Y.S.2d 493, 494 (App. Div. 1995) ("the proceeds of a winning lottery ticket acquired by a spouse during the marriage constitute marital property"). *See also Thomas v. Thomas*, 579 S.E.2d 310 (S.C. 2003) (dividing lottery winnings acquired post-separation).

Answer (B) is not the best answer. While the winnings might be treated as separate property were there an agreement to that effect between the parties, *see Parker v. Parker*, 773 N.Y.S.2d 518, 521 (Sup. Ct. 2003) ("The lottery proceeds in issue are not held in joint name. Accordingly, pursuant to the terms of the June 1987 agreement, the winnings are, *prima facie*, the wife's separate property, not subject to equitable distribution."), they might also be treated as marital property subject to distribution. *See Thomas v. Thomas*, 579 S.E.2d 310 (S.C. 2003).

Answer (C) is not the best answer. Even the winnings distributed after the divorce is final will be marital property and subject to distribution. *See In re Marriage of Morris*, 640 N.E.2d 344, 347 (Ill. App. Ct. 1994) ("The fact that the payments are made solely in petitioner's name and that the majority of the lottery payments would not be received until after entry of the judgment of dissolution of marriage does not change the fact that the winnings are marital property.").

Answer (D) is incorrect. Even those who have been living separate and apart for the necessary period are still married in the eyes of the law and thus the lottery winnings might still be considered marital and subject to distribution. *See In re Marriage of Palacios*, 656 N.E.2d 107, 109 (Ill. App. Ct. 1995) (dividing lottery winnings between parties even though they had already been living apart for the requisite period).

79. **Answer (C) is the best answer.** Property inherited by one of the parties during the marriage is separate property. *See Linville v. Linville*, 2010-Ohio-5736, 2010 Ohio App. LEXIS 4826, at ¶ 7 ("'Separate property' is defined as 'all real and personal property and any interest in real or personal property that is found by the court to be . . . [a]n inheritance by one spouse by bequest, devise, or descent during the course of the marriage.") However, the car is marital, because it was bought with marital funds. *See*, for example, *Brackney v. Brackney*, 682 S.E.2d 401, 404 (N.C. Ct. App. 2009) ("the Ballincourt house was marital property because it had been purchased with funds from the sale of the Century Oaks house, which was wholly marital property").

Answer (A) is incorrect. Property acquired by gift or bequest is separate, *see Avery v. Avery*, 2001 Tenn. App. LEXIS 487, at *13 (July 11, 2001) ('separate property' means 'property acquired by a spouse at any time by gift, bequest, devise or descent' "), whereas property purchased with marital funds is marital. *See Brackney v. Brackney*, 682 S.E.2d 401,

404 (N.C. Ct. App. 2009).

Answer (B) is incorrect. Even property acquired during the marriage may be classified as separate property if acquired by gift or bequest. *See Linville v. Linville*, 2010-Ohio-5736, 2010 Ohio App. LEXIS 4826.

Answer (D) is incorrect. Property acquired with marital funds is marital unless that property is gifted to one of the parties. *See Langston v. Richardson*, 696 S.E.2d 867, 871 (N.C. Ct. App. 2010) (discussing gift from one spouse to another where the intention is to make the gift the latter's separate property).

80.   **Answer (D) is the best answer.** Property bought with marital funds will be characterized as marital, *see*, for example, *Meador v. Meador*, 44 So. 3d 411, 417 (Miss. Ct. App. 2010), unless the property was an interpousal gift. Some states treat interpousal gifts as separate property. *See In re Marriage of Fenton*, 2010 Iowa App. LEXIS 809, at *15 (July 28, 2010) ("Many other states agree that a statute which defines all gifts as separate property must be construed to define interspousal gifts as separate property."). Other states will do so where the intent to make the gift separate property can be established. *McNeely v. McNeely*, 2008 N.C. App. LEXIS 217, at *14 (Feb. 5, 2008) ("The 'interspousal gift' provision . . . provides: '[P]roperty acquired by gift from the other spouse during the course of the marriage shall be considered separate property only if such an intention is stated in the conveyance.' ").

Answer (A) is incorrect. Absent an intent to make an interspousal gift of marital property the recipient's separate property, property bought with marital funds is marital property. *See*, for example, *Meador v. Meador*, 44 So. 3d 411, 417 (Miss. Ct. App. 2010) ("a spouse's business interest is marital property if the interest was . . . purchased with marital funds").

Answer (B) is incorrect. Assuming that no interpousal gifts have been made, the relevant issue is not who uses the items but the source of the funds used to purchase them. *See Jennings v. Jennings*, 327 S.W.3d 21, 23 (Mo. Ct. App. 2010) ("The source of funds theory dictates that the character of property will be determined by the source of funds financing the purchase.").

Answer (C) is not the best answer. While it is true that property bought with marital funds will be characterized as marital, *see*, for example, *Meador v. Meador*, 44 So. 3d 411, 417 (Miss. Ct. App. 2010), that assumes that there have been no interpousal gifts, where the intention was to make the object the separate property of the recipient spouse. Some states treat interpousal gifts as separate property. *See In re Marriage of Fenton*, 2010 Iowa App. LEXIS 809 (July 28, 2010). Other states do so only where the intent to make the gift separate property can be established. *See McNeely v. McNeely*, 2008 N.C. App. LEXIS 217 (Feb. 5, 2008).

81.   **Answer (A) is the best answer.** Separate property brought to the marriage would continue to be separate unless, for example, the house had been gifted to the marital community. However, the possibility of a gift to the marital estate should be considered. *See Storrs v. Storrs*, 463 S.E.2d 853, 855 (W. Va. 1995) ("a presumption of gift to the marital estate does exist when separate property is converted to jointly held property").

Answer (B) is incorrect. Merely because the couple lived in the home during the marriage would not make the home marital property. *See McCoy v. McCoy*, 868 P.2d 527, 533 (Idaho

Ct. App. 1994) (home in which couple lived during marriage was wife's separate property).

Answer (C) is not the best answer. While it is true that separate property brought to the marriage would continue to be separate unless, for example, the house had been gifted to the marital community, *see Storrs v. Storrs*, 463 S.E.2d 853, 855 (W. Va. 1995), the possibility of a gift to the marital estate should be considered.

Answer (D) is not the best answer. Absent a gift to the marital estate or use of marital funds to maintain or improve the home, *see Mackey v. Mackey*, 2002 UT App 349 ("After Husband and Wife moved into the Home, Husband's labor added to the Home's value and marital funds were invested in the Home. Thus, the trial court did not abuse its discretion by finding all appreciation in equity while the parties lived in the Home to be marital property."), the home's status as separate property would continue.

82. **Answer (B) is the best answer.** If, indeed, funds were commingled and there is no way to trace them, then the home *might* be recharacterized as marital property. *See Gleaves v. Gleaves*, 2008 Tenn. App. LEXIS 702 (Nov. 13, 2008) ("The four most common factors, or conduct of the parties, courts look for in determining whether property has been transmuted are: (1) the use of the property as a marital residence; (2) the ongoing maintenance and management of the property by both parties; (3) placing the title to the property in joint ownership; and (4) using the credit of the non-owner spouse to improve the property."). *See also Von Raab v. Von Raab*, 494 S.E.2d 156, 160 (Va. Ct. App. 1997) ("we conclude that the entirety of husband's separate interest in the Prince Street property was transmuted to marital property during the parties' marriage").

Answer (A) is not the best answer. While the house was separate property, the fact that marital funds were used to maintain and improve it could result in a change of its characterization from separate to marital. *See Mackey v. Mackey*, 2002 UT App 349 ("After Husband and Wife moved into the Home, Husband's labor added to the Home's value and marital funds were invested in the Home. Thus, the trial court did not abuse its discretion by finding all appreciation in equity while the parties lived in the Home to be marital property.").

Answer (C) is not the best answer. While one way for separate property to be transformed into marital property would be as a result of a gift, *see Storrs v. Storrs*, 463 S.E.2d 853, 855 (W. Va. 1995) ("a presumption of gift to the marital estate does exist when separate property is converted to jointly held property"), that is not the only way such a transformation can occur. *See Mackey v. Mackey*, 2002 UT App 349 (investment of marital funds and marital time can cause separate property to be recharacterized as marital).

Answer (D) is incorrect. Merely because the house was used as the marital domicile would not suffice to justify recharacterizing it as marital. *See McCoy v. McCoy*, 868 P.2d 527, 533 (Idaho Ct. App. 1994) (home in which couple lived during marriage was wife's separate property).

83. **Answer (D) is the best answer.** A jurisdiction that treats property as partially marital and partially separate would then split the marital portion equitably. *See Doublier v. Doublier*, 2001 Va. Cir. LEXIS 375 (July 10, 2001) ("The parties share in the non-marital and marital contributions is then ascribed based upon the proportion that each party's separate non-marital advances have to the total non-marital advances. Since only that portion of a mortgage payment reducing loan principal increases the parties' equity in real estate, only

the curtailment of the principal balance of a mortgage loan may be treated as a contribution made toward the acquisition of or increase to the value of the encumbered property.") However, it might be noted that such a method is not without fault, because it may inadequately account for the contribution made when the contribution goes to interest rather than a decrease in the principal owed. *See Keeling v. Keeling*, 624 S.E.2d 687, 690 (Va. Ct. App. 2006) (noting that under a literal application of the formula, "any increase in equity in the property is wholly separate property, despite the fact that marital funds were used to hold the property for the period during which it appreciated; none of the increase in equity is classified as marital because the principal loan balance has not been reduced.").

Answer (A) is not the best answer. While jurisdictions will consider that marital funds were used to reduce a mortgage, they likely will not say that the house therefore became marital property, assuming that that the separate and marital contributions are traceable. *Moran v. Moran*, 512 S.E.2d 834, 835 (Va. Ct. App. 1999) (suggesting that the property then becomes partly separate and partly marital).

Answer (B) is incorrect. Donald's contribution will likely either make the house partly marital, *see Doublier v. Doublier*, 2001 Va. Cir. LEXIS 375 (July 10, 2001) (describing formula to determine extent to which the house is marital property subject to distribution) or at least may entitle him to a credit for his contribution. *See P.D. v. L.D.*, 28 Misc. 3d 1232A (N.Y. Sup. Ct. 2010) ("where marital funds are used to pay off the separate debt of the titled spouse on the separate property, the nontitled spouse may be entitled to a credit").

Answer (C) is incorrect. A jurisdiction that views the marital contribution as creating a marital interest in the home would likely not award the entire marital share to Donald. Rather, he would be entitled to an equitable share of the marital interest. *See Doublier v. Doublier*, 2001 Va. Cir. LEXIS 375 (July 10, 2001).

84.   **Answer (C) is the best answer.** Mary is a passive investor who has expended neither marital funds nor marital time in the upkeep or improvement of her apartment building. The building is thus likely to be viewed as separate. *See In re Binge's Estate*, 105 P.2d 689, 703 (Wash. 1940) ("We also held that the status of the separate property of the husband is not affected by the erection of buildings and the payment of the balance of the purchase price after marriage, where the rentals of the property alone had turned back more than sufficient to pay the balance of the purchase price and the cost of the improvements and upkeep.") On the other hand, Tom has been spending marital time and effort in managing the building. Further, he did not receive a salary, and the salary would normally have been marital property, so Mary should be entitled to some kind of share or credit for the amount that would have been marital had he been receiving a salary. *See Jones v. Jones*, 356 P.2d 231, 234 (N.M. 1960) (where party paid reasonable salary, no reason to assume that time and effort in running separate business would require recharacterizing it as marital). *Cf. Glenn v. Glenn*, 930 S.W.2d 519, 525 (Mo. Ct. App. 1996) (no reason for characterization of separate property to be modified where husband paid reasonable salary).

Answer (A) is incorrect, because Tom has used marital time and effort in maintaining and improving his building. *See Moran v. Moran*, 512 S.E.2d 834, 835 (Va. Ct. App. 1999) ("Property that is acquired by either party before the marriage is separate property, . . . subject to being transmuted into hybrid property — that is, part marital and part separate — by virtue of an increase in value due to personal efforts.").

Answer (B) is incorrect, because Mary's apartment building was separate property, and has been maintained and improved with funds derived from that separate property. *See In re Binge's Estate*, 105 P.2d 689, 703 (Wash. 1940) (refusing to recharacterize property which had been separate and had been maintained and improved with separate funds).

Answer (D) is incorrect. Even if the parties are well off, that would be no reason for the court to treat the marriage as if it had never existed. *See,* for example, *In re Marriage of Bush*, 547 N.E.2d 590, 592 (Ill. Ct. App. 1989) (deciding division of property among other issues when two doctors divorced).

85.   **Answer (D) is the best answer.** Many courts will consider the acquisition of a degree when calculating what would be fair, although they differ with respect to the best way to account for the acquisition of that degree. *See Downs v. Downs*, 574 A.2d 156, 158 (Vt. 1990) (noting that many "courts hold that a professional degree is not an asset subject to property distribution upon divorce, but, in the interest of justice and equity, fashion a maintenance award using the increased earning potential of the spouse with the degree as a relevant factor in determining an appropriate award.").

Answer (A) is incorrect. Some jurisdictions treat professional degrees as marital property subject to distribution. *See McSparron v. McSparron*, 662 N.E.2d 745, 748 (N.Y. 1995) (medical degree treated as marital property where defendant was the primary provider of economic support and the primary caretaker of the children).

Answer (B) is incorrect. While jurisdictions differ as to how to compensate the spouse who did not receive the degree, *see Stevens v. Stevens*, 492 N.E.2d 131, 131 (Ohio 1986) ("the future value of a professional degree or license acquired by one of the parties during the marriage is an element to be considered in reaching an equitable award of alimony"); *Mahoney v. Mahoney*, 453 A.2d 527, 533 (N.J. 1982) ("Several courts, while not treating educational degrees as property, have awarded the supporting spouse an amount based on the cost to the supporting spouse of obtaining the degree. In effect, the supporting spouse was reimbursed for her financial contributions used by the supported spouse in obtaining a degree."), courts have tended not to use the opportunity cost theory with respect to the amount that the degreed spouse would have been making had that spouse not pursued the degree.

Answer (C) is incorrect. While courts do point to the difficulty of valuing the degree, *see Woodworth v. Woodworth*, 337 N.W.2d 332, 336 (Mich. Ct App. 1983) ("The third argument against including an advanced degree as marital property is that its valuation is too speculative"), they nonetheless suggest that it should be included in the calculation of what the non-degreed spouse should receive. *See Downs v. Downs*, 574 A.2d 156, 158 (Vt. 1990).

86.   **Answer (D) is the best answer.** The pension benefits earned during the marriage are marital property. That marital property is to be distributed to both parties. *Laing v. Laing*, 741 P.2d 649, 657 (Alaska 1987) ("The court determines a fraction of the present value representing the marital contribution to the accrued pension benefits. The numerator of this fraction is the number of years the pension has accrued during the marriage; the denominator is the total number of years during which the employee spouse's pension has accrued.").

Answer (A) is incorrect. Pension benefits earned during the marriage are marital property subject to distribution. *See Flynn v. Flynn*, 491 A.2d 156, 164 (Pa. Super. Ct. 1985) (discussing different ways to distribute "the marital property portion of the pension benefits entitlement").

Answer (B) is incorrect. While some of the pension benefits were earned during the marriage, not all of them were. Jurisdictions tend to award a percentage of the pension benefits earned during the marriage. *See Flynn v. Flynn*, 491 A.2d 156, 164 (Pa. Super. Ct. 1985) ("To determine the percentage of the pension benefits entitlement ascribable to the marriage, the court must apply a coverture fraction whose numerator is the period of the employee-spouse's pension plan participation during the parties' marriage from the date of marriage to the date of separation and whose denominator is the total period of the employee-spouse's participation in the pension plan.").

Answer (C) is incorrect. The pension benefits are marital property subject to distribution. *Laing v. Laing*, 741 P.2d 649, 655 (Alaska 1987) ("Alaska thus follows the majority rule that 'vested' pension and retirement benefits are subject to division by a divorce court.").

87. **Answer (D) is the best answer.** Basically, property acquired during the marriage that is not classified as separate property will be viewed as community property. *See* Nev. Rev. Stat. § 123.220 (suggesting that all property acquired during a marriage is community property unless there is an agreement to the contrary, there is an applicable court decree, or the property is defined as separate as specified elsewhere in the code).

Answer (A) is incorrect. Such property would be considered separate property. *See* Tex. Fam. Code Ann. § 3.001(2) ("A spouse's separate property consists of . . . the property acquired by the spouse during marriage by gift, devise, or descent").

Answer (B) is incorrect. Use of separate property does not transform it into marital property. *See Rogers v. Rogers*, 754 S.W.2d 236, 240 (Tex. Ct. App. 1988) (discussing condominium, which remained the separate property of the wife, notwithstanding that it was used by the husband).

Answer (C) is incorrect, because property acquired by gift during the marriage would be separate property. *See* Tex. Fam. Code Ann. § 3.001(2).

88. **Answer (D) is the best answer.** Quasi-community property is property that would have been characterized as community property had it been acquired while domiciled in a community property state. *See* Cal. Fam. Code § 125(a) (" 'Quasi-community property' means all real or personal property, wherever situated, acquired . . . [b]y either spouse while domiciled elsewhere which would have been community property if the spouse who acquired the property had been domiciled in this state at the time of its acquisition.").

Answer (A) is incorrect. Quasi-community property is not a hybrid of community and separate property, *cf. Duva v. Duva*, 685 S.E.2d 842, 846 (Va. Ct. App. 2009) (describing hybrid property as part marital and part separate), but instead is property that would have been characterized as community property had it been acquired while domiciled in a community property state. *See* Cal. Fam. Code § 125(a).

Answer (B) is incorrect. Quasi-community property does not refer to property that is a combination of separate and community property where the separate property is (almost) no longer traceable, *cf. Nichols v. Nichols*, 648 P.2d 780, 786–87 (N.M. 1982) ("when the separate property cannot be traced, the evidence of the separate status is insufficient to overcome the presumption of community property and transmutation is deemed by operation of law to have been proven by clear and convincing evidence.") Instead, it is property that would be considered community property had the couple acquired it while domiciled in a community property state. *See* Cal. Fam. Code § 125(a).

Answer (C) is incorrect. Property belonging to a non-marital couple would not be considered community property unless there were a separate statutory specification making such property community property. *See* Wash. Rev. Code § 64.28.040 (discussing community property interests of domestic partners).

89.   **Answer (C) is the best answer.** While the Monoming court had jurisdiction to grant the divorce, *see Gage v. Gage*, 89 F. Supp. 987, 990 (D.D.C. 1950) ("A divorce decree based on a bona fide domicil and procedural due process is valid and entitled to recognition in other states."), it did not have jurisdiction over Bernice and thus should not be deciding property rights over property not in the jurisdiction. *See Vanderbilt v. Vanderbilt*, 354 U.S. 416, 418 (1957) ("It has long been the constitutional rule that a court cannot adjudicate a personal claim or obligation unless it has jurisdiction over the person of the defendant."); *Snider v. Snider*, 551 S.E.2d 693, 701 (W. Va. 2001) ("We hold, therefore, that under the divisible divorce doctrine, where a foreign jurisdiction does not have personal jurisdiction over both parties to a marriage, the personal and property rights of the parties may be litigated in West Virginia separately from a divorce decree issued in another jurisdiction.").

Answer (A) is incorrect. The divorce would be valid. *See Gage v. Gage*, 89 F. Supp. 987, 990 (D.D.C. 1950) ("A divorce decree based on a bona fide domicil and procedural due process is valid and entitled to recognition in other states.").

Answer (B) is incorrect. Merely because the court had jurisdiction to grant the divorce would not also mean that it had jurisdiction to distribute the marital property. *See Snider v. Snider*, 551 S.E.2d 693, 697 (W. Va. 2001) ("if a court has jurisdiction over only one spouse but not the other, 'the "divisible divorce" concept permits the court to dissolve the marital relationship of the parties . . . without addressing the property rights and obligations of the parties'").

Answer (D) is incorrect. While Bernice could have gone to Monoming, her not having done so would not somehow give the Monoming court jurisdiction to adjudicate her property rights in their Calidaho belongings. *See Snider v. Snider*, 551 S.E.2d 693, 697 (W. Va. 2001).

90.   **Answer (B) is the best answer.** Courts can grant the divorce. *See Gage v. Gage*, 89 F. Supp. 987, 990 (D.D.C. 1950) ("A divorce decree based on a bona fide domicil and procedural due process is valid and entitled to recognition in other states."). However, courts are split with respect to whether they can distribute property in an ex parte divorce if that property is located in the forum. *Compare Fox v. Fox*, 559 S.W.2d 407, 410 (Tex. Civ. App. 1977) ("Even though the spouses are domiciled in different states, a Texas court may grant an ex parte divorce . . . if one of the parties falls within the statute. . . . Under these circumstances a court may even divide property within its jurisdiction.") *with Singh v. Gomar*, 33 Va. Cir. 284 (1994) ("Based on the domicile of the plaintiff, and lacking personal jurisdiction over the defendant, this Court is limited to an in rem proceeding addressing only the marriage itself, not any property or support issues arising from it.").

Answer (A) is incorrect. The divorce can be granted even if the state does not have jurisdiction over John. *See In re Marriage of Kimura*, 471 N.W.2d 869 (Iowa 1991) (affirming granting of divorce when the state had jurisdiction over only one of the parties to the marriage).

Answer (C) is incorrect. John did not lose any opportunity to contest the decision by virtue of his refusing to go to East Virginton. Had the court divided up property in New Carington, John would have been able to contest that property division. *See Schroeder v. Vigil-Escalera Perez*, 664 N.E.2d 627, 635 (Ohio Com. Pl. 1995) (noting that foreign court had jurisdiction to grant divorce but not to distribute property).

Answer (D) is not the best answer. While it is clear that the court could grant the divorce, it is not clear that the court was precluded from distributing marital property located in the forum. *See Fox v. Fox*, 559 S.W.2d 407, 410 (Tex. Civ. App. 1977) (court granting ex parte divorce can distribute property located in the jurisdiction).

91.   Notwithstanding that Donna originally acquired the property by paying the down payment herself and notwithstanding that she used separate funds (her inheritance) to pay off the mortgage, the property might well be considered marital. Her having put title in both of their names might well be considered as establishing a gift of the house to the marital estate. *See Koontz v. Koontz*, 396 S.E.2d 439, 442 (W. Va. 1990) ("the joint titling of the real property in this case is presumed to be a gift to the *marital estate*"). Further, she used marital funds (her salary during the marriage) to help pay down the mortgage. His failure to reciprocate does not establish that she did not make such a gift, although she might argue that her making the gift was predicated on his doing something similar, so the house should not be considered a gift to the marital estate. *See Burnside v. Burnside*, 460 S.E.2d 264, 267 (W. Va. 1995) ("presumption may be rebutted by competent evidence offered by the transferring spouse showing lack of intent to make a gift or by circumstances showing fraud, coercion, or duress").

92.   The appropriate characterization of these items will depend upon donor intent. Jewelry purchased with marital funds may be considered marital property subject to equitable distribution, *see Ruiz v. Ruiz*, 548 So. 2d 699, 700 (Fla. Ct. App. 1989) ("[I]t is uncontroverted that the jewelry was purchased during the marriage and with marital funds. As such, it became subject to equitable distribution."), or may be considered a gift to one of the parties *See Moore v. Moore*, 2004 WL 2677032, *5 (Ky. App. 2004) (treating jewelry as separate property of wife). By the same token a car may be considered separate property, *see Shramek v. Shramek*, 901 A.2d 593, 599 (R.I. 2006) (affirming trial court determination that husband's gift of car should be treated as separate property) or marital property. *See Weber v. Weber*, 1999 Ohio App. LEXIS 3113 (June 30, 1999) (affirming that car given as a gift was marital property).

93. **Answer (D) is the best answer.** Custody determinations are based on what would promote the best interests of the child. *See Watson v. Watson*, 46 So. 3d 218, 220 (La. Ct. App. 2010) ("the paramount consideration in any determination of child custody is the best interest of the child").

Answer (A) is incorrect. Merely because a different parent is more likely to promote the best interests of the child does not establish that the parent at issue is unfit. Unfitness is determined in light of a variety of factors, for example, cruelty, abandonment, etc. *See* 750 Ill. Comp. Stat. 50/1(D) (specifying a variety of factors to establish unfitness).

Answer (B) is incorrect. Child support is determined in light of child support tables which establish how much should be paid in light of the parents' income. *See State ex rel. M.M.G. v. Graham*, 152 P.3d 1005, 1006 (Wash. 2007) ("The basic child support obligation is generally determined from an economic table in the child support schedule and is based on the parents' combined monthly net income and the number and age of the children.").

Answer (C) is incorrect. Deference must be given to a parent's medical decision-making for her child, so a court's disagreeing with a parent about what would promote the best interests of the child would not justify court interference. That said, the parent does not have absolute discretion with respect to medical decision-making for her child. *See In re Eli H.*, 871 N.Y.S.2d 846, 850 (Fam. Ct. 2008) ("A court must afford great deference to a parent's choice of medical care and providers, but it may not permit a parent to deny a child all treatment for a condition which threatens his life.").

94. **Answer (D) is the best answer.** The tender years presumption is a presumption that it is better to award custody of a young child to the child's mother, However, this presumption is rebuttable and is only one of many factors to consider when making a custody decision. *See Street v. Street*, 936 So. 2d 1002, 1010 (Miss. Ct. App. 2006).

Answer (A) is incorrect. While the tender years presumption does favor a mother having custody in the case of a small child, the presumption is not irrebuttable and is only one factor among many to consider. *See Johnson v. Adair*, 884 So. 2d 1169, 1171 (Fla. Ct. App. 2004) ("The 'tender years' doctrine gives a preference to the mother of a child of tender years in matters of custody determination. Under the doctrine, with other essential factors being equal, the mother of the infant of tender years should receive prime consideration for custody.").

Answer (B) is incorrect. The tender years presumption focuses on the age of the child rather than that of the parent. *See Street v. Street*, 936 So. 2d 1002, 1010 (Miss. Ct. App. 2006).

Answer (C) is incorrect. While the expressed preferences of a very young child with regard to custody are often given little or no weight, *see*, for example, *Lindberg v. Lindberg*, 770 N.W.2d 252, 260 (N.D. 2009) ("The district court properly disregarded the parties' testimony about the children's preference because the children were too young to express a reasonable preference."), the tender year's presumption instead refers to something else, namely, the presumption that a mother should be awarded custody of a very young child. *See Johnson v. Adair*, 884 So. 2d 1169, 1171 (Fla. Ct. App. 2004).

95.   **Answer (D) is the best answer.** This a factor to be weighed along with many other factors. *See*, for example, 23 Pa. Stat. Ann. § 5303(a)(2) ("In making an order for custody, partial custody or visitation to either parent, the court shall consider, among other factors, which parent is more likely to encourage, permit and allow frequent and continuing contact and physical access between the noncustodial parent and the child.").

       Answer (A) is incorrect. The willingness to promote contact with the noncustodial parent may be one of the factors used to determine who will have custody. *See* Mo. Rev. Stat. § 452.375(4) ("The court shall consider all relevant factors including . . . [w]hich parent is more likely to allow the child frequent, continuing and meaningful contact with the other parent").

       Answer (B) is incorrect. As a general matter, it is better for a child to maintain contact with both parents. *See Cooper v. Cooper*, 491 A.2d 606, 621 (N.J. 1984) ("psychological and sociological studies have similarly pointed to a continued, significant relationship with both parents as critical to a child's development"). Nonetheless, this is one of many factors to consider in awarding custody. *See* Mo. Rev. Stat. § 452.375. Further, the refusal to promote contact with the noncustodial parent may be justified, for example, when continued contact between the child and the noncustodial parent would be harmful to the child. *See In re M.B.*, 647 A.2d 1001, 1006 (Vt. 1994) ("Public policy, however, does not dictate that the parent-child bond be maintained regardless of the cost to the child.").

       Answer (C) is incorrect. This is one of many factors to consider in the calculation and is not only considered when the other factors are in equipoise. *See* Mo. Rev. Stat. § 452.375.

96.   **Answer (D) is the best answer.** A mature child's preferences, when supported by reasons, will be given substantial weight. *See*, for example, *Goldstein v. Goldstein*, 264 So. 2d 49, 52 (Fla. Ct. App. 1972) (giving great weight to high schooler's expressed desire to live with his father, where that desire was supported with reasons). However, if there is reason to believe the preference is based on a consideration of improper factors, *see Butterick v. Butterick*, 506 A.2d 335, 338 (N.H. 1986) (discussing whether "the minor's preference was based on undesirable or improper influences"), that undercuts the weight that should be given to the preference.

       Answer (A) is incorrect. While the test for custody involves what will best promote the interests of a child, *see Watson v. Watson*, 46 So. 3d 218, 220 (La. Ct. App. 2010) ("the paramount consideration in any determination of child custody is the best interest of the child"), the expressed preference of a mature child may be an important consideration when determining what would promote that child's interests. *See Swanson v. Swanson*, 274 N.E.2d 465, 466 (Ill. Ct. App. 1971) ("the preferences of a minor child are important factors to be considered in custodial arrangements").

       Answer (B) is incorrect. While a mature minor's expressed preferences are important to consider, *see Doherty v. Dean*, 337 S.W.2d 153, 156 (Tex. Civ. App. 1960) ("expressed wishes of the minor are to be considered provided that he is of sufficient maturity to judge for himself"), that preference will not be granted when it is thought to run counter to the interests of the child. *See*, for example, *McCrocklin v. McCrocklin*, 430 N.Y.S.2d 320, 321 (App. Div. 1980) ("Colleen's custodial preference was premised, in part, on the laxity of discipline obtaining at her mother's house.").

Answer (C) is incorrect. A mature child's expressed preference can be given great weight. *See Butterick v. Butterick*, 506 A.2d 335, 337 (N.H. 1986) ("the judge may then give substantial weight to the preference of the mature minor as to the parent with whom he wants to live"). However, the judge must be convinced that the preference is backed by good reasons. *See Carr v. Carr*, 17 Phila. Co. Rptr. 581, 589 (Pa. Com. Pl. 1988) ("where no reason or a very inadequate reason for the preference is proffered, we give no weight thereto"). If Miranda cannot offer any reason for her preference, custody might be awarded to Yolanda, even if William is a fit parent.

97. **Answer (D) is the best answer.** A material change involves a significant modification of circumstances that was not known and thus not considered in the initial custody decision. *See Cowan v. Hatmaker*, 2006 Tenn. App. LEXIS 154 (Mar. 3, 2006) ("when a decree awarding custody of children has been entered, that decree is . . . conclusive in a subsequent application to change custody unless some new fact has occurred which has altered the circumstances in a material way so that the welfare of the child requires a change of custody").

Answer (A) is incorrect. While a material change in income might be relevant with respect to whether child support should change, *see McKee v. McKee*, 820 P.2d 1362, 1364 (Okla. Ct. App. 1991) ("any subsequent substantial increase in the income of one or both parents constitutes a sufficient change in circumstances to support a modification of child support"), that alone would not suffice to establish that custody should be revisited. *See*, for example, *McKenzie v. McKenzie*, 860 So. 2d 316 (Miss. Ct. App. 2003) (father's increased income did not warrant modification of custody).

Answer (B) is incorrect. The material change cannot merely be something that a child thinks important, e.g., that the noncustodial parent has just purchased a new television set, but must actually affect the welfare of the child. *See Schenk v. Schenk*, 564 N.E.2d 973, 977 (Ind. Ct. App. 1991) ("the trial court must determine that the changed circumstances warranting modification must be of a decisive nature and such changed circumstances will support a modification order only if such order is necessary for the welfare of the child or children involved").

Answer (C) is incorrect. Merely changing residences will not constitute a material change in circumstance unless it can also be shown that the change undermines the child's interests. *See In re Marriage of Heuberger*, 963 P.2d 153, 157 (Or. Ct App. 1998) (mother's changes in residence did not constitute substantial change in circumstances — they were reasonable and the child did not seem to have been adversely affected).

98. **Answer (D) is the best answer.** Parental alienation involves one parent trying to alienate the child from the other parent. *See F.S.-P. v. A.H.R.*, 844 N.Y.S.2d 644, 645 (Fam. Ct. 2007) (describing "parental alienation as the extreme denigration by one parent of the other parent, or the indoctrination and brainwashing of the child to turn him against the parent").

Answer (A) is incorrect. Parents may voluntarily surrender their parental rights for any number of reasons including a belief that their child's interests would thereby be promoted. Indeed, state courts might seek to determine whether a parental rights termination would promote the best interests of the child. *See Henriquez v. Adoption Centre*, 641 So. 2d 84, 93 (Fla. Ct. App. 1994) ("the courts of Florida are empowered to entertain a proceeding to determine whether it is in the child's best interests that the signor's parental rights be terminated").

Answer (B) is incorrect. While many individuals do not have warm feelings for their ex-spouses, *see*, for example, *In re Marriage of Heuberger*, 963 P.2d 153, 157 (Or. Ct. App. 1998) ("it appears from the record that the hostility between the parties is mutual"), parental alienation involves an attempt by one parent to alienate the child from the other parent. *See Eisenhardt v. Anderson*, 181 Vt. 649 (2007) (discussing case in which mother was poisoning the child's relationship with her father).

Answer (C) is incorrect. While parents may need to take a breather from their parenting responsibilities, *see Bonilla v. Bonilla*, 2004 Conn. Super. LEXIS 889 (Apr. 5, 2004) (discussing the "benefits derived from each parent having a periodic break from the duties of parenting"), that is not what parental alienation involves. *See F.S.-P. v. A.H.R.*, 844 N.Y.S.2d 644, 645 (Fam. Ct. 2007).

99.   **Answer (D) is the best answer.** Because the children and one parent continue to have significant connections with the state issuing the initial decree, Vermshire rather than Oklexio has jurisdiction to modify custody. *See In re Marriage of Nurie*, 98 Cal. Rptr. 3d 200, 212 (Cal. Ct. App. 2009) ("A court that properly acquires initial jurisdiction has exclusive, continuing jurisdiction unless . . . there is a judicial determination . . . that the child, the child's parents, and any person acting as a parent do not presently reside in the issuing state.").

Answer (A) is incorrect. The merits of this case should not be addressed by the Oklexio court, because it does not have jurisdiction to grant the custody modification. *See In re Marriage of Nurie*, 98 Cal. Rptr. 3d 200, 212 (Cal. Ct. App. 2009).

Answer (B) is incorrect. As a general matter, a state is not required to give full faith and credit to a child custody order if that order is modifiable in the issuing state. *See Padron v. Lopez*, 220 P.3d 345, 354 (Kan. 2009) ("full faith and credit is not required when a decree is interlocutory or subject to modification under the law of the rendering state"). Nonetheless, the Oklexio would not have jurisdiction to grant the custody modification. *See In re Marriage of Nurie*, 98 Cal. Rptr. 3d 200, 212 (Cal. Ct. App. 2009).

Answer (C) is incorrect. The Uniform Interstate Family Support Act (UIFSA) is the analog of the Uniform Child Custody Jurisdiction and Enforcement Act, although the subject of the former is support rather than custody. *See McQuade v. McQuade*, 2010 Tenn. App. LEXIS 747 (Aug. 4, 2010) ("The correlative to the UCCJEA is the Uniform Interstate Family Support Act ("UIFSA"), which governs interstate jurisdiction questions involving child support.").

100. **Answer (D) is the best answer.** While Zachary's change in circumstances would likely not justify a modification of custody, *see*, for example, *Lewis v. Lewis*, 974 So. 2d 265, 267 (Miss. Ct. App. 2008) (noncustodial parent's remarriage and ability to provide more stable environment did not establish a substantial change in circumstances), custody might be modified if Zachary could show a change in circumstances in the home provided by Alice that was having an adverse effect on the children. *See Savell v. Morrison*, 929 So. 2d 414, 418 (Miss. Ct. App. 2006) ("Normally, it must be shown that a material change in circumstances

in the child's custodial home has a present adverse effect on the child or is detrimental to the child [or] . . . if it is shown that it is reasonably foreseeable that the child will suffer adverse effects because the child's present custodial environment is clearly detrimental to his or her well being.").

Answer (A) is not the best answer. Many states do not view the noncustodial parent's remarriage as a substantial change in circumstances justifying a modification of custody. *See Key v. Fite*, 2000 Ark. App. LEXIS 199 (Mar. 1, 2000) (discussing "the majority view that a change in circumstances of the noncustodial parent, including a claim of an improved life because of a recent marriage, is not sufficient to justify modifying custody").

Answer (B) is incorrect. The UCCJEA does not apply to intrastate custody disputes, *see Seamans v. Seamans*, 37 S.W.3d 693, 696 (Ark. App. 2001) ("the UCCJEA has no application to intrastate custody disputes") and, in any event, is a jurisdiction-setting act. *See Stephens v. Fourth Judicial Dist. Court*, 128 P.3d 1026, 1029 (Mont. 2006) ("The drafters intended that the UCCJEA should be construed to promote one of its primary purposes of avoiding the jurisdictional competition and conflict that flows from hearings in competing states.").

Answer (C) is incorrect. A change in the noncustodial parent's salary would be unlikely to establish a substantial change in circumstances justifying a modification of custody. *See*, for example, *McKenzie v. McKenzie*, 860 So. 2d 316 (Miss. Ct. App. 2003) (father's increased income did not warrant modification of custody).

101. **Answer (C) is the best answer.** Eastlandia, the children's new domicile and home state, is the jurisdiction that should be hearing the suit requesting a custody modification. *See Michael McC. v. Manuela A.*, 848 N.Y.S.2d 147, 151 (N.Y. App. Div. 2007) ("under New York's UCCJEA, a New York court has jurisdiction to modify a child custody determination made by a court of another state if this state is the 'home state' of the child").

Answer (A) is incorrect. Delacut no longer has any connection to any of the parties and thus would not be the appropriate jurisdiction to determine whether the custody modification request should be granted. *See Jamil v. Jahan*, 760 N.W.2d 266, 268 (Mich. App. 2008) ("the Mississippi court no longer had exclusive, continuing jurisdiction over the matter because neither the children nor either parent currently resided in Mississippi, nor did they have a substantial connection to the state").

Answer (B) is incorrect. While Delacut no longer has continuing, exclusive jurisdiction because none of the parties lives there, *See In re Marriage of Nurie*, 98 Cal. Rptr. 3d 200, 212 (Cal. App. 2009) ("A court that properly acquires initial jurisdiction has exclusive, continuing jurisdiction unless . . . there is a judicial determination . . . that the child, the child's parents, and any person acting as a parent do not presently reside in the issuing state."), West Marylania is also not the appropriate forum, because the children have been living in Eastlandia for the past year. *See Michael McC. v. Manuela A.*, 848 N.Y.S.2d 147, 151 (App. Div. 2007) ("under New York's UCCJEA, a New York court has jurisdiction to modify a child custody determination made by a court of another state if this state is the 'home state' of the child").

Answer (D) is incorrect. First, the requisite period is not eighteen months but six. *See In re L.S.*, 226 P.3d 1227, 1232 (Colo. Ct. App. 2009) ("where a child with home-state status in one state is moved for any reason to a second state, the child will not lose home-state status in the first state or gain it in the second for another six months"). Second, other provisions permit a state to exercise jurisdiction when it might not normally be allowed to do so. *See In* *re State ex rel. M.C.*, 94 P.3d 1220, 1223 (Colo. Ct. App. 2004) ("the UCCJEA specifies various circumstances when a court outside the home state may exercise temporary emergency jurisdiction to protect a child from the threat of immediate mistreatment or abuse").

102.   **Answer (D) is the best answer.** States will permit a custodial parent to relocate if doing so would be in the best interests of the child. *See Rozborski v. Rozborski*, 686 N.E.2d 546, 547 (Ohio App. 1996) ("Whether a motion to relocate will be granted turns on whether the relocation is in the best interest of the children.").

   Answer (A) is incorrect. While the effect on the relationship between the noncustodial parent and the children will be considered, it is not dispositive. *See In re Pfeuffer*, 837 A.2d 311, 314 (N.H. 2003). As a general matter, a custodial parent will not be precluded from relocating if such a relocation would promote the best interests of the children, even if that would mean that alternate visitation arrangements would have to be made. *See Boyer v. Schake*, 799 A.2d 124, 128 (Pa. Super. 2002) ("A change in visitation arrangements necessitated by geographical distances will not defeat a move which has been shown to offer real advantages to the custodial parent and the children.").

   Answer (B) is incorrect. While the custodial parent cannot be prevented from moving, the parent can be precluded from bringing the children out of state if the relocation would be detrimental to their interests. *See Bartosz v. Jones*, 197 P.3d 310, 324 (Idaho 2008) ("[T]he best interest of the child standard is the most appropriate way to fairly balance parents' competing constitutional rights in relocation cases and is a compelling government interest. In this case, the magistrate determined that it was not in Sydney's best interest to move to Hawaii, which provides the state a compelling reason for restricting Julie's right to travel.").

   Answer (C) is incorrect. As a general matter, states permit a relocation if the children's interests would thereby be promoted. *See Rozborski v. Rozborski*, 686 N.E.2d 546, 547 (Ohio App. 1996) ("Whether a motion to relocate will be granted turns on whether the relocation is in the best interest of the children.") While court will consider the parents' reasons for supporting and opposing the move, *see Tropea v. Tropea*, 665 N.E.2d 145, 150 (N.Y. 1996) ("These factors include, but are certainly not limited to each parent's reasons for seeking or opposing the move"), a number of factors are considered to determine whether the relocation is in the best interests of the child. *See*, for example, *Flynn v. Flynn*, 92 P.3d 1224, 1227 (Nev. 2004) (listing such factors as "(1) whether the move will likely improve the quality of life for the child and the parent, (2) whether the custodial parent's motives are to frustrate visitation with the noncustodial parent, (3) whether the custodial parent will comply with visitation orders, (4) whether the noncustodial parent's opposition is honorable, and (5) whether there will be an adequate alternative visitation schedule available to preserve the parental relationship.").

103.   **Answer (C) is the best answer.** The nexus test suggests that the adultery of one parent is only relevant for determination of custody purposes insofar as the adultery affects the welfare of the child. *See Swain v. Swain*, 406 A.2d 680, 683 (Md. App. 1979) ("adultery of one of the parents should be considered, along with other factors, only insofar as it affects the child's welfare").

   Answer (A) is incorrect. While the behavior of the "innocent" spouse might be relevant insofar as a defense of recrimination is offered, *see Brobst v. Brobst*, 90 A.2d 320, 320 (Pa. Super. 1952) ("We are persuaded that there is ample evidence of a clear and positive nature establishing that the plaintiff was likewise guilty of adultery; that the record is replete with incidents, hereinafter related, showing both opportunity and adulterous inclinations on the part of plaintiff requiring that the decree be reversed and the complaint dismissed."), that would not be relevant in the determination of custody. For a determination of custody the important question is which parent will best promote the interests of the child. *See Watson v. Watson*, 46 So. 3d 218, 220 (La. Ct. App. 2010) ("the paramount consideration in any determination of child custody is the best interest of the child").

Answer (B) is incorrect. The issue of how closely connected in time were the filing for divorce and the discovery of the adultery might be relevant if, for example, condonation were at issue. *See*, for example, *Cutlip v. Cutlip*, 383 S.E.2d 273, 275 (Va. App. 1989) ("[H]e asserts that the wife's actions on December 29, 1986 and thereafter amounted to condonation of his behavior. The wife acknowledges that on December 29, she condoned the husband's actions."). However, absent more, this would not be relevant in determining which parent having custody would best promote the interests of the child.

Answer (D) is incorrect. Extenuating circumstances might be relevant to consider if a spouse were seeking spousal support and such support would be denied in cases of adultery unless rare circumstances obtained. *See Flanagan v. Flanagan*, 311 A.2d 407, 411 (Md. 1973) ("in those suits in which the actions of the party seeking such a pecuniary award constitute the sole cause for the demise of the marriage, and this wrongdoing consists of acts which are either adultery or abandonment, then, except in rare instances where there exist extremely extenuating circumstances, the award of any alimony would be an abuse of discretion"). Here, however, the focus is on the welfare of the child rather than on the cause of break-up of the marriage.

104. To prevail on a motion for a modification of custody, the noncustodial parent must establish that there has been a substantial change in circumstances. *See Reeves-Weible v. Reeves*, 995 S.W.2d 50, 65 (Mo. Ct. App. 1999) ("before a trial court can award custody in order to best serve the interests of the children, it must first be presented with a sufficient evidentiary basis for finding a substantial and continuing change of circumstances"). Further that change must have a detrimental effect on the child. *See Burger v. Burger*, 862 So. 2d 828, 832 (Fla. Ct. App. 2003) ("The party requesting the modification must show first that there has been a substantial change in circumstances and, second, that these changed circumstances have resulted in such a detriment to the child that a modification would be in the best interests of the child.") Mere disapproval of the custodial parent's partner, without more, will not suffice to establish a substantial change in circumstances having a detrimental effect on the child. *See In re Marriage of Collins*, 51 P.3d 691, 693 (Or. App. 2002) ("The fact that mother's companion was of the same sex may have been significant to father; he frankly testified that he disapproved of mother's 'lifestyle.' But it is not and cannot be significant to this court.").

105. The test to determine custody is which parent will best promote the child's welfare. *See Watson v. Watson*, 46 So. 3d 218, 220 (La. Ct. App. 2010) ("the paramount consideration in any determination of child custody is the best interest of the child"). Jill's adulterous behavior is unlikely to provide a basis upon which to deny her custody of Josephina unless that behavior is deemed to have had a detrimental effect on the child. *See Swain v. Swain*, 406 A.2d 680, 683 (Md. App. 1979) ("adultery of one of the parents should be considered, along with other factors, only insofar as it affects the child's welfare"). Nonetheless, it will be

important to determine whether Josephina would do better with her father who, allegedly, is more of a disciplinarian, *see,* for example, *Lagrone v. Lagrone,* 311 So. 2d 290, 292 (La. Ct. App. 1975) (son does better in home where there is more discipline) or with a mother with whom she had a warmer relationship. *See Sorkow v. Grossman,* 852 N.E.2d 1143 (Mass.App. Ct. 2006) (affirming wife's being awarded custody when she had a warmer relationship with the children).

106.   In order for a modification of custody to be granted, it must first be established that there has been a substantial change in circumstances. *See Reeves-Weible v. Reeves,* 995 S.W.2d 50, 65 (Mo. Ct. App. 1999) ("before a trial court can award custody in order to best serve the interests of the children, it must first be presented with a sufficient evidentiary basis for finding a substantial and continuing change of circumstances"). Further, that change must have a detrimental effect on the child. *See Burger v. Burger,* 862 So. 2d 828, 832 (Fla. Dist. Ct. App. 2003) ("The party requesting the modification must show first that there has been a substantial change in circumstances and, second, that these changed circumstances have resulted in such a detriment to the child that a modification would be in the best interests of the child.") A remarriage plus difficulty in getting along with a stepparent or stepsiblings may, but need not, qualify as a substantial change in circumstances. *See In re Marriage of Anderson,* 783 P.2d 1372, 1375 (Mont. 1989) (upholding custody modification because of difficulties in getting along with stepfather); *Elder v. Elder,* 2001 Tenn. App. LEXIS 681 (Sept. 14, 2001) ("Specifically, she asserts that her daughter's difficulties with her stepmother and stepbrother provide ample grounds for changing custody. We disagree.") The trial court will have to make findings of fact with respect to the degree to which the children are adversely affected by the current living arrangements, and the degree to which their lives would improve were custody modified.

107.   Before the Floramba court can even address whether there has been a substantial change in circumstances, it must first establish that it has jurisdiction to hear the case. Donald and Edweena are domiciled in Massacut and they have only been in Floramba for six weeks, which simply is not long enough for the Floramba court to be able to assert jurisdiction. *See In re L.S.,* 226 P.3d 1227, 1232 (Colo. App. 2009) ("where a child with home-state status in one state is moved for any reason to a second state, the child will not lose home-state status in the first state or gain it in the second for another six months"). Unless an exception could be invoked, *see State of N.M., ex rel. CYFD v. Donna J.,* 129 P.3d 167, 170 (N.M. Ct. App. 2006) (discussing UCCJEA emergency exception), the Floramba court simply would not have jurisdiction to address the substantive issues.

108.   Both Billie Jean and Gertrude are Frieda's parents in the eyes of the law, and either might be awarded custody. *See Carter v. Carter,* 546 S.E.2d 220, 221 (Va. App. 2001) ("Once the adoption is final, there is no distinction in law between the biological parent and the adoptive parent; they are parents to that child of equal rank and responsibility."). The determination of custody will be based on who would best promote Frieda's welfare. *Firmin v. Firmin,* 770 So. 2d 930, 932 (La. Ct. App. 2000) ("the best interest of the child remains the paramount concern in making custody determinations"). The best interests analysis might take into account that Gertrude is Frieda's primary caretaker. *See Gantter v. Higgins,* 2009 Minn. App. Unpub. LEXIS 1150 (Oct. 27, 2009). However, that factor need not outweigh other factors. *See Dinius v. Dinius,* 448 N.W.2d 210 (N.D. 1989) (awarding custody to father notwithstanding mother having played primary caretaker role).

109. States differ with respect to whether an individual who stands in an in loco parentis relationship with a child is permitted to seek custody or visitation with that child. *Compare T.B. v. L.R.M.*, 786 A.2d 913, 916 (Pa. 2001) ("A third party has been permitted to maintain an action for custody, however, where that party stands *in loco parentis* to the child.") *with In re Jones*, 2002-Ohio-1748 ("because Dvorak is neither the natural nor the adoptive parent of Cheyenne, she cannot be a 'parent' within the meaning of [the relevant statute] . . . , and she is not entitled to an award of parental rights under the statute without first proving that Jones is unsuitable.")Those states permitting someone with in loco parentis status to seek custody or visitation may require a showing of harm to the child in order for that adult to get custody of the child. *See Riepe v. Riepe*, 91 P.3d 312, 316 (Ariz. Ct. App. 2004) ("in order to obtain in loco parentis *custody*, a petitioning party must establish, among other things, that it would be significantly detrimental to the child to remain or be placed in the custody of either of the child's living legal parents who wish to retain or obtain custody."). The likely result here is that Bob will be awarded at most visitation rights with Norman, absent a showing of probable harm to Norman were Marley awarded custody.

110. While the tender years presumption is no longer employed in many states at least in part because of equal protection worries, *see*, for example, *Ex parte Devine*, 398 So. 2d 686, 695 (Ala. 1981) ("we conclude that the tender years presumption represents an unconstitutional gender-based classification which discriminates between fathers and mothers in child custody proceedings solely on the basis of sex"), that is because it involved a facial classification on the basis of a gender. Mere statistical evidence, without more, would be unlikely to be held sufficient to establish invidious discrimination. *See Personnel Administrator of Massachusetts v. Feeney*, 442 U.S. 256 (1979) (upholding state employment preference for Veterans even though the preference had a disproportionate adverse impact on women). Thus, even were the evidence gathered about the custody decisions of this particular court (rather than courts more generally), one would need more to establish that the court had awarded custody to mothers "at least in part because of, not merely in spite of, its adverse effects upon an identifiable group." *Id.* at 279. Absent some kind of evidence of bias on the part of the court, Bob Gilman's appeal is unlikely to be successful.

111. The enforceability of a surrogacy contract is a matter of state law, so it will depend upon the conditions under which Old Jersey will enforce such agreements. Some states treat such agreements as enforceable, *see* Ark. Code Ann. § 9-10-201, while other states treat them as void and unenforceable. *See* Mich. Comp. Laws Ann. § 722.855 ("A surrogate parentage contract is void and unenforceable as contrary to public policy."). Assuming that Old Jersey does not treat such agreements as unenforceable as a general matter, a separate issue is whether Old Jersey requires that particular procedures be followed, *see*, for example, Va. Code Ann. § 20-160, and, if so, whether those procedures were followed. Even if the court refuses to enforce the surrogacy contract, a separate question will involve the determination of which parent should have custody of the child. *See*, for example, *A.L.S. ex rel. J.P. v. E.A.G.*, 2010 WL 4181449 (Minn. App. 2010) (holding that surrogate was the mother of the child but that the father would have sole physical and legal custody of the child).

112. Some states distinguish between traditional or genetic surrogacy on the one hand and gestational surrogacy on the other. California, for example treats gestational surrogacy contracts as enforceable, *see Johnson v. Calvert*, 851 P.2d 776 (Cal. 1993), but traditional or genetic surrogacy arrangements as voidable by the surrogate. *See In re Marriage of*

Moschetta, 30 Cal. Rptr. 2d 893, 903 (Cal. App. 1994) (affirming judgment in favor of surrogate). Other states do not distinguish and may hold neither agreement is enforceable. *See A.H.W. v. G.H.B.*, 772 A.2d 948, 954 (N.J. Super. Ch. Div. 2000) (refusing to enforce surrogacy agreement against gestational surrogate); *In re Baby M*, 537 A.2d 1227 (N.J. 1988) (traditional surrogacy contract void). If, like California, Old Jersey law distinguishes between the two kinds of contracts, then this contract may be enforceable even if a traditional surrogacy contract would not have been.

113. **Answer (A) is the best answer.** While states differ in their approaches to this problem, at least some suggest that if the marriage was void ab initio, the support payments must resume. *See Watts v. Watts*, 547 N.W.2d 466, 470 (Neb. 1996) ("Since Kilgore's 3-month marriage to Metoyer was a legal nullity, the void marriage standing alone cannot operate to terminate Watts' alimony obligations under the divorce decree.").

Answer (B) is incorrect. No jurisdiction would base the decision on the continued success of Alex's first marriage. For example, Alex and Amy might now divorce based on adultery or desertion, and the Alex and Barbara might then marry, which would then end Carls' support obligation, assuming that the state had adopted the void/voidable distinction. *See Darling v. Darling*, 335 N.E.2d 708 (Ohio App. 1975) (adopting void/voidable distinction for use in determining whether support obligation would be revived).

Answer (C) is not the best answer. The issue at hand is whether Carl can be forced to continue to pay support. Many courts would be loathe to base that determination on whether someone in Alex's position could afford to support Barbara. Insofar as the state must consider that Carl may have reasonably relied on his no longer having the support obligation, *see*, for example, *Joye v. Yon*, 586 S.E.2d 131, 133 (S.C. 2003) ("payor spouse should be able to rely on the expectation that payee spouse's subsequent marriage is not voided due to the actions of payee spouse's subsequent spouse"), that would be true whether or not Alex had won the lottery.

Answer (D) is incorrect. In the eyes of the law, Amy is an innocent spouse. There is no suggestion that she waited too long. *See Sullivan v. Mandigo*, 332 N.Y.S.2d 200, 201 (App. Div. 1972) (action challenging validity of divorce six years later not barred by laches). If the defense of laches were viewed as having merit, then the divorce between Alex and Amy would not have been viewed as invalid.

114. **Answer (B) is the best answer.** While Keith will likely be able to have the marriage annulled, *see Stegienko v. Stegienko*, 295 N.W. 252, 254 (Mich. 1940) (granting annulment based on wife's misrepresentation that she wanted to have children), many jurisdictions will not require the reinstatement of spousal support under these circumstances. A jurisdiction that distinguishes between void and voidable marriages will suggest that because his marriage to Karen was merely voidable, Linda's support obligation will not be reinstated. *See Darling v. Darling*, 335 N.E.2d 708 (Ohio App. 1975).

Answer (A) is incorrect. The question here is not whether they in fact would have been able to conceive but, instead, whether Karen had made a fraudulent misrepresentation going to the essence of marriage. *See Stegienko v. Stegienko*, 295 N.W. 252, 254 (Mich. 1940) ("Marriage may be annulled for fraud of any nature wholly subversive of the true essence of the marriage relationship.").

Answer (C) is incorrect. He will likely be able to have the marriage annulled even if he did not expressly state his desire to have children. *See Stegienko v. Stegienko*, 295 N.W. 252, 254 (Mich. 1940) (suggesting that marriage presumes an ability and willingness to have children).

Answer (D) is incorrect. Many states will not reinstate a support obligation even if the payor spouse has not remarried in the interim. *See*, for example, *Darling v. Darling*, 335 N.E.2d 708 (Ohio App. 1975).

115.   **Answer (B) is the best answer.** Rehabilitative spousal support enables one of the parties to the divorce to acquire or improve skills so that he or she can enter the job market. *Reback v. Reback*, 296 So. 2d 541, 543 (Fla. Dist. Ct. App. 1974) (" 'rehabilitative' alimony is appropriate in those situations where it is possible for the person to develop anew or redevelop a capacity for self-support, and should be limited in amount and duration to what is necessary to maintain that person through his training or education, or until he or she obtains employment or otherwise becomes self-supporting").

Answer (A) is incorrect. While a spouse might be required to cover counseling and medical expenses resulting from abuse during the marriage, *see Garces v. Garces*, 704 So. 2d 1106 (Fla. Dist. Ct. App. 1998), those expenses are not considered part of rehabilitative spousal support. *See Reback v. Reback*, 296 So. 2d 541, 543 (Fla. Dist. Ct. App. 1974).

Answer (C) is incorrect. While required medical treatment due to spouse's mistreatment might be the basis for affording a more favorable division of marital or community property, *see Brinkman v. Brinkman*, 966 S.W.2d 780, 783 (Tex. App. 1998) (plaintiff "allege[d] cruel treatment as grounds for divorce in order to receive a disproportionate share of community property"), rehabilitative spousal support is a term of art. *See Reback v. Reback*, 296 So. 2d 541, 543 (Fla. Dist. Ct. App. 1974).

Answer (D) is incorrect. While there are cases where one spouse would withhold access to a child because of the other spouse's failure to pay support for the ex-spouse and child, *see*, for example, *Rogers v. Rogers*, 593 N.Y.S.2d 299, 301 (App. Div. 1993), that is not permissible without court authorization. *See id.* ("We make it clear, however, that this court does not, and will not, condone the wife's institution of self-help.") In any event, this is not connected to rehabilitative spousal support. *See Reback v. Reback*, 296 So. 2d 541, 543 (Fla. Dist. Ct. App. 1974).

116.   **Answer (A) is the best answer**, because spousal support pendant lite is support for the period during which the proceeding in pending. *See Gerloff v. Gerloff*, 23 Pa. D.& C. 3d 515 (1982) ("The Divorce Code of 1980, in Section 104, defines alimony pendente lite as an 'order for temporary support during the pendency of a divorce or annulment proceeding.' ").

Answer (B) is incorrect. This description more aptly fits rehabilitative spousal support. *See Reback v. Reback*, 296 So. 2d 541, 543 (Fla. Dist. Ct. App. 1974).

Answer (C) is incorrect. Rather than being suspended during this period, this is the support that one of the spouses will be using to pay bills while the divorce issues remain unresolved. *See Maynard v. Maynard*, 399 A.2d 900, 901 (Md. App. 1979) ("an award of alimony pendente lite is a monetary payment pending the outcome of litigation which has been instituted but which has not been concluded").

Answer (D) is incorrect. This is support ordered for one of the spouses while the litigation is still pending. *See Maynard v. Maynard*, 399 A.2d 900, 901 (Md. App. 1979).

117.   **Answer (D) is the best answer.** The ages of children are not relevant when considering permanent support if only because as a general matter there is a time in the future when the children will not need support, even if they do need it now. Some of the relevant factors to determine whether permanent support should be ordered include the ages of the parties, their earning ability, the length of marriage, and the standard of living to which the parties had become accustomed. *See Pearson v. Pearson*, 771 N.W.2d 288, 291 (N.D. 2009).

Answer (A) is incorrect, because the ability of the spouse to enter into the job market (possibly after receiving training) is one of the factors to be considered when determining whether permanent spousal support should be awarded. *See In re Marriage of Wargo*, 556 P.2d 1388, 1389 (Or. App. 1976) (wife should be awarded permanent support given her poor job prospects).

Answer (B) is incorrect, because the ability of the ex-spouse to be able to establish a standard of living "reasonably commensurate with the standard of living established during the marriage" is one of the factors considered when determining whether permanent support should be awarded. *See Zeigler v. Zeigler*, 635 So. 2d 50, 54 (Fla. Dist. Ct. App. 1994).

Answer (C) is incorrect, because the length of the marriage is one of the factors considered when determining whether permanent child support should be awarded. *See In re Marriage of Wann*, 737 P.2d 151, 151 (Or. App. 1987) (permanent support awarded, at least in part, because the couple had been together for 36 years).

118.   **Answer (D) is the best answer.** The parent cannot waive the child's right to support. *See Forrester v. Buerger*, 244 S.E.2d 345, 345 (Ga. 1978). However, the parent can waive spousal support. *See Toni v. Toni*, 636 N.W.2d 396, 401 (N.D. 2001).

Answer (A) is incorrect. While Wayne has the right to seek custody, *see Farnsworth v. Farnsworth*, 756 N.W.2d 522, 526 (Neb. 2008) ("due process of law requires a parent to be granted a hearing on his or her fitness as a parent before being deprived of custody"), a parent does not have the right to waive child support. *See Forrester v. Buerger*, 244 S.E.2d 345, 345 (Ga. 1978).

Answer (B) is incorrect. Absent evidence of fraud, coercion, or duress, courts will approve of agreements to waive spousal support. *See Barber v. Barber*, 38 So. 3d 1046, 1050 (La. Ct. App. 2010) (noting "there is no prohibition against the waiver of post-divorce permanent spousal support").

Answer (C) is incorrect. The parent cannot waive child support, *see Forrester v. Buerger*, 244 S.E.2d 345, 345 (Ga. 1978), even if she can provide adequate support for the child from her own salary.

119.   **Answer (B) is the best answer.** Some state require divorced parents to contribute to their children's college expenses when doing so would not impose an unreasonable burden. *See In re Gilmore*, 803 A.2d 601, 603 (N.H. 2002) ("this court and the legislature, however, have recognized the superior court's jurisdiction to order divorced parents, consistent with their

means, to contribute toward the educational expenses of their adult children"). Assuming that she did not know the answer already, Laura would have to do some research to discover whether New Floraco imposed such a requirement on divorced parents.

Answer (A) is incorrect. Some states require divorced parents to contribute to the college education costs of their children. *See In re Gilmore*, 803 A.2d 601, 603 (N.H. 2002) (recognizing that divorced parents may have this requirement imposed on them).

Answer (C) is incorrect. Some states do not require divorced parents to pay college expenses. *See Curtis v. Kline*, 666 A.2d 265 (Pa. 1995) (striking down such a requirement on state constitutional grounds); *Burtch v. Burtch*, 972 S.W.2d 882, 886 (Tex. App. 1998) ("Absent a contractual agreement, there is no basis for a court to enforce child support for children who have graduated from high school and are over the age of eighteen."). However, a separate question would be presented if the parents had agreed to provide that support. *See Harmer v. Harmer*, 36 Pa. D. & C.4th 146 (1997) ("While the Supreme Court clearly held that divorced, separated, or unmarried parents may no longer be *statutorily*-required to provide post-secondary education support for their adult children, it gave no indication that the decision was also intended to invalidate every voluntarily-assumed child support arrangement involving the payment of post-secondary education expenses.").

Answer (D) is incorrect. The fact that Linda and Alice had both reached eighteen would not preclude the father from being forced to help pay their higher education costs. *See Childers v. Childers*, 575 P.2d 201, 206 (Wash. 1978) ("Where, as here, the children would have most likely remained dependent on their father past 18 while they obtained a college education, it is within the discretion of the trial court to define them as dependents for that purpose.").

120. **Answer (C) is the best answer.** Jurisdictions differ as to whether a failure to specify that the incurred obligation is to pay in-state tuition at a public school will mean that a parent would be responsible for private college tuition. *Compare In re Marriage of Frink*, 409 N.W.2d 477, 481 (Iowa Ct. App. 1987) (suggesting that in-state tuition provides the more appropriate benchmark) *with Kayle v. Kayle*, 565 A.2d 1069, 1071 (N.H. 1989) (suggesting that the failure to specify might make him responsible for private tuition if that would not involve an unreasonable burden).

Answer (A) is incorrect. Such an agreement is enforceable. *See Burtch v. Burtch*, 972 S.W.2d 882 (Tex. App. 1998) (enforcing agreement to provide post-secondary education support).

Answer (B) is incorrect. Jurisdictions differ. Some suggest that the appropriate benchmark involves what an in-state public university would charge, *see In re Marriage of Frink*, 409 N.W.2d 477, 481 (Iowa Ct. App. 1987) (suggesting that in-state tuition provides the more appropriate benchmark). Others suggest that the failure to specify might make him responsible for private tuition if that would not involve an undue burden. *See Kayle v. Kayle*, 565 A.2d 1069, 1071 (N.H. 1989). However, those choosing a public university as providing the benchmark tend to use the state university, because of the lower cost of in-state tuition. *See Medeiros v. Medeiros*, 823 N.Y.S.2d 637, 638 (App. Div. 2006) (holding that the parent was only obligated to pay what would have been required for in-stare tuition).

Answer (D) is incorrect. Because the agreement specified that *he* rather than *they* would pay reasonable college expenses, it is only his obligation is to pay those reasonable expenses. *See Medeiros v. Medeiros*, 823 N.Y.S.2d 637, 638 (App. Div. 2006) (per agreement, only one of the parents was obligated to pay tuition costs, Nancy has no obligation to foot the bill for those expenses).

121. **Answer (C) is the best answer.** Support will likely be order in this case, *see Laura G. v. Peter G.*, 830 N.Y.S.2d 496 (Sup. Ct. 2007) (husband required to pay support for child who was a product of artificial insemination). Visitation may be denied if it would result in harm to the child. *See Pettry v. Pettry*, 486 N.E.2d 213, 215 (Ohio App. 1984).

   Answer (A) is incorrect. Lack of biological connection will not preclude a husband from being required to pay child support. *See Laura G. v. Peter G.*, 830 N.Y.S.2d 496 (Sup. Ct. 2007) (husband required to pay support for child who was a product of artificial insemination).

   Answer (B) is incorrect, because a support order can be entered, lack of biological connection notwithstanding. *See Laura G. v. Peter G.*, 830 N.Y.S.2d 496 (Sup. Ct. 2007).

   Answer (D) is incorrect. Support is likely to be imposed, *see Laura G. v. Peter G.*, 830 N.Y.S.2d 496 (Sup. Ct. 2007), and it is true that as a general matter it is good for the noncustodial parent and the child to have a relationship. *See Bennett v. Bennett*, 617 N.Y.S.2d 931, 932 (App. Div. 1994) ("In most situations, the best interests of children are served by a continuing relationship with both parents.") However, if it is really true that in this case the child would be harmed by the visitation, then visitation would not likely to be ordered, general rule notwithstanding. *See Pettry v. Pettry*, 486 N.E.2d 213, 215 (Ohio App. 1984).

122. **Answer (D) is the best answer.** While the husband would likely not be held liable for child support if the pregnancy resulted from sexual intercourse, *see In re Marriage of Adams*, 701 N.E.2d 1131, 1134 (Ill. App. 1998) (ex-husband not liable for child support when children born through sexual relationship with other men rather than through artificial insemination as agreed), he might well be liable for support if, for example, artificial insemination was performed with a doctor's assistance per their agreement. Liability is sometimes imposed, even where there is some irregularity in the artificial insemination procedure. *Cf. Laura G. v. Peter G.*, 830 N.Y.S.2d 496 (Sup. Ct. 2007) (husband liable for child support when wife artificially inseminated by doctor, notwithstanding failure to obtain husband's written consent).

   Answer (A) is incorrect. A father may well be ordered to pay support, lack of positive feelings for the child notwithstanding. *See H.N.H. v. H.M.F.*, 2005-Ohio-1869 (mother can seek child support from father, notwithstanding lack of relationship between father and child).

   Answer (B) is incorrect. While the husband would be responsible for a child born though artificial insemination when he has agreed to do so, he as a general matter would not be responsible for children born to his wife through sexual intercourse with another man. *See L.M.S. v. S.L.S.*, 312 N.W.2d 853, 855 (Wis. Ct. App. 1981) ("As a general rule, a husband is not liable to support a child born to his wife but not procreated by him.").

   Answer (C) is incorrect. While it may well be in the child's best interest to receive the support, that alone may not suffice to establish that the ex-husband must pay support if the child was not born through artificial insemination. *See In re Marriage of Adams*, 701 N.E.2d 1131, 1134 (Ill. App. 1998) (ex-husband not liable for child support when children born through sexual relationship with other men rather than through artificial insemination as agreed).

123.   **Answer (D) is the best answer.** Jurisdictions differ as to whether a support obligation will be imposed when children were the product of an affair during the marriage. *Compare Amrhein v. Cozad*, 714 A.2d 409 (Pa. Super. 1998) (imposing support obligation) *with In re Marriage of Adams*, 701 N.E.2d 1131, 1134 (Ill. App. 1998) (refusing to impose support obligation).

   Answer (A) is incorrect. A visitation schedule is unlikely to be imposed if his maintaining contact with the children would harm rather than benefit them. *See Pettry v. Pettry*, 486 N.E.2d 213, 215 (Ohio App. 1984).

   Answer (B) is incorrect. He might be ordered to pay support even if the children resulted from an affair during the marriage. *See Amrhein v. Cozad*, 714 A.2d 409 (Pa. Super. 1998) (husband presumed father and liable for support despite ex-wife's paramour being child's biological father).

   Answer (C) is incorrect. While it is of course true that the children are not at fault here, the husband may well not be forced to pay support if the children were not conceived using artificial insemination, relationship with the children over the past several years notwithstanding. *See In re Marriage of Adams*, 701 N.E.2d 1131, 1134 (Ill. App. 1998) (ex-husband not liable for child support when he discovered years later that his wife had not made use of artificial insemination after all).

124.   **Answer (B) is the best answer.** Assuming that Larry wishes to maintain contact with the children, Kim may well be stopped from denying his paternity, *see Hausman v. Hausman*, 199 S.W.3d 38 (Tex. App. 2006) (wife estopped from denying husband's paternity of child, lack of biological link between husband and wife notwithstanding), or he may be held to be the father because a child born into a marriage is presumed to be the child of the parties. *See Amrhein v. Cozad*, 714 A.2d 409 (Pa. Super. 1998). In that event, support and visitation would be determined just as they would be had parentage not been at issue.

   Answer (A) is incorrect. The custodial parent cannot deny visitation to the noncustodial parent merely because the former parent believes that child would be better off not seeing the noncustodial parent. Rather, there must be an objective showing of actual or likely detriment to the child. *See Ware v. Ware*, 2002-Ohio-871 ("The right of visitation should be denied only under extraordinary circumstances, such as the unfitness of the non-custodial parent or a showing that the visitation would cause harm.").

   Answer (C) is incorrect. Visitation and support can be ordered even absent a biological connection to the child. *See Titus v. Rayne*, 1992 Del. Fam. Ct. LEXIS 43 (Nov. 19, 1992) (wife estopped from denying husband's paternity and husband entitled to visitation).

   Answer (D) is incorrect. Notwithstanding Kim's belief that it would be better for the children never to see Larry, she may well be estopped from denying his paternity and a visitation schedule may well be entered. *See Titus v. Rayne*, 1992 Del. Fam. Ct. LEXIS 43 (Nov. 19, 1992).

125.   **Answer (C) is the best answer.** Because Jimmy knew that contraception is not foolproof, he was on notice that sexual relations might result in pregnancy. Further, he could have used additional precautions if he had been worried about fathering a child. *See L. Pamela P. v. Frank S.*, 449 N.E.2d 713, 716 (N.Y. 1983) ("the mother's conduct in no way limited his right

to use contraception").

Answer (A) is incorrect. When a child is born as a result of unprotected sexual relations, the father may have support obligations imposed. *See Inez M. v. Nathan G.*, 451 N.Y.S.2d 607 (Fam. Ct. 1982).

Answer (B) is incorrect. Fathers may be held responsible for child support even if their partners lied about using contraception. *See Wallis v. Smith*, 22 P.3d 682 (N.M. App. 2001) (refusing to afford relief to man responsible for child support who claimed that his sexual partner had affirmatively misrepresented that she was using contraception); *L. Pamela P. v. Frank S.*, 449 N.E.2d 713, 716 (N.Y. 1983) (even if partner lied about contraception, man still responsible for support).

Answer (D) is incorrect. Child support is not only ordered when the noncustodial parent makes more than the custodial parent. *See Goar v. Goar*, 368 N.W.2d 348 (Minn. Ct. App. 1985) (discussing child support of obligation of noncustodial parent who made less than custodial parent).

126. **Answer (D) is the best answer.** Because Alex quit his job to avoid paying support, the court will likely find that there has been no change in circumstances justifying a modification of support. *See Burdette v. Burdette*, 681 So. 2d 862, 863 (Fla. Dist. Ct. App. 1996) ("A change in circumstances does not exist when a parent obligated to pay child support attempts to avoid or reduce that obligation by voluntarily becoming unemployed or underemployed.").

Answer (A) is incorrect. An individual who quits his job in order to avoid his support obligation will not have his obligation lowered merely because he is no longer working. *See Kolosso v. Kolosso*, 516 N.W.2d 22 (Wis. Ct. App. 1994) (upholding support obligation established in light of what individual could be earning rather than what he in fact was earning because individual was found to be intentionally shirking his support obligation).

Answer (B) is incorrect. Alex's support obligation will likely be established in light of what he could be earning rather than what he in fact was earning, whether or not he had another income stream. *See Kolosso v. Kolosso*, 516 N.W.2d 22 (Wis. Ct. App. 1994).

Answer (C) is incorrect. Modifications can be made when there has been a material change in circumstances. *See Sneckenberg v. Sneckenberg*, 616 N.W.2d 68, 73 (Neb. App. 2000). However, that change must not be due to the noncustodial parent's having acted in bad faith to avert the support obligation. *See Kolosso v. Kolosso*, 516 N.W.2d 22 (Wis. Ct. App. 1994).

127. **Answer (D) is the best answer.** Children born in a later marriage should be considered when determining the noncustodial parent's support obligation. *See Hasty v. Hasty*, 828 P.2d 94, 99 (Wyo. 1992) ("consideration can be given to later-born children in setting child support").

Answer (A) is incorrect. Children of a later marriage are appropriately considered when determining a support obligation. *See Moxham v. Moxham*, 1994 Neb. App. LEXIS 55 (Feb. 22, 1994) ("The trial court must consider and determine whether, in the particular case, the obligation to support children of a subsequent marriage justifies a deviation from the guidelines.").

Answer (B) is incorrect. Later-born children are to be considered even when reasonably foreseeable. *See Hasty v. Hasty*, 828 P.2d 94, 99 (Wyo. 1992).

Answer (C) is incorrect. While Verne also has a responsibility to provide for the twins, he is not the *only* person with that responsibility, so they should nonetheless be considered when determining Roni's support obligation. *See Hasty v. Hasty*, 828 P.2d 94, 99 (Wyo. 1992).

128. This is a matter of state law. Some states have a nurturing parent exception that permits a noncustodial parent to stop working without having the income imputed to her that she would have earned had she continued working. *See Reinert v. Reinert*, 926 A.2d 539, 541 (Pa. Super. 2007). However, those states permitting use of the nurturing parent doctrine may well not apply it in particular cases, *see Doherty v. Doherty*, 859 A.2d 811, 813 (Pa. Super. 2004) (upholding trial court imputation of income and refusal to employ nurturing parent doctrine to parent who chose to remain at home to take care of very young children). Further, some states may not recognize the doctrine. *See Snader v. Dudley*, 741 A.2d 17 (Del. 1999) ("Delaware has not adopted the nurturing parent doctrine and we decline to do so on the facts of this case.").

129. **Answer (D) is the best answer.** Under UIFSA, New Vermshire rather than Massecticut has jurisdiction to modify the support order. *See In re Marriage of Hillstrom*, 126 P.3d 315, 318 (Colo. Ct. App. 2005) ("under UIFSA, the issuing tribunal has continuing, exclusive jurisdiction only as long as one of the parties or the child continues to reside in the issuing state, or unless each party consents in writing to a court of another state assuming continuing, exclusive jurisdiction to modify the order").

Answer (A) is incorrect. While there is ample evidence that Bernice was not acting in bad faith, the Massecticut court should not be exercising jurisdiction and thus should not be addressing the merits. *See In re Marriage of Hillstrom*, 126 P.3d 315, 318 (Colo. Ct. App. 2005).

Answer (B) is incorrect. Massecticut should not be exercising jurisdiction. *See In re Marriage of Hillstrom*, 126 P.3d 315, 318 (Colo. Ct. App. 2005). Further, New Vermshire might well modify the support order under these circumstances, Daniella's faultlessness notwithstanding. *See Parker v. Parker*, 645 So. 2d 1327 (Miss. 1994) (upholding modification of child support when individual was not at fault when he lost his job).

Answer (C) is incorrect. While a court addressing the merits might well grant her request, *see Parker v. Parker*, 645 So. 2d 1327 (Miss. 1994), the Massecticut court does not have jurisdiction to reach the merits.

130. **Answer (D) is the best answer.** *See Letellier v. Letellier*, 40 S.W.3d 490, 495 (Tenn. 2001) ("Ms. LeTellier alleges that long-arm personal jurisdiction has been satisfied in this case. Even assuming that to be true, the order she sought to modify was issued by a state other than Tennessee. Tennessee courts lack subject matter jurisdiction to modify out-of-state orders when the provisions of UIFSA are not satisfied.").

Answer (A) is incorrect. While there is no dispute that Henrietta lost her job in good faith, a prior question is whether the Massecticut court has subject matter jurisdiction to hear this case. If under UIFSA the Massecticut court lacks subject matter jurisdiction, then its having personal jurisdiction over Irwin will not suffice to enable the court to hear this case. *See Letellier v. Letellier*, 40 S.W.3d 490, 495 (Tenn. 2001).

Answer (B) is incorrect. The Massecticut court should not be addressing the merits because it lacks subject matter jurisdiction. However, on the merits, the modification might have been granted, because there has been a material change in circumstances affecting Henrietta's ability to pay, and Henrietta cannot be blamed for this occurrence. *See Greenwood v. Greenwood*, 596 N.W.2d 317, 323 (N.D. 1999).

Answer (C) is incorrect. While Henrietta might well have been successful on the merits, *see Greenwood v. Greenwood*, 596 N.W.2d 317, 323 (N.D. 1999), the Massecticut court is unlikely to be found to have subject matter jurisdiction in this case. *See Letellier v. Letellier*, 40 S.W.3d 490, 495 (Tenn. 2001).

131.   **Answer (D) is the best answer.** If Winona is domiciled in Texarkana and has met the residency requirement, then the court has jurisdiction to grant the divorce. *See Hager v. Hager*, 607 N.E.2d 63, 67 (Ohio App. 1992) (upholding validity of divorce when individual was both domiciled in state and resident of state for requisite period). If the court has personal jurisdiction over the husband via the state's long-arm statute, then a support order can be issued as well. *See Cabaniss v. Cabaniss*, 620 S.E.2d 559, 563 (Va. App. 2005) (upholding spousal support order because court had personal jurisdiction over husband via long-arm statute).

Answer (A) is incorrect. The Texarkana court may well have personal jurisdiction over Wylie via its long-arm statute. *See Cabaniss v. Cabaniss*, 620 S.E.2d 559, 563 (Va. App. 2005) (upholding spousal support order because court had personal jurisdiction over husband via long-arm statute).

Answer (B) is incorrect. The Texarkana court could both grant the divorce and issue the support order because it had personal jurisdiction over the husband via the long-arm statute and jurisdiction to grant the divorce assuming that the wife was domiciled in Texarkana. *See Cabaniss v. Cabaniss*, 620 S.E.2d 559, 563 (Va. App. 2005).

Answer (C) is incorrect. While the court could grant the divorce and issue the support order, that was because it had jurisdiction over both parties (and the marriage), *see Cabaniss v. Cabaniss*, 620 S.E.2d 559, 563 (Va. App. 2005), rather than despite its lack of jurisdiction over one of the parties.

132.   **Answer (B) is the best answer.** Child support can be increased if the noncustodial parent's standard of living improves after the divorce. *See In re Marriage of Kerr*, 91 Cal. Rptr. 2d 374, 380 (Cal. App. 1999) ("Unlike spousal support awards requiring consideration of the parties' standard of living during marriage, child support awards must reflect a minor child's right to be maintained in a lifestyle and condition consonant with his or her parents' position in society after dissolution of the marriage.").

Answer (A) is incorrect. Even if the children's needs are being met, an increase in support may well be ordered if the noncustodial parent's income has increased substantially. *See Smith v. Edelman*, 814 N.E.2d 764 (Mass. App. Ct. 2004) ("children's needs are to be defined, at least in part, by their parents' higher standard of living and that children are entitled to participate in the noncustodial parent's higher standard of living when available resources permit").

Answer (C) is incorrect. Courts might be more sympathetic to the disincentive argument in a case where the noncustodial parent was working two jobs, *see In re Marriage of Fini*, 31 Cal. Rptr. 2d 749, 754 n.10 (Cal. App. 1994), because the noncustodial parent would only be expected to have one job. However, as a general matter, courts interpret the support acts to require that the children be supported in a way that is commensurate with the parents' current income, *see In re Marriage of Singleteary*, 687 N.E.2d 1080, 1087 (Ill. App. 1997) ("The Act was intended to protect the rights of children to be supported by their parents in an amount commensurate with their income."), which might well mean that support should increase when the noncustodial parent's income increases. *See id.*

Answer (D) is incorrect. Support will be determined in light of a number of factors that include the child's needs and the incomes of the parents. However, the refusal to exercise full visitation rights will not be a justification for decreasing support. *See Kurts v. Parrish*, 2004 Tenn. App. LEXIS 771 (Nov. 17, 2004) (discussing how decreasing the support for a parent not exercising visitation would violate public policy).

133. **Answer (D) is the best answer.** A minor having fathered a child is not enough to emancipate the minor. The bases for becoming emancipated include joining the armed services, marrying, or being self-supporting while living away from one's parents. *See Dunson v. Dunson*, 769 N.E.2d 1120, 1124 (Ind. 2002).

Answer (A) is incorrect. Joining the United States Armed Forces is a basis for having a child declared emancipated. *See Borders v. Noel*, 800 N.E.2d 586, 589 (Ind. Ct. App. 2003).

Answer (B) is incorrect. Marriage is a basis for having a child declared emancipated. *See Borders v. Noel*, 800 N.E.2d 586, 589 (Ind. Ct. App. 2003).

Answer (C) is incorrect. A child may be declared emancipated if living away from her parents and self-supporting. *See Robles v. Robles*, 855 N.E.2d 1049, 1054 (Ind. Ct. App. 2006).

134. **Answer (C) is the best answer.** During the minor's marriage, the father is not obligated to pay support. However, when the minor marriage is annulled and the minor is dependent on the other parent, the father's support obligation is reinstated. *See In re Marriage of Fetters*, 584 P.2d 104, 106 (Colo. Ct. App. 1978).

Answer (A) is incorrect. When the child marries, the support obligation ends, and the parent will not be required to pay support while the marriage is recognized. However, when the marriage is annulled, the support obligation recommences. *See State ex rel. Dept. of Economic Sec. v. Demetz*, 130 P.3d 986, 991 (Ariz. Ct. App. 2006).

Answer (B) is incorrect. *See*, for example, *State ex rel. Dept. of Economic Sec. v. Demetz*, 130 P.3d 986, 991 (Ariz. Ct. App. 2006) ("upon entry of a decree annulling that marriage during the child's minority, or before she would have otherwise become emancipated, her unemancipated status revives and the parent's support obligation recommences").

Answer (D) is incorrect. The father may well be required to resume support payments, lack of willingness notwithstanding. *See In re Marriage of Fetters*, 584 P.2d 104 (Colo. Ct. App. 1978) (reinstituting father's support obligation when his minor daughter's marriage was annulled).

135. **Answer (A) is the best answer.** While service at the last known address may meet due process requirements, *Crumpler v. State, Dept. of Revenue*, 117 P.3d 730, 732 (Alaska 2005) (due process requirements met for child support modification purposes when notice sent to father's last known address), that does not mean that the state has jurisdiction under UIFSA, which would require some further connection with the state. *See Chisholm-*

Brownlee v. Chisholm, 676 N.Y.S.2d 818, 820 (Fam. Ct. 1998).

Answer B is incorrect, because the parent's having resided with the child in the jurisdiction is a basis for the assertion of personal jurisdiction under UIFSA. *See Chisholm-Brownlee v. Chisholm*, 676 N.Y.S.2d 818, 820 (Fam. Ct. 1998).

Answer (C) is incorrect, because the parent's having likely conceived the child in the jurisdiction is a basis for asserting personal jurisdiction. *See Chisholm-Brownlee v. Chisholm*, 676 N.Y.S.2d 818, 820 (Fam. Ct. 1998).

Answer (D) is incorrect, because the parent being personally served in the jurisdiction is a basis for the assertion of personal jurisdiction over the parent. *See Chisholm-Brownlee v. Chisholm*, 676 N.Y.S.2d 818, 820 (Fam. Ct. 1998).

136. **Answer (C) is the best answer.** Even if the divorce decree does not specify that support will end upon cohabitation, some states will treat remarriage and cohabitation as equivalent for these purposes as a matter of law, *see* Ala. Code 1975 § 30-2-55 (ending support upon remarriage or cohabitation), while others do not. *See Cermak v. Cermak*, 569 N.W.2d 280 (N.D. 1997) (refusing to find that a support obligation no longer exists merely because the ex-spouse is cohabiting with someone).

Answer (A) is incorrect. While a cohabitation clause could be incorporated into the support agreement, *see Clark v. Clark*, 860 N.E.2d 1080 (Ohio App. 2006) (holding that following the support agreement the ex-husband no longer had to pay spousal support because his ex-wife was now cohabiting with someone else) and some states will not treat cohabitation as triggering an end to the support obligation absent such a provision in the support agreement, see *Cermak v. Cermak*, 569 N.W.2d 280, 284 (N.D. 1997), other states will treat cohabitation as the equivalent of remarriage for purposes of ending support, even without such a provision in the support agreement. *See*, for example, Ala. Code 1975 § 30-2-55 (ending support upon remarriage or cohabitation).

Answer (B) is incorrect. Some states will not treat cohabitation as the equivalent of marriage absent an agreement to that effect. *See Cermak v. Cermak*, 569 N.W.2d 280, 284 (N.D. 1997).

Answer (D) is incorrect. Courts may well not interpret local law to treat remarriage and cohabitation as equivalent. *See Cermak v. Cermak*, 569 N.W.2d 280 (N.D. 1997). However, a different result obtains where there is legislation to that effect. *See* 23 Pa. Stat. Ann. § 3706 ("No petitioner is entitled to receive an award of alimony where the petitioner, subsequent to the divorce pursuant to which alimony is being sought, has entered into cohabitation with a person of the opposite sex who is not a member of the family of the petitioner within the degrees of consanguinity."). Sometimes, states specifically authorize courts to modify support in light of provisions included in the decree. *See*, for example, Ohio Rev. Code § 3105.18(E)(1) (discussing what happens in "the case of a divorce, the decree or a separation agreement of the parties to the divorce that is incorporated into the decree contains a provision specifically authorizing the court to modify the amount or terms of alimony or spousal support").

137. **Answer (B) is the best answer.** Some states specify that cohabitation with a member of the opposite sex will trigger an end to the support obligation, *see* Ala. Code 1975 § 30-2-55 ("Any decree of divorce providing for periodic payments of alimony shall be modified by the court to provide for the termination of such alimony upon petition of a party to the decree and

proof that the spouse receiving such alimony has remarried or that such spouse is living openly or cohabiting with a member of the opposite sex."), whereas other states specify that cohabitation with someone else regardless of the latter's sex can trigger an end to the support obligation. *See* Ga. Code Ann. § 19-6-19 (b) ("Subsequent to a final judgment of divorce awarding periodic payment of alimony for the support of a spouse, the voluntary cohabitation of such former spouse with a third party in a meretricious relationship shall also be grounds to modify provisions made for periodic payments of permanent alimony for the support of the former spouse. As used in this subsection, the word 'cohabitation' means dwelling together continuously and openly in a meretricious relationship with another person, regardless of the sex of the other person.").

Answer (A) is incorrect. Georgia, for example, does not recognize same-sex marriage but does permit cohabitation with a same-sex partner to trigger the cessation of a spousal support obligation. *See* Ga. Code Ann. § 19-6-19 (b) ("As used in this subsection, the word "cohabitation" means dwelling together continuously and openly in a meretricious relationship with another person, regardless of the sex of the other person.").

Answer (C) is incorrect. Whether or not the parties would marry if they could, some states would end the support obligation. *See* Ga. Code Ann., § 19-6-19 (b).

Answer (D) is incorrect. Cohabitation tends not to be viewed as a matter of official status but, instead, as a matter of fact. *See Clark v. Clark*, 860 N.E.2d 1080, 1084 (Ohio App. 2006) ("whether two parties are cohabiting is a question of fact for the trial court").

138.   While Rachel's decision to help the needy is commendable, her decision to do so may well be viewed as voluntary, which may mean that she will have additional income imputed to her. *See Pribble v. Pribble*, 800 So. 2d 743, 746 (Fla. Dist. Ct. App. 2001) ("Income will be imputed to an underemployed parent when such employment is found to be voluntary on that parent's part, absent physical or mental incapacity or other circumstances over which the parent has no control.") It is not necessary to show that the reduction in income was due to bad faith and simply involved an attempt to avoid paying as much child support as had been owed before. *See Arnal v. Arnal*, 636 S.E.2d 864, 866 (S.C. 2006) ("a parent seeking to impute income to the other parent need not establish a bad faith motivation to lower a support obligation in order to prove voluntary underemployment"). That said, however, where it is clear that Rachel is doing this in good faith, she may not have income imputed to her. *See*, for example, *Dunn v. Dunn*, 307 N.W.2d 424, 426 (Mich. App. 1981) (determining child support in terms of parent's actual income after he made vow of poverty and joined religious order). *But see Rohloff v. Rohloff*, 411 N.W.2d 484, 488–89 (Mich. App. 1987) ("where a party voluntarily reduces his or her income, or, as in this case, voluntarily eliminates his or her income, and the trial court concludes that the party has the ability to earn an income and pay child support, we do not believe that the trial court abuses its discretion by entering a support order based upon the unexercised ability to earn").

139.   While child support may well be increased post-divorce if the standard of living of the noncustodial parent improves substantially, spousal support is often not treated in the same way. *See Wright v. Quillen*, 83 S.W.3d 768, 773 (Tenn. Ct. App. 2002) ("An award of alimony in futuro is not a guarantee that the recipient spouse will forever be able to enjoy a lifestyle equal to that of the obligor spouse.") Certainly, it can be increased if the divorce decree includes a provision that spousal support may be increased under certain conditions, *see McHenry v. McHenry*, 2004 WL 1728518, *3 (Ohio App. 2004) (noting that support can be

increased pursuant to provisions in the decree). However, where these is no such specification, many jurisdiction will not increase the spousal award if the existing award enables the supported spouse to live in the style to which he or she had become accustomed during the marriage. *See Ederer v. Ederer*, 900 So. 2d 420, 422 (Ala. Civ. App. 2003). Courts have suggested that there is no right for a spouse to an improved standard of living after the divorce. *See Lee v. Lee*, 460 N.E.2d 710 (Ohio App. 1983).

140. While courts have rejected the right of a supported spouse to an improved standard of living after the divorce, *see Harris v. Harris*, 2001 WL 36132451, *3 (Vt. 2001) ("Many other courts have also concluded that increases in the supporting spouse's income do not support a finding of changed circumstances relative to the receiving spouse's ability to meet his or her reasonable needs at the standard established during the marriage."), courts have not adopted that view with respect to children born of the marriage. Child support obligations are geared to help the child maintain the standard of living that she would have had if there had been no divorce, which might well mean that she should benefit if the noncustodial parent's income substantially increases after the divorce. *See Hubert v. Hubert*, 465 N.W.2d 252, 257 (Wis. Ct. App. 1990).

141. Many states will preclude a sperm donor from having rights or responsibilities with respect to any child born using his sperm via artificial insemination, absent agreement to the contrary. *See*, for example, *McIntyre v. Crouch*, 780 P.2d 239 (Or. App. 1989) (suggesting that the sperm donor would have parental rights and responsibilities only if he could establish that this was the agreement beforehand). Here, if Peter can show that Martha's lover is the father and that they conceived via coital relations, Peter will likely be relieved of any obligation of support. If the child was born through artificial insemination and Martha's lover did not provide the sperm, then Peter may well be estopped from denying his parental obligations. *See*, for example, *In re Parentage of M.J.*, 787 N.E.2d 144, 146 (Ill. 2003) (man estopped from denying parental obligations to children born to nonmarital partner through use of artificial insemination). As to whether Peter will be responsible if Martha's lover provided the sperm for the artificial insemination, this may well depend upon the conditions upon which the sperm was donated and whether implicit or explicit conditions had been agreed upon by Peter and Martha with respect to the identity of the sperm donor.

142. Lottery winnings can be considered when determining child support. *See County of Contra Costa v. Lemon*, 252 Cal. Rptr. 455, 456 (Cal. App. 1988). When determining the appropriate level of support, courts should consider both parents' incomes. *See Owens v. Owens*, 489 So. 2d 321, 324 (La. Ct. App. 1986) If the lottery winnings are sufficiently substantial as to constitute a material and permanent change in circumstances, *see Fuller v. Fuller*, 607 P.2d 1314, 1317 (Idaho 1980) ("a modification of child support payments can be made only where there is shown to be a material, permanent, and substantial change in conditions and circumstances"), then there might be a modification in light of the custodial parent's lottery winnings.

143. **Answer (B) is the best answer.** The doctrine of necessaries when applied in a gender-neutral fashion may be the basis upon which an individual will be required to pay for needed medical services provided to a spouse. *Moses H. Cone Memorial Hosp. Operating Corp. v. Hawley*, 672 S.E.2d 742, 744 (N.C. App. 2009).

Answer (A) is incorrect. The doctrine of necessaries does not require that the spouse approve of the procedure in order for that spouse to be obligated to pay the expenses. *See North Carolina Baptist Hospitals, Inc. v. Harris*, 354 S.E.2d 471, 472 (N.C. 1987) (requiring wife to pay deceased husband's medical debt, notwithstanding that she "neither requested her husband's admission to the hospital, anticipated that he would be admitted, nor agreed to pay for the services").

Answer (C) is incorrect. The doctrine of necessaries can be applied to medical expenses. *See Moses H. Cone Memorial Hosp. Operating Corp. v. Hawley*, 672 S.E.2d 742, 744 (N.C. App. 2009).

Answer (D) is incorrect. The question would not be which services Penny thought best, but whether the needed, uncompensated services were provided to promote the spouse's health and well-being. *See Moses H. Cone Memorial Hosp. Operating Corp. v. Hawley*, 672 S.E.2d 742, 744 (N.C. App. 2009).

144. Assuming that Nancy is not trying to retire early, she may well be permitted to reduce her level of support. *See In re Marriage of Reynolds*, 74 Cal. Rptr. 2d 636, 639 (Cal. App. 1998) ("no one may be compelled to work after the usual retirement age of 65 in order to pay the same level of spousal support as when he was employed"). As long as Nancy's retirement is viewed by the court as reasonable, that decision will likely not be viewed as her becoming voluntarily underemployed. *See Bogan v. Bogan*, 60 S.W.3d 721, 729 (Tenn. 2001) ("we hold that when an obligor's retirement is objectively reasonable, it does constitute a substantial and material change in circumstances — irrespective of whether the retirement was foreseeable or voluntary — so as to permit modification of the support obligation").

<table>
<tr><td>

TOPIC 16:

FAMILY PRIVACY AND THE CONSTITUTION

</td><td>

ANSWERS

</td></tr>
</table>

145. **Answer (D) is the best answer.** Because the United States Constitution does not protect the biological parent in this kind of case, *see In re Adoption of Baby Girl H.*, 635 N.W.2d 256, 262 (Neb. 2001) ("when a biological father has not taken the opportunity to form a relationship with his child, the constitution does not afford him an absolute right to notice and opportunity to be heard before a child may be adopted"), Barry would have to base his claim upon a state statute or state constitutional provision. *Cf. In re J.W.T.*, 872 S.W.2d 189 (Tex. 1994) (recognizing that biological fathers have more expansive rights under the Texas Constitution than under the United States Constitution).

 Answer (A) is incorrect. The biological father may well have great difficulty in having the adoption annulled. *See*, for example, *K.L.V. v. Florida Dept. of Health and Rehabilitative Services*, 684 So. 2d 253, 254 (Fla. Dist. Ct. App. 1996) (reversing trial court annulment of adoption).

 Answer (B) is incorrect. Because the biological father never had a relationship with the child, he may well be held not to have parental rights. *See Lehr v. Robertson*, 463 U.S. 248 (1983).

 Answer (C) is incorrect. Assuming that Linda's consent to the adoption was valid and that Barry does not have parental rights because he never established a relationship with the child, *see In re Adoption of Baby Girl H.*, 635 N.W.2d 256, 262 (Neb. 2001) ("when a biological father has not taken the opportunity to form a relationship with his child, the constitution does not afford him an absolute right to notice and opportunity to be heard before a child may be adopted"), Linda and Barry might well be precluded from raising the child because of the importance in maintaining the finality of adoptions. *See In re Adoption of A.A.T.*, 196 P.3d 1180, 1197 (Kan. 2008) (discussing the importance of having prompt and certain adoption procedures).

146. **Answer (D) is the best answer.** Because Terry has never established a relationship with Barbara, he will likely be unable to block the adoption. *See Petition of Steve B.D.*, 730 P.2d 942, 943 (Idaho 1986). Wanda would have to agree to the adoption, *see* Mont. Code Ann. § 42-4-304, and the adoption would have to be in the interests of Barbara. *See*, for example, *In re Adoption of Clark*, 183 N.W.2d 179, 184 (Iowa 1971) (refusing to approve stepparent adoption because it was not clear that the adoption would promote the interests of the children).

 Answer (A) is incorrect. Because Terry never established any relationship at all with his daughter, his consent may be unnecessary. *See In re Adoption of TMP*, 2003-Ohio-2404 (father's failure to have any relationship with child for over a year made his consent to the adoption unnecessary).

 Answer (B) is incorrect. It would not have sufficed that the custodial parent, Wanda, approved of the adoption if the biological parent, Terry, had established a relationship with

199

and provided support for his daughter. *See In re Adoption of C.R.B.*, 990 P.2d 316, 318 (Okla. Civ. App. 1999) (father's consent to adoption required where he had significant relationship with children).

Answer (C) is incorrect. Merely because the state refuses to recognize that a child might have three legal parents would not preclude the state from recognizing the adoption. If indeed Terry never established a relationship with Barbara, his consent to the adoption might well be unnecessary. *See Petition of Steve B.D.*, 730 P.2d 942, 943 (Idaho 1986) (consent of biological father to adoption not required when he had never established a relationship with the child).

147.   The United States Constitution does not provide protection to the biological father in this case, *see Michael H. v. Gerald D.*, 491 U.S. 110 (1989) (refusing to recognize parental interest of biological child with respect to child born into a marriage between the mother and her husband). Any rights of the biological father would have to be a result of the state constitution, *see In re J.W.T.*, 872 S.W.2d 189 (Tex. 1994) (recognizing that biological fathers have more expansive rights under the Texas Constitution than under the United States Constitution) or local law. *See Smith v. Jones*, 566 So. 2d 408, 411 (La. Ct. App. 1990) (local law permits biological father to seek visitation with child born into a marriage between his former paramour and her husband).

148.   **Answer (D) is the best answer.** The United States Constitution affords a pregnant woman the right to make a decision regarding whether or not to terminate her pregnancy. *See Planned Parenthood of Central Missouri v. Danforth*, 428 U.S. 52, 71 (1976) ("The obvious fact is that when the wife and the husband disagree on this decision, the view of only one of the two marriage partners can prevail. Inasmuch as it is the woman who physically bears the child and who is the more directly and immediately affected by the pregnancy, as between the two, the balance weighs in her favor.") The analysis would be no different were the parties not married. *See Jones v. Smith*, 278 So. 2d 339, 340 (Fla. Dist. Ct. App. 1973) (rejecting would-be non-marital father's attempt to enjoin his pregnant girlfriend from securing an abortion).

Answer (A) is incorrect. Even if the pregnancy posed no unusual risk to the mother, it is unlikely that an injunction would be granted, *see Jones v. Smith*, 278 So. 2d 339, 340 (Fla. Dist. Ct. App. 1973). The state's interest cannot tip the scales against the mother as long as the fetus is not viable. *See Planned Parenthood of Southeastern Pennsylvania v. Casey*, 505 U.S. 833, 878 (1992) ("An undue burden exists, and therefore a provision of law is invalid, if its purpose or effect is to place a substantial obstacle in the path of a woman seeking an abortion before the fetus attains viability.").

Answer (B) is incorrect. The state can impose substantial obstacles on obtaining abortions once the fetus is viable, as long as the state is not thereby putting the mother's life or health at risk. *See Planned Parenthood of Southeastern Pennsylvania v. Casey*, 505 U.S. 833, 879 (1992).

Answer (C) is incorrect. The pregnant woman has the ultimate decision whether to terminate the pregnancy of a pre-viable fetus. *See Planned Parenthood of Central Missouri v. Danforth*, 428 U.S. 52, 71 (1976).

149.   **Answer (D) is the best answer.** Current law requires the states to include a judicial bypass option. *See Bellotti v. Baird*, 443 U.S. 622, 647 (1979) ("every minor must have the

opportunity — if she so desires — to go directly to a court without first consulting or notifying her parents. If she satisfies the court that she is mature and well enough informed to make intelligently the abortion decision on her own, the court must authorize her to act without parental consultation or consent").

Answer (A) is incorrect. States must afford minors a judicial bypass option whereby they can bypass their parents to obtain abortion authorization. *See Bellotti v. Baird*, 443 U.S. 622, 647 (1979).

Answer (B) is incorrect. While minors do have constitutional rights, states can impose special limitations on their rights to obtain abortions, e.g., require the consent of a parent as long as a judicial bypass option is available. *See Planned Parenthood of Southeastern Pennsylvania v. Casey*, 505 U.S. 833, 899 (1992) ("State may require a minor seeking an abortion to obtain the consent of a parent or guardian, provided that there is an adequate judicial bypass procedure.").

Answer (C) is incorrect. The state must also include a judicial bypass option in order for the requirement to pass constitutional muster. *See Bellotti v. Baird*, 443 U.S. 622, 647 (1979).

150. **Answer (D) is the best answer.** Where there has been no agreement, there has been a tendency for the right not to be a parent against one's will to prevail. *See*, for example, *J.B. v. M.B.*, 783 A.2d 707, 717 (N.J. 2001). That might mean that the embryos will be destroyed or, perhaps, that the embryos will continue to be cryopreserved until the parent opposing their implantation has a change of heart. *See id.* at 720.

Answer (A) is incorrect. Courts will not make an embryo award based on the gender of the parties, but will instead consider the parties' previously expressed intentions, *see*, for example, *Cwik v. Cwik*, 2011 Ohio 463 ("the trial court did not abuse its discretion by awarding the frozen embryos in accordance with the signed contact"), or other factors such as the right not to be a parent against one's will. *See Davis v. Davis*, 842 S.W.2d 588, 604 (Tenn. 1992) ("Ordinarily, the party wishing to avoid procreation should prevail, assuming that the other party has a reasonable possibility of achieving parenthood by means other than use of the preembryos in question.").

Answer (B) is incorrect. The court is unlikely to award the embryos to Francisco merely because he is more likely to have them implanted. *See Davis v. Davis*, 842 S.W.2d 588, 604 (Tenn. 1992) ("Ordinarily, the party wishing to avoid procreation should prevail, assuming that the other party has a reasonable possibility of achieving parenthood by means other than use of the preembryos in question.").

Answer (C) is incorrect. Precisely because the embryos are not simply property, the court is unlikely to simply divide them up. The court is more likely to award them to the party wishing to have them destroyed, absent some agreement to the contrary or some other unusual circumstance. *See Davis v. Davis*, 842 S.W.2d 588, 604 (Tenn. 1992) ("Ordinarily, the party wishing to avoid procreation should prevail, assuming that the other party has a reasonable possibility of achieving parenthood by means other than use of the preembryos in question.").

151. **Answer (D) is the best answer.** The statute is likely to be upheld because it is seeking to protect children from exposure to harmful substances in utero. *See Whitner v. State*, 492

S.E.2d 777 (S.C. 1997).

Answer (A) is incorrect. The law is likely to be upheld, *see Whitner v. State*, 492 S.E.2d 777 (S.C. 1997), at least in part, because the law is not imposing a limit on which abortions will occur but, instead, is meant to protect children from potential harms resulting from exposure to certain substances during the pregnancy.

Answer (B) is incorrect. At least in part because the statute is not trying to target abortion, the statute would be unlikely to be examined with strict scrutiny. While the state has a compelling interest in the life of the viable fetus, *see Planned Parenthood of Central Missouri v. Danforth*, 428 U.S. 52, 100 (1976), that does not mean that strict scrutiny would be triggered when reviewing the statute at issue.

Answer (C) is incorrect. At issue here is the life and health of the fetus as well as the life and health of the mother. Even were the state precluded from regulating drug use, *but see Gonzales v. Raich*, 545 U.S. 1, 15 (2005) (upholding Congress's power to prohibit the use of marijuana for medical purposes), the state would still have the power to protect viable fetuses. *See Planned Parenthood of Central Missouri v. Danforth*, 428 U.S. 52, 100 (1976).

152.   The Court has struck down a partial birth abortion statute that did not include an exception for the preservation of the life or health of the mother. *See Stenberg v. Carhart*, 530 U.S. 914, 931 (2000). However, the Court has subsequently upheld a federal partial birth abortion statute, notwithstanding the lack of such a provision. *See Gonzales v. Carhart*, 550 U.S. 124, 134 (2007). While there are different ways to reconcile these cases, it is simply unclear whether the Court would strike down the statute hypothesized here. It might depend, for example, on whether the Court accepted that there were other available procedures that would be as effective, so that prohibiting this method in particular would not adversely affect the life or health of anyone seeking to terminate her pregnancy.

153.   **Answer (D) is the best answer.** The Court suggests that the state can protect marriage without violating federal guarantees. *See Lawrence v. Texas*, 539 U.S. 558, 567 (2003) (cautioning states against setting boundaries to relationships "absent injury to a person or *abuse of an institution the law protects*") (italics added). Arguably, marriage is one institution the law may protect. Unless the state constitution offers additional protections, *cf. In re J.W.T.*, 872 S.W.2d 189 (Tex. 1994) (recognizing that privacy rights are more expansive under the Texas Constitution than under the United States Constitution), this statute is unlikely to be struck down. Further, some states still permit spousal support to be denied to a spouse who committed adultery during the marriage. *See* N.C. Gen. Stat. Ann. § 50-16.2A (d) ("At a hearing on postseparation support, the judge shall consider marital misconduct by the dependent spouse occurring prior to or on the date of separation in deciding whether to award postseparation support and in deciding the amount of postseparation support.").

Answer (A) is incorrect. While the Court has suggested that individuals who are married and individuals who are unmarried must be treated alike with respect to access to contraception, *see Eisenstadt v. Baird*, 405 U.S. 438, 453 (1972) ("If the right of privacy means anything, it is the right of the individual, married or single, to be free from unwarranted governmental intrusion into matters so fundamentally affecting a person as the decision whether to bear or beget a child."), the Court has not suggested that the state is precluded from protecting marriage. *See Lawrence v. Texas*, 539 U.S. 558, 567 (2003) (discussing "abuse of an institution the law protects").

Answer (B) is incorrect. States do not have plenary power over who can marry. *See Loving v. Virginia*, 388 U.S. 1 (1967) (striking down interracial marriage ban); *Zablocki v. Redhail*, 434 U.S. 374 (1978) (striking down limitation on marriage for indigent, noncustodial parents).

Answer (C) is incorrect. While the Court has struck down limitations on voluntary sexual relations between individuals who are married to each other, *see Griswold v. Connecticut*, 381 U.S. 479 (1965), and limitations on individuals who are unmarried, *see Lawrence v. Texas*, 539 U.S. 558, 567 (2003), the *Lawrence* Court's suggestion that starts can prevent abuse of an institution the law protects, *see id.* at 567, suggests that the Court would not strike down statutes disincentivizing adultery.

154. **Answer (D) is the best answer.** The state's desire to minimize fraud coupled with the residency requirement merely delaying rather than denying the divorce were held to justify a one year residency requirement. *See Sosna v. Iowa*, 419 U.S. 393, 408–10 (1975).

Answer (A) is incorrect. While the right to marry is fundamental, *see Zablocki v. Redhail*, 434 U.S. 374, 384 (1978) ("the right to marry is part of the fundamental 'right of privacy' "), a separate question is whether the state may impose reasonable restrictions on the condition under which individuals may divorce. *See Sosna v. Iowa*, 419 U.S. 393, 407 (1975) ("A State such as Iowa may quite reasonably decide that it does not wish to become a divorce mill for unhappy spouses who have lived there as short a time as appellant had when she commenced her action in the state court after having long resided elsewhere.").

Answer (B) is incorrect. States are not free to impose substantial burdens on the right to travel. *See Memorial Hospital v. Maricopa County*, 415 U.S. 250, 255 (1974) ("The right of interstate travel has repeatedly been recognized as a basic constitutional freedom.").

Answer (C) is incorrect. States do not have plenary power over divorce. For example, they cannot require that indigents pay certain fees before being able to divorce. *See Boddie v. Connecticut*, 401 U.S. 371 (1971).

155. **Answer (D) is the best answer.** The Court has struck down a zoning ordinance as applied to a family all related by blood, *see Moore v. City of East Cleveland*, 431 U.S. 494, 496 (1977), and has upheld an ordinance as applied to a group of unrelated students. *See Village of Belle Terre v. Boraas*, 416 U.S. 1 (1974). However, the Court has not addressed a zoning ordinance applied to a functional family like the one at issue here.

Answer (A) is incorrect. While the Court has upheld a similar statute, *see Village of Belle Terre v. Boraas*, 416 U.S. 1, 2 (1974), as applied to a group of college students, the Court has not upheld such a statute as applied to two cohabiting adults living with one of the adult's children.

Answer (B) is incorrect. While the Court struck down an ordinance that limited family too narrowly, *see Moore v. City of East Cleveland*, 431 U.S. 494, 496 (1977), that ordinance was being applied to individuals who were all related by blood. Here, not all members of the family are related by blood, adoption, or marriage.

Answer (C) is incorrect. Ordinances defining family will be upheld under certain conditions, burdens on association notwithstanding. *See Village of Belle Terre v. Boraas*, 416 U.S. 1 (1974).

156.   **Answer (D) is the best answer.** Because she is competent and this is invasive, her decision will likely be respected. *See In re Baby Boy Doe*, 632 N.E.2d 326, 330 (Ill. Ct. App. 1994) ("a woman's competent choice in refusing medical treatment as invasive as a cesarean section during her pregnancy must be honored, even in circumstances where the choice may be harmful to her fetus"). It is simply unclear whether her decision would have been respected had the procedure been less invasive. *See In re Brown*, 689 N.E.2d 397, 405 (Ill. Ct. App. 1997) ("the circuit court erred in ordering Brown to undergo the transfusion on behalf of the viable fetus").

    Answer (A) is incorrect. She might well be successful even without testimony that the fetus is in no danger. *See In re Baby Boy Doe*, 632 N.E.2d 326, 330 (Ill. Ct. App. 1994) ("a woman's competent choice in refusing medical treatment as invasive as a cesarean section during her pregnancy must be honored, even in circumstances where the choice may be harmful to her fetus").

    Answer (B) is incorrect. The court would likely suggest that because this is an invasive procedure, the competent woman must be allowed to decide for herself, even if it could plausibly be argued that both she and the fetus would be better off were a cesarean performed. *See In re Baby Boy Doe*, 632 N.E.2d 326, 330 (Ill. Ct. App. 1994).

    Answer (C) is incorrect. Her decision might well have been respected even if the procedure had been less invasive. *See In re Brown*, 689 N.E.2d 397, 405 (Ill. Ct. App. 1997) ("the circuit court erred in ordering Brown to undergo the transfusion on behalf of the viable fetus").

157.   **Answer (D) is the best answer.** The United States Constitution does not immunize parents from prosecution if they cause their children severe harm or death, even if pursuant to sincere religious convictions. *See Prince v. Massachusetts*, 321 U.S. 158, 170 (1944) ("Parents may be free to become martyrs themselves. But it does not follow they are free, in identical circumstances, to make martyrs of their children before they have reached the age of full and legal discretion when they can make that choice for themselves.").

    Answer (A) is incorrect. The United States Constitution would not offer them protection in this kind of case. *See Prince v. Massachusetts*, 321 U.S. 158, 170 (1944).

    Answer (B) is incorrect. Even if the child agrees with the parents, the Constitution still would not afford them immunity, assuming that the child has not yet reached an age where she could make a competent and informed decision. *See Prince v. Massachusetts*, 321 U.S. 158, 170 (1944).

    Answer (C) is incorrect. The state must give some deference to a parent's decision about what is best for her child. *Cf. Troxel v. Granville*, 530 U.S. 57, 70 (2000) ("if a fit parent's decision of the kind at issue here becomes subject to judicial review, the court must accord at least some special weight to the parent's own determination").

158.   **Answer (D) is the best answer.** Some courts require that the individual herself, if competent, would have chosen sterilization, *see Matter of Moe*, 432 N.E.2d 712, 721 (Mass. 1982) ("the court is to determine whether to authorize sterilization when requested by the parents or guardian by finding the incompetent would so choose if competent"), whereas other courts will approve the sterilization if it can be established that performance of the procedure would promote the best interests of the incompetent. *See In re Penny N.*, 414 A.2d 541, 543 (N.H. 1980) ("a probate judge may permit a sterilization after making specific written findings from clear and convincing evidence, that it is in the best interests of the

incapacitated ward, rather than the parents' or the public's convenience, to do so").

Answer (A) is incorrect. An incompetent person may be sterilized if, for example, doing so would be in that person's best interests, notwithstanding that person's inability to give informed consent. *See Lulos v. State*, 548 N.E.2d 173, 174 (Ind. Ct. App. 1990) ("The proper standard of proof requires clear and convincing evidence that the judicially appointed guardian brought the petition for sterilization in good faith and the sterilization is in the best interest of the incompetent adult.").

Answer (B) is incorrect. The reason that sterilization might be permitted would be based on the interests of the person to be sterilized rather than those of the incompetent person's parents. *See In re C.D M.*, 627 P.2d 607, 612 (Alaska 1981) ("The advocates of the proposed operation bear the heavy burden of proving by clear and convincing evidence that sterilization is in the best interests of the incompetent.").

Answer (C) is incorrect. While there may be cases in which both the incompetent and her child would need help from the state, that would not justify sterilization. Instead, it would have to be shown that the individual herself would be benefited were the sterilization procedure performed. *See In re Penny N.*, 414 A.2d 541, 543 (N.H. 1980) ("a probate judge may permit a sterilization after making specific written findings from clear and convincing evidence, that it is in the best interests of the incapacitated ward, rather than the parents' or the public's convenience, to do so").

159. **Answer (D) is the best answer.** A guardian will likely not be appointed if Timothy is sufficiently mature and informed. *See In re E.G.*, 549 N.E.2d 322, 327–28 (Ill. 1989) ("If the evidence is clear and convincing that the minor is mature enough to appreciate the consequences of her actions, and that the minor is mature enough to exercise the judgment of an adult, then the mature minor doctrine affords her the common law right to consent to or refuse medical treatment."). However, a guardian might well be appointed if the minor is not thought capable to make the relevant decision. *Cf. State v. Planned Parenthood of Alaska*, 171 P.3d 577, 582 (Alaska 2007) ("the State has a special, indeed compelling, interest in the health, safety, and welfare of its minor citizens and may properly take affirmative steps to safeguard minors from their own immaturity").

Answer (A) is incorrect. A guardian might well be appointed, notwithstanding the child's opposition, if the child is not viewed as sufficiently competent to make the medical decision herself. *See Prince v. Massachusetts*, 321 U.S. 158, 170 (1944) ("Parents may be free to become martyrs themselves. But it does not follow they are free, in identical circumstances, to make martyrs of their children before they have reached the age of full and legal discretion when they can make that choice for themselves.").

Answer (B) is incorrect. If Timothy is viewed as a mature minor who has the judgment and knowledge to make a competent and informed decision, then he may be allowed to do so, notwithstanding that he may thereby be undermining his own chances of survival. *See In re E.G.*, 549 N.E.2d 322, 327–28 (Ill. 1989) ("If the evidence is clear and convincing that the minor is mature enough to appreciate the consequences of her actions, and that the minor is mature enough to exercise the judgment of an adult, then the mature minor doctrine affords her the common law right to consent to or refuse medical treatment.").

Answer (C) is incorrect. Even if Timothy were incurring greater opportunity costs by refusing treatment, he still might be allowed to do so if he possessed the requisite maturity and understanding. *See In re E.G.*, 549 N.E.2d 322, 327–28 (Ill. 1989).

160.   **Answer (C) is the best answer.** This is strictly a matter of state law, and the state laws vary greatly. California, for example, enforces gestational but not traditional surrogacy contracts. *See Johnson v. Calvert*, 851 P.2d 776 (Cal. 1993) (gestational surrogacy contract enforceable) and *In re Marriage of Moschetta*, 30 Cal. Rptr. 2d 893, 903 (Ct. App. 1994) (traditional surrogacy contract unenforceable). New York suggests that a surrogacy contract may not be used to defeat the parental rights of the birth mother. *See* McKinney's N.Y. Dom. Rel. Law § 124(1) ("In any action or proceeding involving a dispute between the birth mother and (i) the genetic father, (ii) the genetic mother, (iii) both the genetic father and genetic mother, or (iv) the parent or parents of the genetic father or genetic mother, regarding parental rights, status or obligations with respect to a child born pursuant to a surrogate parenting contract: the court shall not consider the birth mother's participation in a surrogate parenting contract as adverse to her parental rights, status, or obligations.").

   Answer (A) is incorrect. This is a matter of state law. While Lori may be forced to relinquish the child, *see Raftopol v. Karma A. Ramey*, 299 Conn. 681 (2011) (forcing surrogate to relinquish custody to commissioning same-sex couple), the mere fact that she otherwise would not have gotten pregnant does not require such a result, since that same rationale would require that a traditional surrogate relinquish custody. *But see In re Baby M*, 537 A.2d 1227 (N.J. 1988) (holding traditional surrogacy agreement unenforceable).

   Answer (B) is incorrect. This is strictly a matter of state law, and the state laws vary greatly. California, for example, enforces gestational but not traditional surrogacy contracts. *See Johnson v. Calvert*, 851 P.2d 776 (Cal. 1993) (gestational surrogacy contract enforceable). However, New Jersey may refuse to enforce even a gestational surrogacy arrangement. *Cf. A.H.W. v. G.H.B.*, 772 A.2d 948, 954 (N.J. Super. Ch. Div. 2000) (suggesting that parentage of child born by gestational surrogate may depend, in part, on whether surrogate changes her mind about giving up any parental rights that she may have).

   Answer (D) is incorrect. Not all jurisdictions treat such contracts are unenforceable. *See Johnson v. Calvert*, 851 P.2d 776 (Cal. 1993) (gestational surrogacy contract enforceable).

161.   Arnold is unlikely to prevail at least with respect to the denial of federal constitutional rights, at least in part, because the state did not play a role in causing the child to be abused. *See DeShaney v. Winnebago County Dept. of Social Services*, 489 U.S. 189, 202 (1989) ("Because, as explained above, the State had no constitutional duty to protect Joshua against his father's violence, its failure to do so-though calamitous in hindsight-simply does not constitute a violation of the Due Process Clause."). A separate issue would be implicated were state law to impose an affirmative duty of protection on the state under these circumstances. *See id.* at 201–02 (noting that state law may provide a remedy even where the Federal Constitution does not).

162.   While state statutes once provided that individuals could not be convicted of marital rape, many of those statutes have been declared unconstitutional. *See*, for example, *People v. Liberta*, 474 N.E.2d 567 (N.Y. 1984). *But see People v. Brown*, 632 P.2d 1025 (1981) (suggesting that the marital exemption did not violate constitutional guarantees). John is claiming that the United States constitution protects marital rape. However, as the New York Court of Appeals suggested, the "marital exemption simply does not further marital privacy because this right of privacy protects consensual acts, not violent sexual assaults." *See People v. Liberta*, 474 N.E.2d 567, 574 (N.Y. 1984).

163. First, states differ as to who owns the privilege. *See*, for example, Mich. Comp. Laws Ann. § 600.2162(2) ("In a criminal prosecution, a husband shall not be examined as a witness for or against his wife without his consent or a wife for or against her husband without her consent."). Even were the marital privilege thought applicable as a general matter, it might well be thought inapplicable in a case involving spousal abuse. *See*, for example, Tenn. Code Ann. § 24-1-201(2) ("Upon a finding that a marital communication is privileged, it shall be inadmissible if either spouse objects. Such communication privileges shall not apply to proceedings concerning abuse of one (1) of the spouses or abuse of a minor in the custody of or under the dominion and control of either spouse."). Thus, it is unlikely that John would be able to prevent Mary from testifying against him were she to desire to do so.

164. **Answer (B) is the best answer.** While states can impose "reasonable regulations that do not significantly interfere with decisions to enter into the marital relationship," *see Zablocki v. Redhail*, 434 U.S. 374, 386–87 (1978), the Court has nonetheless made clear that a marriage restriction is unconstitutional unless important interests are implicated and unless the restriction is closely tailored to promote those interests. *See id.* at 388 ("When a statutory classification significantly interferes with the exercise of a fundamental right, it cannot be upheld unless it is supported by sufficiently important state interests and is closely tailored to effectuate only those interests.").

Answer (A) is incorrect. States have broad discretion to regulate marriage, fundamental nature of the implicated interest notwithstanding. *See Goodridge v. Department of Public Health*, 798 N.E.2d 941, 969 (Mass. 2003) (discussing "the Legislature's broad discretion to regulate marriage").

Answer (C) is incorrect. Traditionally, the domicile determines the validity of a marriage. *See In re Farraj*, 900 N.Y.S.2d 340, 341 (App. Div. 2010) (New York law governs the validity of the marriage, because New York was the intended and actual domicile of the couple).

Answer (D) is incorrect. A marriage need not be recognized if it contravenes an important public policy of the domicile at the time of the marriage. *See In re Estate of Toutant*, 633 N.W.2d 692, 697 (Wis. Ct. App. 2001) (marriage declared void because violating an important public policy of the domicile at the time of the marriage).

165. Thomas is unlikely to be successful in his attempt to have Howard tested. As a general rule, children will not be donors unless the donation would benefit the donor as well as the donee, and there is no evidence here that the donor would be helped by providing bone marrow for a transplant. *See Curran v. Bosze*, 566 N.E.2d 1319, 1331 (Ill. 1990) ("We hold that a parent or guardian may give consent on behalf of a minor daughter or son for the child to donate bone marrow to a sibling, only when to do so would be in the minor's best interest.").

166. While parents are entitled to their own religious beliefs, they are not permitted to make martyrs of their children. *See Prince v. Massachusetts*, 321 U.S. 158, 170 (1944) ("Parents may be free to become martyrs themselves. But it does not follow they are free, in identical circumstances, to make martyrs of their children before they have reached the age of full and legal discretion when they can make that choice for themselves."). Here, Amy has been harmed. As the Maryland Supreme Court has pointed out, the state need not stand idly by while parents harm their children, even if their doing so is in accord with their sincere religious beliefs. *See Kirchner v. Caughey*, 606 A.2d 257, 261 (Md. 1992) ("When the welfare

of a child is threatened, however, the task of intervention cannot be avoided, and under some circumstances actions based upon the sincerely held religious beliefs of one parent or both parents must give way to the safety and welfare of the child.").

167.   **Answer (D) is the best answer.** *See Potter v. Murray City*, 585 F. Supp. 1126 (D. Utah 1984) (upholding polygamy prohibition under strict scrutiny).

      Answer (A) is incorrect. The court is likely to uphold the constitutionality of a law banning plural marriage. *See Reynolds v. United States*, 98 U.S. 145 (1878).

      Answer (B) is incorrect. While the court may well uphold the statute, the implicated interest — marriage — triggers close scrutiny. *See Zablocki v. Redhail*, 434 U.S. 374, 388 (1978) ("When a statutory classification significantly interferes with the exercise of a fundamental right, it cannot be upheld unless it is supported by sufficiently important state interests and is closely tailored to effectuate only those interests."). The court is not likely to subject the classification to mere rational basis review.

      Answer (C) is incorrect. The court is unlikely to hold that the statute violates free exercise guarantees. *See State v. Holm*, 137 P.3d 726, 746 (Utah 2006) ("Utah's prohibition on polygamous behavior does not run afoul of constitutional guarantees protecting the free exercise of religion.").

168.   Mary's challenge is likely to be successful. While the Wiskegan attempt to save money is a legitimate state interest, *see C & A Carbone, Inc. v. Town of Clarkstown*, 511 U.S. 383, 429 (1994) ("Protection of the public fisc is a legitimate local benefit"), the state is attempting to save money by restricting marriage. For such a restriction to pass muster, the state must have more than a merely legitimate interest at stake. *See Zablocki v. Redhail*, 434 U.S. 374, 388 (1978) ("When a statutory classification significantly interferes with the exercise of a fundamental right, it cannot be upheld unless it is supported by sufficiently important state interests and is closely tailored to effectuate only those interests."). The state interest here is unlikely to be viewed as sufficiently important and, further, the classification is unlikely to be held sufficiently closely tailored to meet the requisite standard. *See id.* at 390–91.

169. **Answer (B) is the best answer.** In a state that does not recognize de facto or psychological parent status, Alvin may well not be awarded custody or visitation rights. *See Jones v. Barlow*, 154 P.3d 808, 817–18 (Utah 2007). He would have been more likely to have been awarded such rights had he adopted Carole or had he married Barbara before Carole's birth.

Answer (A) is incorrect. Even if artificial insemination is employed, an individual will be presumed to be the father of a child if that child is born into an existing marriage and the husband has consented to the use of artificial insemination. *See Laura G. v. Peter G.*, 830 N.Y.S.2d 496, 497 (Sup. Ct. 2007) ("Any child born to a married woman by means of artificial insemination performed by persons duly authorized to practice medicine and with the consent in writing of the woman and her husband, shall be deemed the legitimate, natural child of the husband and his wife for all purposes.").

Answer (C) is incorrect. Merely because a child views an adult as a parent may not make that person a parent in the eyes of the law. *See*, for example, *Jones v. Barlow*, 154 P.3d 808, 813 (Utah 2007) ("a legal parent may freely terminate the in loco parentis status by removing her child from the relationship, thereby extinguishing all parent-like rights and responsibilities vested in the former surrogate parent").

Answer (D) is incorrect. *See Jones v. Barlow*, 154 P.3d 808, 817–18 (Utah 2007) (refusing to recognize plaintiff as a de facto or psychological parent and refusing to order visitation for a nonparent even if it were true that such visitation would be in the child's best interests).

170. **Answer (C) is the best answer.** Gerald will likely be held responsible for child support because he will likely be found to be the father. *See In re Baby Doe*, 353 S.E.2d 877, 878 (S.C. 1987) ("a husband who consents for his wife to conceive a child through artificial insemination, with the understanding that the child will be treated as their own, is the legal father of the child born as a result of the artificial insemination and will be charged with all the legal responsibilities of paternity, including support"). Or, in the alternative, he will be estopped from denying his paternity. *See Laura G. v. Peter G.*, 830 N.Y.S.2d 496, 503 (Sup. Div. 2007) ("defendant is estopped from refusing to pay child support as between him and his wife because she relied on his representations to her detriment").

Answer (A) is incorrect. The jurisprudence suggesting that fatherhood depends upon both a biological connection and an established relationship with the child only applies to non-marital father. *See Lehr v. Robertson*, 463 U.S. 248, 261 (1983). Here, because Gerald and Henrietta are married, the case will be analyzed differently.

Answer (B) is incorrect. Because Gerald consented in writing to his wife's being artificially inseminated, he will be treated as the father, subsequent change of heart after the birth notwithstanding. *See Laura G. v. Peter G.*, 830 N.Y.S.2d 496, 497 (Sup. Ct. 2007).

Answer (D) is incorrect. A husband would be able to challenge that he is the father of a child born during the marriage if he was sterile and had never consented to artificial insemination. *See* West's Ann. Cal. Fam. Code § 7630(a)(2) ("For the purpose of declaring the nonexistence of the father and child relationship presumed under subdivision (a), (b), or (c) of Section 7611 only if the action is brought within a reasonable time after obtaining knowledge of relevant facts. After the presumption has been rebutted, paternity of the child by another man may be determined in the same action, if he has been made a party.").

171.   **Answer (A) is the best answer.** If Byron and Susan had so agreed, then the court might well find that Byron was the father. *See In Interest of R.C.*, 775 P.2d 27, 35 (Colo. 1989) ("If no such agreement was present at the time of insemination, then section 19-4-106(2) operates to extinguish J.R.'s parental rights and duties concerning R.C. If such an agreement was present, then section 19-4-106(2) does not operate to extinguish J.R.'s parental rights and duties concerning R.C., and the juvenile court must determine paternity.").

   Answer (B) is incorrect. If indeed Byron and Susan had agreed that he would be the child's father, then their having used artificial insemination would not be a bar to his paternity. *See In Interest of R.C.*, 775 P.2d 27, 35 (Colo. 1989).

   Answer (C) is incorrect. If the understanding had been that Susan would raise the child alone, then his having a genetic connection to the child would not entitle him to be recognized as the child's father. *See In Interest of R.C.*, 775 P.2d 27, 35 (Colo. 1989).

   Answer (D) is incorrect. If, indeed, Byron is recognized as the father, then he might well be granted visitation rights, Susan's wishes to the contrary notwithstanding. *See C.M. v. C.C.*, 377 A.2d 821, 824 (N.J. Juv. & Dom. Rel. 1977) (granting known donor visitation rights over mother's objection).

172.   **Answer (B) is the best answer.** There would be the danger that the involuntary termination would be granted because of the superior parenting abilities of the would-be adoptive family rather than because the parent had been guilty of abandonment or neglect or was in some way unfit. *See Kingsley v. Kingsley*, 623 So. 2d 780, 788 (Fla. Dist. Ct. App. 1993) ("Trying these two matters separately avoids an impermissible comparison between the natural parent's parenting skills and those of the prospective parents, a comparison which could impact greatly the outcome of any termination proceeding where the focus must remain on issues such as abandonment, neglect, or abuse.").

   Answer (A) is incorrect. While a state may well consider a child's preferences if the child has reached a certain age, *see* McKinney's N.Y. Dom. Rel. Law § 111(1)(a) (child 14 years of age consulted with respect to adoption unless certain conditions obtain), such a requirement is not employed for young children and, as a general matter, delaying the adoption until the child is older would not promote the child's best interests.

   Answer (C) is incorrect. If indeed, Anita's parental rights should have been terminated, then it would benefit Bobby to be placed with the family with whom he has already developed a good relationship. *Cf. Matter of Guardianship and Custody of Jonathan E. G.*, 436 N.Y.S.2d 546, 555 (Fam. Ct. 1980) (discussing "the close familial ties between the child and the foster-adoptive parents").

   Answer (D) is incorrect. A parent's expressed preference with respect to adoption placement need not be honored if that placement would be detrimental to the interests of the child. *See In re Dependency of J.S.*, 46 P.3d 273, 275 (Wash. Ct. App. 2002).

173. **Answer (C) is the best answer.** States differ greatly with respect to the enforceability of open adoption agreements. Some treat them as enforceable subject to the best interests of the child. *See Michaud v. Wawruck*, 551 A.2d 738 (Conn. 1988). Other states treat them as unenforceable. *See Quets v. Needham*, 682 S.E.2d 214 (N.C. Ct. App. 2009).

Answer (A) is incorrect. An open adoption involves an arrangement by which a parent will either be able to visit with or receive information about the child even after parental rights have been terminated. *See In re Doe*, 978 P.2d 166, 176 n.11 (Haw. Ct. App. 1999).

Answer (B) is incorrect. An open adoption permits visitation or the receipt of information even after the parental rights have been terminated. *See In re Doe*, 978 P.2d 166, 176 n.11 (Haw. Ct. App. 1999). The biological parent does not retain her parental rights in an open adoption.

Answer (D) is incorrect. This is a mischaracterization of the nature of an open adoption. *See In re Doe*, 978 P.2d 166, 176 n.11 (Haw. Ct. App. 1999).

174. **Answer (B) is the best answer.** The stepparent exception permits the stepparent to establish an adoptive relationship with the marital partner's child without that partner being forced to give up parental rights. *See In re M.M.D.*, 662 A.2d 837, 859–60 (D.C. 1995) ("when a natural parent remarries and plans to live with his or her children and new spouse as a family unit, the statutory 'cut off' requirement — terminating the birth parent's rights so that the adopting parent and child can begin a new family without interference by the birth parent — does not apply").

Answer (A) is incorrect. As a general matter, a stepparent will not be financially responsible for a marital partner's child should the marriage end. *See Weinand v. Weinand*, 616 N.W.2d 1, 7 (Neb. 2000) ("absent exceptional circumstances that invoke equitable principles, an ex-stepparent generally does not have a duty to support an ex-stepchild after the termination of the marriage to the child's biological parent").

Answer (C) is incorrect. While each might want to be respected, that desire has nothing to do with the content of the stepparent exception. *See In re M.M.D.*, 662 A.2d 837, 859–60 (D.C. 1995).

Answer (D) is incorrect. Here, the parties seek to establish a formal legal status through adoption. *See In re M.M.D.*, 662 A.2d 837, 859–60 (D.C. 1995) De facto parental status involves an equitable remedy where the adult is neither a biological nor adoptive parent. *See In re Parentage of M.F.*, 170 P.3d 601, 606 (Wash. Ct. App. 2007).

175. **Answer (C) is the best answer.** A variety of reasonable expenses will be permitted. *See 23 Pa. Cons. Stat. Ann. § 2533(d) (permitted expenses included medical and hospital expenses, reasonable counseling expenses, and attorney fees).

Answer (A) is incorrect. While all states prohibit baby-selling, some money exchanges are not thought to violate that prohibition. For example, the would-be adoptive parents can pay the medical expenses associated with the birth of the child that they will adopt. *See Gorden v. Cutler*, 471 A.2d 449 (Pa. Super. Ct. 1983).

Answer (B) is incorrect. This would violate the strong public policy against having a baby market. *See State v. Runkles*, 605 A.2d 111, 118 (Md. 1992) (discussing the importance of preventing babies from being sold on an open market).

Answer (D) is incorrect. Payment of exorbitant attorney fees might also be construed as offending the law against baby-selling. *See Adoption of Baby Boy L.*, 27 Pa. D. & C. 3d 584, 590 (Pa. Com. Pl. 1983) ("A payment for a baby disguised as an attorney's fee will also be a violation of this act.").

176.   **Answer (B) is the best answer.** An equitable adoption permits the adoptee to inherit from the parties who had agreed to adopt the child but who never satisfactorily completed the formal process. *See Lankford v. Wright*, 489 S.E.2d 604, 606 (N.C. 1997) ("The doctrine is not intended to replace statutory requirements or to create the parent-child relationship; it simply recognizes the foster child's right to inherit from the person or persons who contracted to adopt the child and who honored that contract in all respects except through formal statutory procedures.").

Answer (A) is incorrect. When foster parents adopt a child, they are the child's legal parents with all of the rights and responsibilities attendant on that status. *See State of Kansas/State of Iowa ex rel. Secretary of Social and Rehabilitation Services v. Bohrer*, 189 P.3d 1157, 1166–67 (Kan. 2008) (making clear that an adoptive parent has all of the rights and responsibilities of the biological parent).

Answer (C) is incorrect. The concern with respect to payments in the context of adoption is that the receipt of payments does not amount to baby-selling. *See In re Adoption of Baby C*, 47 Pa. D. & C. 3d 47 (Pa. Comm. Pl. 1987) ("This court has consistently held that any fees paid by adoptive parents to biological parents for *any reason* other than a reimbursement for medical expenses (and reasonable other expenses attendant thereto) were impermissible, and disallowed by this court.") There is no analogous worry with respect to the biological parent's receiving too little for her child.

Answer (D) is incorrect. While it is preferable not to separate twins in an adoption, *cf. In re Adoption of Dennis*, 405 N.Y.S.2d 584, 586 (Sur. Ct. 1978) (describing the separation of siblings as "unfortunate"), there is no requirement that they not be separated if, for example, separate adoptions would be in their best interest. *See id.*

177.   Barbara may well be able to inherit if South Floramba recognizes equitable adoption. The paradigmatic case of equitable adoption involves a parent who relinquishes custody of her child on the understanding that those receiving the child would adopt her. The couple treats the child as their own including, for example, giving the child their last name, but never formally adopts the child. *See Lankford v. Wright*, 489 S.E.2d 604, 606 (N.C. 1997). Assume further that the couple or, perhaps, the surviving member of the couple dies intestate. The issue at hand is whether the child will be permitted to assert intestate succession rights. *See Curry v. Williman*, 834 S.W.2d 443, 444 (Tex. Ct. App. 1992) ("the parent's promises and conduct can create an equitable adoption which allows the child to assert intestate succession rights to the parent's estate"). Here, if a court were to find that Barbara had been equitably adopted by the Andersons, Winona would not be able to preclude Barbara from receiving her share of the estate.

178.   An equitable adoption allows an individual to inherit from the individuals who failed to formally adopt the child. *See Curry v. Williman*, 834 S.W.2d 443, 444 (Tex. Ct. App. 1992). However, the child is not viewed by the law as having been legally adopted and, for example, would not be able to inherit from other members of the adoptive family absent having been

expressly named in a will. *See Goldberg v. Robertson*, 615 S.W.2d 59, 62 (Mo. 1981) ("An equitably adopted child is not an heir of the collateral kin of the equitably adopted parent."). But this also means that the child might still be able to inherit from her natural parent. *See Gardner v. Hancock*, 924 S.W.2d 857, 859 (Mo. Ct. App. 1996) ("an equitably adopted child . . . [can] inherit from both the adoptive parents and from the natural parents because the doctrine of equitable adoption does not change the child's status to that of a legally adopted person.").

179.   **Answer (D) is the best answer.** *See In re Bonfield*, 780 N.E.2d 241, 244 (Ohio 2002) ("Second parent adoption is a process by which a partner in a cohabiting and nonmarital relationship may adopt his or her partner's biological or adoptive child, without requiring the parent to relinquish any parental rights.").

Answer (A) is incorrect. The process described here is a stepparent adoption rather than a second parent adoption. *See In re M.M.D.*, 662 A.2d 837, 859–60 (D.C. 1995) ("when a natural parent remarries and plans to live with his or her children and new spouse as a family unit, the statutory 'cut off' requirement — terminating the birth parent's rights so that the adopting parent and child can begin a new family without interference by the birth parent — does not apply").

Answer (B) is incorrect. The child here is more aptly described a "twice-adopted child." *See In re Luckey's Estate*, 291 N.W.2d 235, 238 (Neb. 1980).

Answer (C) is incorrect. While an adoptive parent might adopt again, this is not what second parent adoption describes. That said, an adoptive parent might attempt a second parent adoption if he or she wishes to establish a legal relationship with his or her nonmarital partner's child. *See In re Bonfield*, 780 N.E.2d 241, 244 (Ohio 2002).

180.   The attorney's response will depend upon whether Famuvania recognizes second-parent adoptions. If it does, then Ken may well be able to adopt Oscar, assuming that Jill consents and that the adoption would promote Oscar's best interests. However, if Famuvania does not permit second parent adoption, then Ken will not be able to adopt Oscar unless Jill is willing to have her own parental rights terminated. *See In re Adoption of Luke*, 640 N.W.2d 374, 382 (Neb. 2002) ("With the exception of stepparent adoptions, which are statutorily permitted, the Nebraska adoption statutes provide that an eligible child is one over whom parental rights have been relinquished or terminated and with respect to whom, upon entry of the adoption decree, a new relationship between the child and adoptive parent is created and the natural parents are relieved of all parental duties."). Or, Jill and Ken could marry, in which case Ken would be able to adopt Oscar via a stepparent adoption. *See id.*

181.   **Answer (B) is the best answer.** *See* Mont. Code Ann. § 42-4-402(1) ("An adult may adopt another adult or an emancipated minor pursuant to this section.").

Answer (A) is incorrect in that it too severely limits what would constitute an adult adoption. *See* Mont. Code Ann. § 42-4-402(1).

Answer (C) is incorrect as a definition, although it does provide an example of an adult adoption. *See* Ohio Rev. Code § 3107.02(B)(2).

Answer (D) is incorrect because too limited, although this might be an instance of an adult adoption. *See* Ohio Rev. Code § 3107.02(B)(3) ("If the adult had established a child-foster caregiver or child-stepparent relationship with the petitioners as a minor, and the adult consents to the adoption.").

182. **Answer (B) is the best answer.** *See In re J.W.*, 11 S.W.3d 699, 704 (Mo. Ct. App. 1999) (mother found to have abandoned children when she "rarely visited her children and provided little or no support for them").

Answer (A) is incorrect. A parent can be found to have abandoned a child if he only pays support sporadically and has very little contact with the child. *See In re Adoption of H.G.C.*, 761 N.W.2d 565, 570 (N.D. 2009).

Answer (C) is incorrect. It will not be necessary to establish that Karen subjectively intended never to see the children again. *See Michael J. v. Arizona Dept. of Economic Sec.*, 995 P.2d 682, 685–86 (Ariz. 2000) ("abandonment is measured not by a parent's subjective intent, but by the parent's conduct: the statute asks whether a parent has provided reasonable support, maintained regular contact, made more than minimal efforts to support and communicate with the child").

Answer (D) is incorrect. Sporadic support and occasional contact may not suffice to avoid a finding of abandonment. *See In re J.W.*, 11 S.W.3d 699, 704 (Mo. Ct. App. 1999).

183. **Answer (C) is the best answer.** Carl is likely to be awarded custody under these circumstances. *See In re A.R.A.*, 919 P.2d 388 (Mont. 1996) (reversing grant of custody to stepparent rather than noncustodial parent after the death of the custodial parent); *Dodge v. Dodge*, 505 S.E.2d 344, 348 (S.C. Ct. App. 1998) ("there exists a rebuttable presumption that the right to custody of a minor child automatically reverts to the surviving parent when the custodial parent dies").

Answer (A) is incorrect. Under exceptional circumstances a third party may be awarded custody over a fit parent. *See Edwards v. Edwards*, 777 N.W.2d 606, 609 (N.D. 2010) ("custody may be awarded to a third party in exceptional circumstances in order to prevent serious harm or detriment to a child").

Answer (B) is incorrect. Able is not likely to be awarded custody merely because doing so might be thought to better promote the interests of the children. *See In re A.R.A.*, 919 P.2d 388 (Mont. 1996) (reversing grant of custody to stepparent rather than noncustodial parent after the death of the custodial parent).

Answer (D) is incorrect. Here, Carl is likely to be awarded custody. *See In re A.R.A.*, 919 P.2d 388 (Mont. 1996); *Dodge v. Dodge*, 505 S.E.2d 344, 348 (S.C. Ct. App. 1998).

184. **Answer (B) is the best answer.** As a general matter, a stepparent will not have a duty of support for the ex-spouse's children once that marriage has been dissolved. *See Ruben v. Ruben*, 461 A.2d 733, 735 (N.H. 1983) ("The majority of those jurisdictions imposing an obligation to support stepchildren by statute have held that the obligation is collateral to the existence of a valid marriage and hold that once the marriage is dissolved the stepparent relationship ceases and with it the obligation to support the stepchild.").

Answer (A) is incorrect. Many states impose a duty of support on a stepparent while that individual is married to the child's parent and while the child is living in the home. *See State ex rel. D.R.M. v. Wood*, 34 P.3d 887, 893–94 (Wash. Ct. App. 2001) ("A stepparent is liable to third parties for support of a stepchild while married to and living with the child's mother. However, the obligation terminates as a matter of law on decree of dissolution, decree of legal separation, or death.").

Answer (C) is incorrect. While stepparents may well have a duty of support during the marriage, *see State ex rel. D.R.M. v. Wood*, 34 P.3d 887, 894 (Wash. Ct. App. 2001), they generally will not have a duty of support imposed even after the marriage has ended. *See Ruben v. Ruben*, 461 A.2d 733, 735 (N.H. 1983).

Answer (D) is incorrect. Good relationship with the children notwithstanding, a stepparent usually must do much more before having a duty of support imposed when the marriage has ended. *See Miller v. Miller*, 478 A.2d 351 (N.J. 1984) (suggesting that more than a good relationship with the children is required before such a support obligation can be imposed).

185.   **Answer (C) is the best answer.** A stepparent who has acquired de facto parent or psychological parent status might well be awarded visitation without also having a duty of support imposed. *See Weinand v. Weinand*, 616 N.W.2d 1 (Neb. 2000) (stepparent can be given visitation privileges without an accompanying order of child support).

Answer (A) is incorrect. A Stepparent might be awarded visitation rights without also having a duty of support imposed. *See Weinand v. Weinand*, 616 N.W.2d 1 (Neb. 2000).

Answer (B) is incorrect. A stepparent might be awarded visitation if she has de facto or psychological parent status. *See Weinand v. Weinand*, 616 N.W.2d 1 (Neb. 2000).

Answer (D) is incorrect. The general rule is that a stepparent will not have a duty to support the children of an ex-spouse. *See Com. ex rel. McNutt v. McNutt*, 496 A.2d 816, 817 (Pa. Super. Ct. 1985) ("The general rule is that no legal duty rests upon the stepparent to support after the termination of the marriage.").

186.   **Answer (B) is the best answer.** While Nancy cannot be forced to instruct the children about Oscar's beliefs and thus is not in danger of losing custody merely because of her refusal to do so, *see LeDoux v. LeDoux*, 452 N.W.2d 1, 5 (Neb. 1990) ("The custodial parent normally has the right to control the religious training of the child."), Oscar would normally be afforded the right to instruct the children with respect to his own religious beliefs. *See Marjorie G. v. Stephen G.*, 592 N.Y.S.2d 209, 211 (Sup. Ct. 1992) (noncustodial father permitted to teach children about his own religious beliefs).

Answer (A) is incorrect. The custodial parent normally has the right to control the children's religious training, *see LeDoux v. LeDoux*, 452 N.W.2d 1, 5 (Neb. 1990), and so Nancy will not be risking a change in custody merely because she refuses to teach the children about Oscar's religious beliefs.

Answer (C) is incorrect. The court could not require the custodial parent to teach her children about a contrary faith. *See Abbo v. Briskin*, 660 So. 2d 1157, 1158 (Fla. Dist. Ct. App. 1995) (reversing a lower court that had "preclude[d] the custodial parent of one religious faith from actively influencing the training of the child inconsistently with the different religious faith of the other parent, and requir[ing] the custodial parent to raise the child in the other parent's faith and cooperate with the other parent in effecting the result").

Answer (D) is incorrect. As a general matter, the custodial parent determines the religious upbringing of the children, *see LeDoux v. LeDoux*, 452 N.W.2d 1, 5 (Neb. 1990), although in many cases the noncustodial parent can teach the children about other religious beliefs. *See Marjorie G. v. Stephen G.*, 592 N.Y.S.2d 209, 211 (Sup. Ct. 1992). That there was a prior agreement about the children's religious education does not alter the custodial parent's rights to determine their religious training. *See In re Landis*, 448 N.E.2d 845, 848 (Ohio Ct. App. 1982) ("prior agreements seeking to control the religious training of children will not be enforced against such a custodial parent").

187. **Answer (D) is the best answer.** The noncustodial parent's right to educate the children in religious matters can be limited if significant harm would thereby be caused. *See Khalsa v. Khalsa*, 751 P.2d 715, 721 (N.M. Ct. App. 1988) ("although the courts are reluctant to enjoin a non-custodial parent from practicing his religion with his children, the courts can and will enjoin such practice where the testimony concerning physical or emotional harm to the child is detailed and the best interests of the child will be served through the prohibition").

      Answer (A) is incorrect. While the custodial parent can determine the children's religious education, *see LeDoux v. LeDoux*, 452 N.W.2d 1, 5 (Neb. 1990), that parent cannot preclude the noncustodial parent from also instructing the children about religious matters unless the children would thereby be harmed. *See In re Marriage of Mentry*, 190 Cal. Rptr. 843, 845 (Ct. App. 1983).

      Answer (B) is incorrect. A noncustodial parent's religious instruction of his or her children can be limited if the instruction is causing the children serious harm. *See Khalsa v. Khalsa*, 751 P.2d 715, 720–21 (N.M. Ct. App. 1988) (discussing the degree of harm that would justify imposing restrictions on the noncustodial parent).

      Answer (C) is incorrect. A noncustodial parent's religious instruction of his or her children can be limited if the instruction is causing the children serious harm. *See Khalsa v. Khalsa*, 751 P.2d 715, 720–21 (N.M. Ct. App. 1988).

188. Benjamin is not likely to be successful. Because Benjamin was not married to Alexandra, provided no support for Alexandra during the pregnancy, and has not developed or even attempted to develop any relationship with the child before the child's placement, he is unlikely to be successful in his attempt to undo the adoption. This is both because the final adoption is presumptively valid, *see K.L.V. v. Florida Dept. of Health and Rehabilitative Services*, 684 So. 2d 253, 254 (Fla. Dist. Ct. App. 1996), and because he had done nothing even when he knew that he might become a father. *Cf. Adoption of Michael H.*, 898 P.2d 891, 902 (Cal. 1995) (discussing how a nonmarital, biological father could protect his parental interests).

189. John may well be successful in establishing his parental interests by timely establishing his paternity and his desire to take custody of the child. *See In re Adoption of BBC*, 831 P.2d 197, 200 (Wyo. 1992). An additional issue that might have to be resolved would be whether John would be a fit parent. *See id.* at 202 (refusing to grant custody to father where the trial court had found that the father was not fit to raise the child).

190.   **Answer (A) is the best answer** because it describes the tort, which involves sexual intercourse between a spouse and a third party. *See Albertini v. Veal*, 357 S.E.2d 716, 718 (S.C. Ct. App. 1987) ("The tort of criminal conversation is premised upon a plaintiff's loss of the consortium of his spouse. . . . It is a violation of a spouse's right to the exclusive privilege of sexual intercourse.").

   Answer (B) is incorrect. A court may take account of one spouse's using family monies for his or her own benefit when distributing property in a divorce, *see Lowrey v. Lowrey*, 25 So. 3d 274, 287 (Miss. 2009) (wife's dissipation of marital assets through gambling is appropriately considered when dividing up the marital estate), but criminal conversation does not address such wasting of assets. *See Albertini v. Veal*, 357 S.E.2d 716, 718 (S.C. Ct. App. 1987).

   Answer (C) is incorrect. While a state may choose to criminalize adultery, *see* Idaho Code § 18-6601 (setting fines and terms of imprisonment for the commission of adultery), criminal conversation is a tort. *See Albertini v. Veal*, 357 S.E.2d 716, 718 (S.C. Ct. App. 1987).

   Answer (D) is incorrect. Criminal conversation does not involve a conspiracy to make improper use of family funds but instead involves a married individual having sexual relations with someone other than a spouse. *See Albertini v. Veal*, 357 S.E.2d 716, 718 (S.C. Ct. App. 1987).

191.   **Answer (B) is the best answer.** The tort of alienation of affections requires that the tortfeasor turned the spouse away from the other spouse. *Nelson v. Jacobsen*, 669 P.2d 1207, 1218 (Utah 1983) ("In order to sustain a cause of action for alienation of affections, the plaintiff must show the following facts: (1) that she and her husband were happily married and that a genuine love and affection existed between them; (2) that the love and affection so existing was alienated and destroyed; (3) that the wrongful and malicious acts of defendant produced and brought about the loss and alienation of such love and affection.") If the spouses no longer cared for each other before the tortfeasor got involved, then there would be no recovery. *Booth v. Krouse*, 65 N.E.2d 89, 92 (Ohio Ct. App. 1946) ("if it appear that there is no affection to alienate, recovery may not be had").

   Answer (A) is incorrect. It is not necessary in all states recognizing the tort to show that the defendant had sexual relations with the spouse in order for an alienation of affections claim to be maintained. *See Nelson v. Jacobsen*, 669 P.2d 1207, 1217 (Utah 1983) ("sexual relations are not a necessary element of alienation of affections").

   Answer (C) is incorrect. Merely because a spouse fell in love with someone else would not establish that the alleged tortfeasor had intentionally acted to alienate the spouse's affections. *See State Farm Fire & Cas. Co. v. Harbert*, 741 N.W.2d 228, 235 (S.D. 2007) ("specific intent to alienate one spouse's affections from the other spouse is required to sustain an action for alienation of affections").

Answer (D) is incorrect. The tort focuses on the spouse's alienation rather than on the children's alienation. *See Nelson v. Jacobsen*, 669 P.2d 1207, 1218 (Utah 1983) ("the love and affection so existing [between the married parties] was alienated and destroyed").

192. **Answer (D) is the best answer.** Many states permit children to bring an action for loss of consortium, *see Reagan v. Vaughn*, 804 S.W.2d 463, 467 (Tex. 1990) ("children may recover for loss of consortium when a third party causes serious, permanent, and disabling injuries to their parent"), but do not permit any and all individuals having a sexual relationship with the victim to bring a loss of consortium claim. *See Sostock v. Reiss*, 415 N.E.2d 1094, 1099 (Ill. Ct. App. 1980) ("a cause of action does not extend in favor of a plaintiff where the injury to his wife occurred shortly before their marriage, notwithstanding that the couple was then engaged to be married").

Answer (A) is incorrect. Although this depends upon the state, many jurisdictions permit children to recover for loss of consortium with a parent. *See Reagan v. Vaughn*, 804 S.W.2d 463, 467 (Tex. 1990) ("children may recover for loss of consortium when a third party causes serious, permanent, and disabling injuries to their parent").

Answer (B) is incorrect. While this is a matter of state law, many states do not allow a fiance, for example, to recover for loss of consortium. *See Sostock v. Reiss*, 415 N.E.2d 1094, 1099 (Ill. Ct. App. 1980).

Answer (C) is incorrect. Some states permit children to bring an action for loss of consortium. *See Reagan v. Vaughn*, 804 S.W.2d 463, 467 (Tex. 1990).

193. **Answer (A) is the best answer.** Some jurisdictions require the ring to be returned if the marriage does not take place, *see McIntire v. Raukhorst*, 585 N.E.2d 456, 457 (Ohio Ct. App. 1989) ("When the condition [marriage] is not fulfilled, the ring or its value should be returned to the donor, no matter who broke the engagement or caused it to be broken."), although other jurisdictions consider who called off the engagement and why. *Lyle v. Durham*, 473 N.E.2d 1216, 1218 (Ohio Ct. App. 1984) ("The majority rule is that the engagement ring may be recovered by the donor if the engagement is broken by mutual agreement or by the donee without justification, but if the donor breaks off the engagement without justification, then he is not entitled to recover.").

Answer (B) is incorrect. Terry may well be forced to give the ring back. *See Lindh v. Surman*, 702 A.2d 560, 564 (Pa. Super. Ct. 1997) ("the gift of the ring to Janis at the time of their betrothal was subject to an implied condition requiring its return if the marriage did not take place").

Answer (C) is incorrect. Courts would instead suggest that because given in anticipation of marriage, the ring must be returned if the marriage is not celebrated. *See McIntire v. Raukhorst*, 585 N.E.2d 456, 457 (Ohio Ct. App. 1989).

Answer (D) is incorrect. Most jurisdictions would require that a ring be returned if, for example, the individual who received the ring was at fault for the breakdown of the marriage. *See Lyle v. Durham*, 473 N.E.2d 1216, 1218 (Ohio Ct. App. 1984) (describing approach where ring will be returned if recipient of the ring breaks off the engagement without justification) and *McIntire v. Raukhorst*, 585 N.E.2d 456, 457 (Ohio Ct. App. 1989) (describing approach whereby ring should be returned regardless of fault).

194.   **Answer (A) is the best answer.** The genetic counselor will likely be liable for damages as long as the Eversons can show that the test results mix up played a causal role in their conceiving a child, e.g., because they otherwise would have used contraception. *See*, for example, *Molloy v. Meier*, 660 N.W.2d 444, 453 (Minn. Ct. App. 2003) (physician held liable for failure to diagnose genetic condition, thereby contributing to the birth of another child with the same genetic difficulties).

    Answer (B) is incorrect. Liability may well be imposed when a child with severe difficulties is born and the parents would not have had that child but for the negligence of a medical professional. *See Molloy v. Meier*, 660 N.W.2d 444, 453 (Minn. Ct. App. 2003).

    Answer (C) is incorrect. It is precisely because of the family medical history that the plaintiffs sought genetic testing in the first place, and the defendant's negligence should not be excused because the plaintiffs were acting responsibly in light of their known family medical history. *See Findley-Smith v. Smith*, 2008 Tex. App. LEXIS 1466 (Feb. 28, 2008) (permitting cause of action of proceed where individuals sought genetic counseling because of family history and were misled about the possible difficulties that their child might have).

    Answer (D) is incorrect. Wrongful birth actions are recognized, *see*, for example, *Keel v. Banach*, 624 So. 2d 1022 (Ala. 1993) (recognizing action for wrongful birth), and the elements of that action include both that the child would not have been born but for the negligence of someone and that the parents were harmed by the birth. *See id.* at 1027 ("It has been recognized that the birth of a seriously deformed child results in injury to the child's parents.").

195.   **Answer (A) is the best answer.** Most jurisdictions do not recognize the cause of action, *see Rich v. Foye*, 976 A.2d 819, 834 (Conn. Super. Ct. 2007). Further, even if the action is recognized in some instances, there would be some difficulty in meeting the high burden of establishing that it would have been better for the child never to have lived at all. *Cf. Elliott v. Brown*, 361 So. 2d 546, 548 (Ala. 1978) (wondering "what criteria would be used to determine the degree of deformity necessary to state a claim for relief?").

    Answer B is incorrect. The Eversons are claiming that they themselves have been harmed both financially and emotionally as a result of Edward's having the disease. *See Naccash v. Burger*, 290 S.E.2d 825, 832 (Va. 1982) (affirming award of emotional and financial damages to parents in wrongful birth case).

    Answer (C) is incorrect. Some jurisdictions recognize a claim for wrongful life. *See Willis v. Wu*, 362 S.C. 146, 160, 607 S.E.2d 63, 70 (2004) ("Three states — California, New Jersey, and Washington — have recognized a wrongful life action by judicial opinion.").

    Answer (D) is not the best answer. While there might be a case in which the wrongful birth claim was time-barred but the wrongful life claim was not, *see Procanik by Procanik v. Cillo*, 478 A.2d 755 (N.J. 1984) (action by parents on their own behalf time-barred but action by parents on behalf of child not time-barred), the applicable statute of limitations did not bar the Eversons from bringing an action in this case.

196.   **Answer (D) is the best answer.** Jurisdictions tend to permit limited recovery under these circumstances. *See Hitzemann v. Adam*, 518 N.W.2d 102, 106 (Neb. 1994) ("[T]he majority of jurisdictions have held that parents of a healthy, normal child born after an unsuccessful sterilization operation may not recover child-rearing costs, but may recover damages for such child for prenatal and delivery medical expenses; for emotional distress, loss of wages,

pain and suffering, and loss of consortium caused by the failed sterilization, pregnancy, and childbirth.").

Answer (A) is incorrect. Some jurisdictions will award damages if negligence can be established in this kind of case. *See Zehr v. Haugen*, 871 P.2d 1006, 1013 (Or. 1994) (reversing and remanding case for determination of damages where a child was born due to an improperly performed tubal ligation).

Answer (B) is incorrect. Courts have rejected as a matter of public policy that there is a duty in these circumstances to mitigate by having an abortion. *See Morris v. Sanchez*, 746 P.2d 184, 189 (Okla. 1987) ("the concept of requiring abortion or adoption under these circumstances is, as a matter of law, unreasonable").

Answer (C) is incorrect. The majority of jurisdictions do not permit parents to recover the expenses of raising a child through majority under these circumstances. *See Morris v. Sanchez*, 746 P.2d 184, 187 (Okla. 1987) ("The majority of jurisdictions having considered this matter have concluded that, as a matter of law, the costs of raising the unplanned child may not be recovered in a medical malpractice action for negligent sterilization.").

197.   **Answer (A) is the best answer.** Melinda will likely be successful if she can establish that the doctor was negligent in failing to tell her of the risks posed by exposure to German Measles during the first trimester and that she would have aborted had she been told of the risks. *See Dumer v. St. Michael's Hospital*, 233 N.W.2d 372, 377 (Wis. 1975) ("[T]he doctor was negligent in not diagnosing the rubella the plaintiff-wife was suffering and inquiring as to pregnancy. If the doctor is found at the trial to have been negligent in those respects, it follows he had a duty to inform the plaintiff-mother of the effects of rubella. To complete a cause of action the plaintiffs must then convince the trier of fact that they would have sought and submitted to an abortion of the wife and that the abortion was legally available to them.").

Answer (B) is incorrect. Here, the physician's negligence lies in failing to warn about the risks of exposure to German Measles rather than in allegedly causing the exposure. *See Dumer v. St. Michael's Hospital*, 233 N.W.2d 372, 377 (Wis. 1975) (discussing the physician's duty to warn of the risks of exposure).

Answer (C) is incorrect. Here, the claimed negligence is in failing to warn about the risks to the fetus in being exposed to German measles rather than in the doctor's failure to mitigate the harm caused by the exposure. *See Dumer v. St. Michael's Hospital*, 233 N.W.2d 372, 377 (Wis. 1975).

Answer (D) is incorrect. The harm here is in the physician's failure to inform Melinda about the risks of exposure. *See Dumer v. St. Michael's Hospital*, 233 N.W.2d 372, 377 (Wis. 1975). She is not claiming that the physician negligently caused the exposure.

198.   **Answer (B) is the best answer.** Some states have abolished parental immunity. *See*, for example, *Broadbent by Broadbent v. Broadbent*, 907 P.2d 43, 50 (Ariz. 1995) (abolishing doctrine of parental immunity). The possibility that the parent might be insured means that the family purse might not be depleted even where such actions are permitted. However, it might be noted that an exclusion within the insurance policy might mean that the insurance company would not have to provide coverage for the injuries resulting from the negligent supervision. *See American Family Mut. Ins. Co. v. Ryan*, 330 N.W.2d 113, 116 (Minn. 1983)

(upholding policy exclusion).

Answer (A) is incorrect. Some jurisdictions have abolished parental immunity. *See,* for example, *Broadbent by Broadbent v. Broadbent,* 907 P.2d 43, 50 (Ariz. 1995) (abolishing doctrine of parental immunity).

Answer (C) is incorrect. Some states still recognize parental immunity. *See Crotta v. Home Depot, Inc.,* 732 A.2d 767, 774 (Conn. 1999) ("the doctrine of parental immunity operates to preclude the parent of a minor plaintiff from being joined as a third party defendant for purposes of apportionment of liability, contribution or indemnification based on the parent's allegedly negligent supervision of the minor plaintiff").

Answer (D) is incorrect. Just as a tortfeasor might seek contribution from a father who has negligently supervised his child, *see Meier v. Morrison,* 655 N.E.2d 449, 451 (Ohio Com. Pl. 1995), Steve might be held liable for Virginia's injuries and he might seek contribution from the dog owner once identified.

199.   **Answer (A) is the best answer.** Many states recognizing parental immunity do not extend its protections to intentional torts. *See Henderson v. Woolley,* 644 A.2d 1303, 1305 (Conn. 1994) ("many states either limited parental immunity to suits alleging parental negligence or were unwilling to extend it to acts of willful, intentional or wanton parental misconduct").

Answer (B) is incorrect. Many states recognizing parental immunity for negligence do not extend that immunity to intentional torts. *See Henderson v. Woolley,* 644 A.2d 1303, 1305 (Conn. 1994).

Answer (C) is incorrect. There is no requirement that the alleged tortfeasor be successfully prosecuted. Parental immunity was recognized to preserve family harmony and there is good reason to believe that such harmony might well not exist if the parent has committed an intentional tort against his or her child. *See Herzfeld v. Herzfeld,* 781 So. 2d 1070, 1078 (Fla. 2001) ("If indeed the principal reason for the parental immunity doctrine is to preserve family harmony, then it appears that the immunity can have no justification in such cases of intentional and malicious sexual abuse, for in those cases the inescapable conclusion is that the family fabric has already been tragically disrupted by the serious misconduct alleged.").

Answer (D) is incorrect. Courts have refused to permit parental immunity to extend to intentional torts even without express direction to that effect from the Legislature. *See,* for example, *Herzfeld v. Herzfeld,* 781 So. 2d 1070 (Fla. 2001).

200.   **Answer (C) is the best answer.** Where interspousal immunity has been abrogated, the third-party tortfeasor, Sarah, will likely be permitted to seek contribution from the negligent spouse, Joan. *See Noone v. Fink,* 721 P.2d 1275, 1276 (Mont. 1986) ("Since we have abrogated the doctrine of interspousal tort immunity, the contribution statute, § 27-1-703, MCA, controls.").

Answer (A) is incorrect. Sarah may well be permitted to sue Joan for contribution. *See Wirth v. City of Highland Park,* 430 N.E.2d 236, 242 (Ill. Ct. App. 1981).

Answer (B) is incorrect. Because Joan is partially responsible, Bonnie's recovery from Sarah is likely to be diminished rather than barred. *See Wirth v. City of Highland Park,* 430 N.E.2d 236, 242 (Ill. Ct. App. 1981).

Answer (D) is not the best answer. Sarah will likely be able to seek contribution from Joan.

See Noone v. Fink, 721 P.2d 1275, 1276 (Mont. 1986).

201.   **Answer (D) is the best answer.** *See Boyd v. Watson*, 680 N.E.2d 251, 253 (Ohio Com. Pl. 1996) ("A parent may also be liable for negligent supervision when the parent fails to exercise proper parental control over his child, and the parent knows, or should know from his knowledge of habits or tendencies of the child, that failure to exercise such control poses unreasonable risk that the child will injure others.").

   Answer (A) is incorrect. Parents tend not to be liable for the injuries caused by their children. *See Boyd v. Watson*, 680 N.E.2d 251, 253 (Ohio Com. Pl. 1996) ("Parents are generally not liable for the wrongful conduct of their children.").

   Answer (B) is incorrect. The parent will not be liable merely because her child was negligent. Rather, the parent might be liable for her own negligence with respect to the child. *See Boyd v. Watson*, 680 N.E.2d 251, 253 (Ohio Com. Pl. 1996) ("A parent can be liable for his own negligent act when the injury caused by the child is foreseeable to the parent.").

   Answer (C) is incorrect. The parent can be liable for her child's negligent or intentional torts even if the parent did not encourage the child to commit those torts. For example, the parent might be liable if she negligently failed to exercise proper control over her child. *See Boyd v. Watson*, 680 N.E.2d 251, 253 (Ohio Com. Pl. 1996) ("A parent may also be liable for negligent supervision when the parent fails to exercise proper parental control over his child, and . . . [should have known that the] failure to exercise such control poses unreasonable risk that the child will injure others.").

202.   **Answer (A) is the best answer.** *See Ross v. Louise Wise Services, Inc.*, 777 N.Y.S.2d 618, 622 (Sup. Ct. 2004) ("this Court is constrained to limit plaintiffs' potential recovery of compensatory damages in this case to the extraordinary out-of-pocket expenses of raising Anthony Ross to age 21").

   Answer (B) is incorrect. While it is true that adoption agencies do not guarantee that parents will be completely satisfied with their adopted child, *see M.H. v. Caritas Family Services*, 488 N.W.2d 282, 286 (Minn. 1992) ("an adoption agency cannot be expected to be a guarantor of the infant's future good health"), agencies may nonetheless be liable if they intentionally or negligently provide inaccurate information. *See Gibbs v. Ernst*, 647 A.2d 882, 891 (Pa. 1994) ("Adoption agencies must merely use reasonable care to insure that the information they communicate is accurate, and the parents must show that any negligently communicated information is causally related to their damages.").

   Answer (C) is incorrect. The Cunninghams are likely to recover the extraordinary expenses incurred in raising Shawn. *See Ross v. Louise Wise Services, Inc.*, 777 N.Y.S.2d 618, 622 (Sup. Ct. 2004). They would have incurred ordinary expenses in raising him, even if everything had gone as they had hoped.

   Answer (D) in incorrect. The Cunninghams will likely only be able to recover extraordinary expenses associated with raising Shawn. *See Ross v. Louise Wise Services, Inc.*, 777 N.Y.S.2d 618, 622 (Sup. Ct. 2004).

203.   **Answer (C) is the best answer.** An adoption can be set aside when there has been a fraudulent misrepresentation of material information. *See In re Adoption of T.B.*, 622 N.E.2d 921, 925 (Ind. 1993) ("In order to set aside the order of adoption based on fraud, there must be a material misrepresentation of past or existing fact made with knowledge or reckless

disregard for the falsity of the statement, and the misrepresentation must be relied upon to the detriment of the relying party."). However, states tend not to permit a revocation based on mere negligent misrepresentation. *See Juman v. Louise Wise Services*, 608 N.Y.S.2d 612, 616 (Sup. Ct. 1994) ("public policy so favors adoption that only lack of jurisdiction or fraud will cause a court to set aside an order of adoption").

Answer (A) is incorrect. Adoptions can be undone under the proper circumstances. *See C.C.K. v. M.R.K.*, 579 So. 2d 1368, 1370 (Ala. Civ. App. 1991) (undoing stepparent adoption that had been based on a fraudulent promise).

Answer (B) is incorrect. Courts are reluctant to undo adoptions precisely because a child rather than a mere product is involved. *Cf. Migues v. Fountain*, 203 So. 2d 483, 485 (Miss. 1967) (considering whether an adoption revocation would promote the best interests of the child).

Answer (D) is incorrect. Adoptions can be set aside when there has been an intentional misrepresentation of material information. *See In re Adoption of T.B.*, 622 N.E.2d 921, 925 (Ind. 1993).

204. **Answer (B) is the best answer.** Both Rob and his father may be liable here if it can be shown that they without excuse intentionally interfered with Sarah's custodial relationship with Chastity. *See Kessel v. Leavitt*, 511 S.E.2d 720, 765–66 (W. Va. 1998) (listing elements of the tort).

Answer (A) is incorrect. If Rob's grandfather conspired with Rob to intentionally deprive Sarah of custody, then he too may be liable. *See Stone v. Wall*, 734 So. 2d 1038 (Fla. 1999) (grandparent is potentially liable for interference with parent's custodial relationship).

Answer (C) is incorrect. Because Rob is not the custodial parent, he is also potentially subject to liability for intentional interference. *See Khalifa v. Shannon*, 945 A.2d 1244, 1245 (Md. 2008) (affirming that one parent can sue the other parent for intentional interference with custodial relationship).

Answer (D) is incorrect. Such suits are recognized in several jurisdictions. *See, for example, Khalifa v. Shannon*, 945 A.2d 1244, 1245 (Md. 2008).

205. **Answer (C) is the best answer.** While some of the jurisdictions recognizing intentional interference with custodial relationship also recognize a cause of action for intentional interference with parental relationship even when the parent does not have custody of the child, *see Khalifa v. Shannon*, 945 A.2d 1244, 1245 (Md. 2008), many do not. *See Cosner v. Ridinger*, 882 P.2d 1243, 1246 (Wyo. 1994) ("The jurisdictions recognizing this tort [intentional interference with custodial relationship] have limited the cause of action to the custodial parent and have not extended it to a non-custodial parent who is somehow deprived of visitation privileges.").

Answer (A) is not the best answer, because many jurisdictions do not recognize a tort for interference with parental visitation rights. *See Cosner v. Ridinger*, 882 P.2d 1243, 1246 (Wyo. 1994).

Answer (B) is incorrect. Many jurisdictions recognizing a cause of action for intentional interference with custodial relationship do not in addition recognize a tort action for intentional interference with visitation rights. *See Cosner v. Ridinger*, 882 P.2d 1243, 1246

(Wyo. 1994).

Answer (D) is incorrect. While a custodial parent's interference with visitation might in some cases justify a change in custody, *see Martin v. Martin*, 90 P.3d 981, 981–82 (Nev. 2004) ("a custodial parent's substantial or pervasive interference with a noncustodial parent's visitation could give rise to changed circumstances warranting a change in custody"), a separate issue is whether the jurisdiction recognizes a tort action for intentional interference with visitation rights, and many jurisdictions do not. *See Cosner v. Ridinger*, 882 P.2d 1243, 1246 (Wyo. 1994).

206.   Many states have abolished the tort actions of criminal conversation and alienation of affections. *See*, for example, *Speer v. Dealy*, 495 N.W.2d 911, 914 (Neb. 1993) ("claims for alienation of affections and criminal conversation have been abolished in this state by statute"). Let us assume, however, that Missamba recognizes these causes of action. To establish alienation of affections, Thomas will have to show that Wilhemina still had feelings for Thomas when she started to date Stan and that Stan caused Wilhemina to lose her affections for Thomas. *See Bland v. Hill*, 735 So. 2d 414, 417 (Miss. 1999) ("To prove an alienation of affections claim, the plaintiff must show: (1) wrongful conduct of the defendant; (2) loss of affection or consortium; and (3) causal connection between such conduct and loss.") Unless Wilhemina's loss of affection for Thomas was due to Stan, Thomas will be unsuccessful. *See Pankratz v. Miller*, 401 N.W.2d 543, 549 (S.D. 1987) ("the evidence fails to support an action for alienation of affections because there was no causal connection between Winston's conduct and Elke's loss of affection for her husband"). To prove criminal conversation, Thomas will have to establish that Stan and Wilhemina committed adultery. *See Helsel v. Noellsch*, 107 S.W.3d 231, 233 (Mo. 2003) ("The . . . difference between alienation of affection and criminal conversation is that criminal conversation requires proof of an adulterous sexual relationship."). If Missamba still recognizes the tort of criminal conversation and if Thomas can establish that Stan and Wilhemina had sexual relations, then Thomas may be successful, notwithstanding that the couple was separated at the time that the sexual relations took place. *See Nunn v. Allen*, 574 S.E.2d 35, 44 (N.C. Ct. App. 2002) ("the existence of the separation agreement between plaintiff and Mrs. Nunn does not shield defendant from liability for criminal conversation based on his post-separation sexual relationship with Mrs. Nunn").

207.   One issue that must be addressed is whether Tortsylvania recognizes parental immunity for negligent supervision. *See*, for example, *Zellmer v. Zellmer*, 188 P.3d 497, 503 (Wash. 2008) ("parents are immune from suit for negligent parental supervision"). If so, then the Robinsons will not be financially rspoinsible for any of the harm caused to their child. Even if Tortsylvania has abolished parental immunity, a separate question will be whether Tortsylvania recognizes a parental duty to supervise, *see Holodook v. Spencer*, 324 N.E.2d 338, 346 (N.Y. 1974) ("we are not persuaded that a parent's failure to supervise his child is, or on balance should be, a tort actionable by the child") and, if so, whether the Robinsons have negligently failed to fulfill that duty. Many jurisdictions would not impose liability under these circumstances, *see Zellmer v. Zellmer*, 188 P.3d 497, 501 (Wash. 2008) ("the overwhelming majority of jurisdictions hold parents are not liable for negligent supervision of their child, whether stated in terms of a limited parental immunity (among jurisdictions that have partially abrogated the parental immunity doctrine), parental privilege (among those that either abolished the immunity doctrine outright or declined to adopt it in the first instance), or lack of an actionable parental duty to supervise"). That said, it is possible that

Tortsylvania would permit liability to be imposed here. *See Zellmer v. Zellmer*, 188 P.3d 497, 502 (Wash. 2008) ("A minority of states have followed the lead of the California Supreme Court, allowing children to sue parents for negligent supervision under a 'reasonable parent' standard.").

208.   While adultery during a marriage might be held as a matter of law not to be sufficiently outrageous to be the basis of an intentional infliction claim, *see Poston v. Poston*, 436 S.E.2d 854, 856 (N.C. Ct. App. 1993) ("appellant's allegation of adultery does not evidence the extreme and outrageous conduct which is essential to this cause of action"), states split with respect to whether concealment of the fact that the husband is not the father of the children born during the marriage can be the basis of an intentional infliction of emotional distress action. *Compare Koestler v. Pollard*, 471 N.W.2d 7 (Wis. 1991) (action barred under these circumstances) *with Miller v. Miller*, 956 P.2d 887, 891 (Okla. 1998) (permitting such a cause of action to be pursued). As to whether Maurice can bring this intentional infliction of emotional distress claim against Nancy in Texahoma, this will depend upon local law. At least one relevant issue will be whether Texahoma recognizes a cause of action for either criminal conversation or alienation of affections and, if not, whether an intentional infliction of emotional distress action under these circumstances is viewed as basically a kind of alienation of affections claim. *See D.D. v. C.L.D.*, 600 So. 2d 219, 222 (Ala. 1992) (affirming that an intentional infliction of emotional distress action cannot be brought under these circumstances because it was in essence an alienation of affections claim).

209.   In many states, a bystander negligent infliction of emotional distress claim can only be brought by a legally recognized family member, so that a paramour would not be allowed to bring such an action under these circumstances. *See Smith v. Toney*, 862 N.E.2d 656, 660 (Ind. 2007) ("Most courts that have considered this issue have disallowed bystander recovery for negligent infliction of emotional distress by persons engaged to be married or involved in cohabiting but unmarried relationships."). If, however, Georgiana adopts a more functional approach, *cf. Leong v. Takasaki*, 520 P.2d 758, 766 (Haw. 1974) ("the plaintiff should be permitted to prove the nature of his relationship to the victim and the extent of damages he has suffered because of this relationship"), then John may be permitted to bring the bystander action assuming that he can prove the requisite degree of harm. *See Paugh v. Hanks*, 451 N.E.2d 759, 765 (Ohio 1983) ("We believe that where a bystander to an accident states a cause of action for negligent infliction of serious emotional distress, the emotional injuries sustained must be found to be both serious and reasonably foreseeable, in order to allow a recovery.").

210. **Answer (B) is the best answer.** Once Tom represented both parties, he should not have represented either of them without the other's permission. *See Vinson v. Vinson*, 588 S.E.2d 392, 394 (Va. Ct. App. 2003) (suggesting that the attorney should not have represented the wife alone after representing both the husband and wife, unless he secured the husband's permission to do so).

    Answer (A) is incorrect. Tom still would have been subject to discipline even if Alice had called him. *See Forbush v. Forbush*, 485 N.Y.S.2d 898, 902 (App. Div. 1985) (attorney sanctioned for representing one of the parties in a matrimonial action after having represented the family unit).

    Answer (C) is incorrect. Once Tom had represented both parties, he would need the permission of the unrepresented spouse to represent the other spouse individually. *See Forbush v. Forbush*, 485 N.Y.S.2d 898, 902 (App. Div. 1985).

    Answer (D) is incorrect. Tom is subject to discipline on these facts. *See Vinson v. Vinson*, 588 S.E.2d 392, 394 (Va. Ct. App. 2003).

211. **Answer (A) is the best answer.** Some states impose a per se bar on dual representation in a divorce, *see Ware v. Ware*, 687 S.E.2d 382, 389 (W. Va. 2009) ("in the context of a divorce, one attorney can never represent both parties"), whereas other states permit such representation as long as the parties consent after having been fully informed of the implications of the dual representation. *See Rowland v. Rowland*, 599 N.E.2d 315, 319 (Ohio Ct. App. 1991).

    Answer (B) is incorrect. Some states have a per se ban of dual representation in a divorce. *See Ware v. Ware*, 687 S.E.2d 382, 389 (W. Va. 2009).

    Answer (C) is incorrect. Some states bar dual representation in a divorce even after full disclosure. *See Ware v. Ware*, 687 S.E.2d 382, 389 (W. Va. 2009).

    Answer (D) is incorrect. The mere possibility of conflict will not suffice for the imposition of discipline in a state that permits dual representation, although that possibility might be the justification for a state's decision to impose a per se bar on dual representation in divorce matters. *See Walden v. Hoke*, 429 S.E.2d 504, 509 (W. Va. 1993) ("The likelihood of prejudice is so great with dual representation so as to make adequate representation of both spouses impossible, even where the separation is 'friendly' and the divorce uncontested.").

212. **Answer (A) is the best answer.** Contingency fee agreements in the context of divorce are prohibited in some jurisdictions, *see Succession of Butler*, 294 So. 2d 512 (La. 1974) (holding that contingency fee agreement is void as against public policy in divorce context), but permitted in others. *See Alexander v. Inman*, 903 S.W.2d 686, 698–99 (Tenn. Ct. App. 1995) (discussing conditions under which such an arrangement would be permissible in the divorce

context).

Answer (B) is incorrect. Some states preclude such agreements and other states will only rarely approve of them. *See Alexander v. Inman*, 974 S.W.2d 689, 693 (Tenn. 1998) ("Because public policy favors marriage and discourages attorneys from promoting bitter divorce battles for financial gain, contingent fees are subjected to enhanced scrutiny and rarely are found to be justified.").

Answer (C) is not the best answer. Such agreements are sometimes upheld, *see Alexander v. Inman*, 903 S.W.2d 686, 698–99 (Tenn. Ct. App. 1995), and it is inaccurate to suggest that they are never enforceable.

Answer (D) is incorrect. Sometimes, contingency fee arrangements are held unenforceable and the attorney is not allowed any compensation for his services. *See Burns v. Stewart*, 188 N.W.2d 760, 766 (Minn. 1971) ("it has been the position of this court that effectuation of the public policy requires not only that the contract be unenforceable, but also that the attorney entering such an arrangement be barred from recovery in quantum meruit as well").

213.   While a scribe does not have a duty to zealously represent his client, *see Chem-Age Industries, Inc. v. Glover*, 652 N.W.2d 756, 774–75 (S.D. 2002) (contrasting the duties of an attorney representing a client with the duties of an attorney acting as a scrivener), Augustus may nonetheless have a duty to withdraw. *See In re Marriage of Eltzroth*, 679 P.2d 1369, 1373 n.7 (Or. Ct. App. 1984) ("When the proposed 'agreement' between the parties presents obvious inequities on its face and raises questions and conflicts over the disposition of a substantial marital asset, it is the clear duty of the attorney to withdraw and advise the parties to seek independent counsel."). Augustus would not want to be a party to Sandra's attempt to defraud her husband. *Cf. In re Nash*, 568 N.Y.S.2d 936, 936 (App. Div. 1991) (attorney sanctioned for assisting client in make false statements). A separate issue is whether the state would permit or require Augustus to explain to Terence the reason for the withdrawal. *Cf. A. v. B.*, 726 A.2d 924, 929 (N.J. 1999) ("the *Restatement* advises that the lawyer, when withdrawing from representation of the co-clients, may inform the affected co-client that the attorney has learned of information adversely affecting that client's interests that the communicating co-client refuses to permit the lawyer to disclose.").

214. **Answer (B) is the best answer.** The Supreme Court has recognized a domestic relations exception, which "divests the federal courts of power to issue divorce, alimony, and child custody decrees." *See Elk Grove Unified School Dist. v. Newdow*, 542 U.S. 1, 12 (2004).

Answer (A) is incorrect. Federal courts are not precluded from hearing any matter involving family law, especially because some cases involve matters arising under international treaties. *See*, for example, *Antunez-Fernandes v. Connors-Fernandes*, 259 F. Supp. 2d 800 (N.D. Iowa 2003) (analyzing case arising under Hague Convention on the Civil Aspects of International Child Abduction, and the relevant implementing legislation, the International Child Abduction Remedies Act (ICARA)).

Answer (C) is incorrect. The exception does not relax standing requirements but instead precludes federal courts from issuing certain kinds of decrees. *See Elk Grove Unified School Dist. v. Newdow*, 542 U.S. 1, 12 (2004).

Answer (D) is incorrect. Federal courts cannot issue advisory opinions. *See Richardson v. Ramirez*, 418 U.S. 24, 72 (1974) (discussing the "oldest and most consistent thread in the federal law of justiciability . . . that the federal courts will not give advisory opinions.").

215. In order for federal law to displace state family, the latter law "must do major damage to clear and substantial federal interests." *See Franz v. U.S.*, 712 F.2d 1428, 1436 (D.C. Cir. 1983). Bracketing whether equal protection issues are implicated in the federal government's refusal to recognize the marriage valid according to state law, there is a separate federalism jurisprudence that imposes significant burdens on the federal government before it can substitute its own marriage law for that of one or several of the states. As to whether the burden can be met in this instance, that would have to be determined in the courts, although there is reason to believe that such a burden cannot be met. *See Gill v. Office of Personnel Management*, 699 F. Supp. 2d 374 (D. Mass. 2010) (striking down federal definition of marriage using rational basis test).

PRACTICE FINAL EXAM: ANSWERS

216. **Answer (B) is the best answer.** Assuming that New Hampticut treats minor marriages as voidable, then the marriage is likely to be treated as valid and Don will be treated as Gerald's surviving spouse. A voidable marriage is valid until voided by a court, *see Flaxman v. Flaxman*, 273 A.2d 567, 569 (N.J. 1971) (suggesting that a voidable marriage "is treated as valid and binding until its nullity is ascertained and declared by a competent court."), and it cannot be declared void once one of the spouses has died. *Arnelle v. Fisher*, 647 So. 2d 1047, 1048 (Fla. Dist. Ct. App. 1994) ("[A] voidable marriage is good for every purpose and can only be attacked in a direct proceeding during the life of the parties. . . . Upon the death of either party, the marriage is good *ab initio*.").

   Answer (A) is incorrect. Assuming that New Hampticut treats minor marriages as merely voidable, there is no requirement for such a marriage to be ratified after majority in order for it to be treated as valid. Such a marriage is valid until declared void by a court. *See Arnelle v. Fisher*, 647 So. 2d 1047, 1048 (Fla. Dist. Ct. App. 1994).

   Answer (C) is incorrect. There is no requirement that individuals live together before their marriage will be treated as valid. *See Hassan v. Hassan*, 2001 Conn. Super. LEXIS 2959 (Oct. 9, 2001) ("There is no Connecticut law supporting the proposition that failing to cohabit after a marriage renders the marriage void *ab initio*.").

   Answer (D) is incorrect. A marriage valid where celebrated may nonetheless not be recognized by the couple's domicile at the time of the marriage if that marriage violates an important public policy of the latter state. *See*, for example, *Catalano v. Catalano*, 170 A.2d 726, 728–29 (Conn. 1961) ("The marriage of the plaintiff and Fred Catalano, though valid in Italy under its laws, was not valid in Connecticut because it contravened the public policy of this state.").

217. **Answer (A) is the best answer.** If New Hampticut has a very strong public policy against either same-sex marriages or minor marriages, then the marriage will not be recognized under any circumstances and will likely be treated as void ab initio. If it is treated as void ab initio, then Don will not be treated as a surviving spouse. *See In re Mastrogiacomo*, 2003 N.Y. Misc. LEXIS 614, at *5–*6 (Sur. Ct. May 12, 2003) ("a marriage which satisfies the requirements of the state where it was contracted will everywhere be recognized as valid unless it violates the strong public policy of another state which had the most significant relationship to the spouses and the marriage at the time of the marriage").

   Answer (B) is incorrect. Even if minor marriages are treated as voidable, a separate question is whether New Hampticut views same-sex marriages as violating an important public policy of the state. If so, then the marriage is likely not to be recognized for any purpose. *See In re Mastrogiacomo*, 2003 N.Y. Misc. LEXIS 614 (Sur. Ct. May 12, 2003).

   Answer (C) is not the best answer. If, for example, New Hampticut has a very strong public policy against minor marriages, then the marriage will not be treated as valid for any purpose. *Cf. State ex rel. Dept. of Economic Sec. v. Demetz*, 130 P.3d 986, 989 (Ariz. Ct. App. 2006) ("In Arizona, a 'void' marriage . . . never comes into existence, and cannot be ratified.").

Answer (D) is incorrect. The issue is not whether New Hampticut permits the marriages to be celebrated locally but whether it has such a strong public policy against such marriages that it will not recognize such marriages even if validly celebrated elsewhere. *See In re Mastrogiacomo*, 2003 N.Y. Misc. LEXIS 614 (Sur. May 12, 2003).

218. As long as New Mexarkana treats Dolly and Wally's marriage as voidable rather than void, then they can ratify their marriage once they attain majority. *Medlin v. Medlin*, 981 P.2d 1087, 1090 (Ariz. Ct. App. 1999) ("When a marriage is voidable, it can be ratified by the minor once he or she reaches the age of majority."). Ratification will occur if they continue to live together once they are both of age. *See id.* at 1090 ("Ratification of an underage marriage is normally accomplished by the parties merely continuing to live together as husband and wife after the age of majority is attained."). Once the marriage has been validated through ratification, the couple will likely be unable to have it annulled and instead will have to have it dissolved. *See Kuehmsted v. Turnwall*, 138 So. 775, 777 (Fla. 1932) (noting that "there is a vast difference between a decree annulling, and a decree dissolving, a marriage by divorce; the one being grounded on the fact that there was never a valid marriage, while the other concedes that a valid marriage in fact exists but dissolves it").

219. **Answer (B) is the best answer.** Most states do not allow siblings to marry, even if one of them has been adopted. *See*, for example, *In re Marriage of MEW*, 4 Pa. D. & C. 3d 51, 59 (Pa. Com. Pl. 1977) ("To authorize and encourage marriages of brothers and sisters by adoption would undermine the fabric of family life and would be the antithesis of the social aims and purposes which the adoption process is intended to serve."). However there is case law permitting such a marriage where the individuals have not lived together as part of a family unit. *See Israel v. Allen*, 577 P.2d 762, 764 (Colo. 1978) (striking down law precluding a brother from marrying his sister by adoption), so it is possible that Newviewington would follow the minority view.

Answer (A) is incorrect. Even if no one in the family objects to the marriage, it would likely be treated as null and of no legal effect were it challenged by anyone, including a third party. *See In re Davis' Estate*, 640 P.2d 692, 693 (Or. Ct. App. 1982) ("A void marriage, on the other hand, is invalid from the outset and may be challenged by third parties.").

Answer (C) is incorrect. *See*, for example, *In re Marriage of MEW*, 4 Pa. D. & C. 3d 51 (Pa. Com. Pl. 1977) (declaring marriage between brother and adopted sister void).

Answer (D) is incorrect. Many states will treat a marriage between siblings by adoption as void regardless of whether or not they can have a child through their union. *See*, for example, *In re Marriage of MEW*, 4 Pa. D. & C. 3d 51 (Pa. Com. Pl. 1977). However, some states will permit first cousins to marry if they can establish that they cannot have a child through their union. *See Cook v. Cook*, 104 P.3d 857, 858 n.2 (Ariz. Ct. App. 2005) (explaining that in Arizona "first cousins may marry if both are sixty-five years of age or older or if one or both first cousins are under sixty-five years of age, upon approval of any superior court judge in the state if proof has been presented to the judge that one of the cousins is unable to reproduce").

220. The first question is whether Limitania permits first cousins to marry. If so, then the state will of course recognize the marriage validly celebrated elsewhere. Even if the state does not permits such marriages to be celebrated within the state, a separate question is whether it considers such marriages as violating an important public policy. If not, then Limitania might well recognize the marriage validly celebrated elsewhere, even though it could not be celebrated locally. *See*, for example, *In re Loughmiller's Estate*, 629 P.2d 156, 161 (Kan. 1981) ("Although our statutes prohibit first cousin marriages and impose criminal penalties where such marriages are contracted in Kansas, we cannot find that a first cousin marriage validly contracted elsewhere is odious to the public policy of this state.").

221. **Answer (A) is the best answer.** The issue is not whether the two were inebriated but whether they were so inebriated that they did not know what they were doing. *See Christoph v. Sims*, 234 S.W.2d 901, 904 (Tex. Civ. App. 1950) ("A party claiming he was intoxicated at the time of marriage cannot escape liability unless he was incapable at the time of understanding his acts; he must be so drunk that he did not understand what he was doing and the nature of the transaction."). That they kissed after they were pronounced husband and wife suggests that they understood what was taking place. Even were they thought not to have been competent to contract the marriage, a separate issue is whether Famvalington treats marriages celebrated by those temporarily unable to understand what they were doing as voidable or void. If the former, then the marriage will be treated as valid until declared void by a court. *See Flaxman v. Flaxman*, 273 A.2d 567, 569 (N.J. 1971) (suggesting that a voidable marriage "is treated as valid and binding until its nullity is ascertained and declared by a competent court."). Further, the marriage will not be subject to challenge once one of the parties had died. *See Vance v. Hinch*, 261 S.W.2d 412, 415 (Ark. 1953) (refusing to allow challenge to marriage celebrated by someone allegedly incompetent once one of the parties to the marriage had died.). *See also Patey v. Peaslee*, 111 A.2d 194, 198 (N.H. 1955) ("We conclude that the plaintiffs have not stated a cause for annulment which is cognizable in the courts of this state, because the marriage was voidable rather than void, and the proceedings were not brought 'during the lives of both the contracting parties.").

Answer (B) is incorrect. Assuming that the marriage is treated by Famvalington as voidable rather than void, the marriage, even if not ratified, will nonetheless be treated as valid until declared void by a court, *see Flaxman v. Flaxman*, 273 A.2d 567, 569 (N.J. 1971).

Answer (C) is incorrect. The marriage does not have to be consummated before it can be considered valid. *See Berdikas v. Berdikas*, 178 A.2d 468, 470–71 (Del. Super. 1962) ("where the parties have been wed in compliance with the requirements of the statute, . . . a valid marriage is effected and no consummation of the marriage, as by coition is necessary").

Answer (D) is incorrect. If the marriage is considered void because the parties were not competent to contract it, then Wanda is very unlikely to be treated as the surviving spouse. *See*, for example, *Krukowsky v. Krukowsky*, 1970 Pa. Dist. & Cnty. Dec. LEXIS 464 (Del. Com Pl. May 4, 1970) ("a marriage performed while one of the parties is non compos mentis is a void marriage").

222. **Answer (B) is the best answer.** Carol's refraining from filing for divorce constitutes the consideration, *see Gilley v. Gilley*, 778 S.W.2d 862, 864 (Tenn. Ct. App. 1989), and her

threatening her husband with divorce does not constitute coercion as a legal matter. *See id.*

Answer (A) is incorrect. Carol's deciding to remain in the marriage rather than immediately seek a divorce was consideration. *See Gilley v. Gilley*, 778 S.W.2d 862, 864 (Tenn. Ct. App. 1989) (wife's remaining in the marriage was consideration for postnuptial agreement).

Answer (C) is incorrect. Even though Bob felt pressured to sign the agreement to save his marriage, that feeling of pressure does not constitute legal coercion. *See Gilley v. Gilley*, 778 S.W.2d 862, 864 (Tenn. Ct. App. 1989).

Answer (D) is incorrect. Her staying in the marriage was consideration and her threatening to seek a divorce does not constitute legal coercion. *See Gilley v. Gilley*, 778 S.W.2d 862, 864 (Tenn. Ct. App. 1989).

223.   While Edward might get relief from the judgment where Donna intentionally misrepresented the assets, Edward does not seem to have proof that this was a knowing misrepresentation and so seems unlikely to be able to avoid the judgment on that basis. *See, for example, In re McLoughlin v. McLoughlin*, 2006 Ohio 1530, at ¶ 37 (Ohio Ct. App.) ("The evidence does not support a finding that appellee knowingly made any misrepresentation of material fact with the intention of misleading appellant, with the result that appellant actually relied on the alleged misrepresentation. Appellant failed to demonstrate the existence of any fraud, misrepresentation or misconduct in connection with the separation agreement."). But the absence of fraud does not end the matter. If, for example, a significant amount of the assets was not accounted for, that might justify treating the judgment as void. *See In re Murphy*, 461 N.E.2d 910, 915 (Ohio Ct. App. 1983) ("when a separation agreement omits assets that are substantial in relative amount and material to an informed and deliberate agreement about an equitable division of the property, the statutory requirement has not been met and the ensuing decree has a fatal flaw"). In many cases, however, the trial court may be given discretion to decide whether relief should be granted for an alleged omission. *See Lewis v. Lewis*, 2010 Ohio App. LEXIS 881, at *13 (Mar. 18, 2010) ("while such an omission may be sufficient grounds for relief . . . , ultimately, whether equity demands that the judgment be set aside remains a question within the court's discretion.").

224.   **Answer (C) is the best answer.** Many jurisdictions require that the prenuptial agreement not be unconscionable at the time it is made and, in addition, require that its enforcement would not be unfair and unreasonable. *See Hardee v. Hardee*, 585 S.E.2d 501, 504 (S.C. 2003).

Answer (A) is incorrect. Many states will invalidate a prenuptial agreement if it is unconscionable at the time of enforcement. *See, for example, In re Marriage of Ikeler*, 161 P.3d 663, 667 (Colo. 2007).

Answer (B) is not the best answer. While some jurisdictions might suggest that it is foreseeable that one of the parties might become ill so the failure to include that possibility in the prenuptial agreement cannot later be used to invalidate the agreement, *see Simeone v. Simeone*, 581 A.2d 162, 166 (Pa. 1990), others will not. *See, for example, Lakin v. Lakin*, 1999 Conn. Super. LEXIS 3475 (Conn. Super. Dec. 6, 1999) (refusing to enforce prenuptial agreement because of wife's subsequently acquired illness and inability to work).

Answer (D) is incorrect. Some jurisdictions focus on when the agreement was signed rather than when enforcement is sought. *See Donovan v. Donovan*, 51 Va. Cir. 34 (1999) (noting that the relevant time frame is when the agreement is signed).

225. **Answer (B) is the best answer.** Jurisdictions vary with respect to the enforceability of prenuptials that are presented shortly before a wedding. *Compare Hjortaas v. McCabe*, 656 So. 2d 168 (Fla. Dist. Ct. App. 1995) (treating such a prenuptial agreement as unenforceable) *with In re Marriage of Miller*, 2002 WL 31312840 (Iowa App. 2002) (holding such a prenuptial agreement enforceable). A court upholding the validity of such a contract might well note that the wedding could have been delayed. *See*, for example, *Dornemann v. Dornemann*, 850 A.2d 273, 281 (Conn. Super. Ct. 2004) ("She could have delayed the wedding.").

   Answer (A) is not the best answer. While some courts have struck down prenuptial agreements presented shortly before a wedding when in addition there had been no financial disclosure and, furthermore, the agreement was inequitable, *see*, for example, *Hjortaas v. McCabe*, 656 So. 2d 168 (Fla. Dist. Ct. App. 1995), other courts have upheld prenuptial agreements presented shortly before the weddings. *See*, for example, *In re Marriage of Miller*, 2002 WL 31312840 (Iowa App. 2002).

   Answer (C) is not the best answer. It is unlikely that the court would want to decide which tasks could be delegated and which not. *Cf. In re Marriage of Bernard*, 204 P.3d 907, 913 (Wash. 2009) (striking prenuptial after noting that there were many last-minute items to be taken care of, but refusing to address which responsibilities could have been delegated).

   Answer (D) is incorrect. Merely because the agreement was signed would not make it enforceable. *See In re Marriage of Bernard*, 204 P.3d 907, 913 (Wash. 2009).

226. At least part of the prenuptial agreement is unenforceable, because such agreement cannot specify which parent will have custody. *See Edwardson v. Edwardson*, 798 S.W.2d 941, 946 (Ky. 1990) ("[A]ntenuptial agreements may apply only to disposition of property and maintenance. Questions of child support, child custody and visitation are not subject to such agreements."). However, merely because an agreement has an invalid provision does not mean that the whole agreement is unenforceable. *See Sanford v. Sanford*, 694 N.W.2d 283, 291 (S.D. 2005) ("Those portions of a prenuptial agreement that are valid will be enforced despite the presence of invalid provisions within the agreement."). As to whether the provision barring spousal support is enforceable, this will be a matter of state law. Some states preclude such provisions. *See id.* at 293 ("Provisions in a prenuptial agreement purporting to limit or waive spousal support are void and unenforceable as they are contrary to public policy.") Other states will enforce them as long as their enforcement would not be unconscionable or unfair. *See Saari v. Saari*, 2009 Ohio 4940 (Ohio Ct. App.) (enforcing prenuptial agreement that there would be no spousal support).

227. **Answer (B) is the best answer.** A refusal to marry unless the premarital agreement is signed would not alone constitute duress. *See In re Marriage of Miller*, 2002 WL 31312840, *3 (Iowa App. 2002) ("We find insistence on a prenuptial agreement as a condition of marriage is not a threat or unlawful."), and the failure of his business would not alone make enforcement of the prenuptial agreement regarding spousal support unconscionable or unfair. *See Schnitker v. Schnitker*, 2007 Minn. App. Unpub. LEXIS 308 (Apr. 10, 2007).

   Answer (A) is incorrect. Coercion if established will invalidate a prenuptial agreement. *See Gordon v. Gordon*, 25 So. 3d 615, 617 (Fla. Dist. Ct. App. 2009).

   Answer (C) is incorrect, because the failure of William's business would not alone establish that his not receiving support would be unfair or unconscionable. *See Schnitker v. Schnitker*,

2007 Minn. App. Unpub. LEXIS 308 (Apr. 10, 2007).

Answer (D) is incorrect. A refusal to marry without a premarital agreement would not alone constitute duress. *See In re Marriage of Miller*, 2002 WL 31312840, *3 (Iowa App. 2002). Further, the failure of his business would not alone make enforcement of the prenuptial agreement regarding spousal support unconscionable or unfair. *See Schnitker v. Schnitker*, 2007 Minn. App. Unpub. LEXIS 308 (Apr. 10, 2007).

228.   **Answer (D) is the best answer.** If indeed this misrepresentation goes to the essentials of marriage, *see Husband v. Wife*, 257 A.2d 765, 768 (Del. Super. Ct. 1969) ("only such fraud as goes to the very essentials of the marriage relation will suffice as ground for annulment"), then the annulment might be granted. *See Wolfe v. Wolfe*, 378 N.E.2d 1181, 1183 (Ill. Ct. App. 1978) (holding that wife's refusal to admit that her ex-husband was alive provided the basis for annulment, given her second husband's religious beliefs).

   Answer (A) is incorrect. A couple having had children together would not alone preclude the granting of an annulment. *See Stone v. Stone*, 145 P.2d 212, 213 (Okla. 1944) (affirming annulment of minor marriage notwithstanding that a child was born to that marriage).

   Answer (B) is not the best answer. Some jurisdictions might permit an annulment of the marriage under these conditions, *see Wolfe v. Wolfe*, 378 N.E.2d 1181, 1183 (Ill. Ct. App. 1978) (holding that wife's refusal to admit that her ex-husband was alive provided the basis for annulment, given her second husband's religious beliefs). Other jurisdictions might not. *See Villasenor v. Villasenor*, 107 N.Y.S.2d 951, 952–53 (Sup. Ct. 1951) (refusing to allow annulment when husband had falsely claimed that his previous marriage had been annulled when he in fact had gotten a divorce).

   Answer (C) is incorrect. The relevant question is not whether Patrick believed in good faith that Colleen would never discover his misrepresentation nor whether he overestimated the degree to which he could convince her to remain in the marriage if she discovered the misrepresentation. Instead, the relevant question is whether the fraud goes to an essential of the marriage. *See Husband v. Wife*, 257 A.2d 765, 768 (Del. Super. Ct. 1969) ("only such fraud as goes to the very essentials of the marriage relation will suffice as ground for annulment").

229.   **Answer (B) is the best answer.** A court might well hold that a third party cannot challenge the presumed parentage of a husband when the child was born into a marriage. *See CW v. LV*, 788 A.2d 1002, 1005 (Pa. Super. Ct. 2001).

   Answer (A) is incorrect. States distinguish between a biological father and a legal father. Those two concepts may but need not pick out the same individual. *See In re C.N.W.*, 560 S.E.2d 1, 3 (Ga. 2002) (discussing a biological father who is not the child's legal father).

   Answer (C) is not the best answer. Here, the question involves a presumption of paternity rather than an adoption. *See CW v. LV*, 788 A.2d 1002, 1005 (Pa. Super. Ct. 2001).

   Answer (D) is not the best answer. While parental rights may be terminated because of a failure to support the mother during the pregnancy, *see In re Adoption of D.M.M.*, 955 P.2d 618, 619 (Kan. 1997) (upholding termination of rights because of failure to support mother during pregnancy), the issue here involves Karl's presumed parentage. John's parental rights are not recognized and thus do not have to be terminated.

230. **Answer (B) is the best answer.** The facts here provide a paradigmatic example of an equitable parent. *See York v. Morofsky*, 571 N.W.2d 524, 526 (Mich. Ct. App. 1997) ("A husband who is not the biological father of a child born or conceived during the marriage may be considered the natural father of that child where (1) the husband and the child mutually acknowledge a relationship as father and child, or the mother of the child has cooperated in the development of such a relationship over a period of time prior to the filing of the complaint for divorce, (2) the husband desires to have the rights afforded to a parent, and (3) the husband is willing to take on the responsibility of paying child support.").

Answer (A) is incorrect, because it mischaracterizes what the term "equitable parent" means. An equitable parent would include the situation described in this question. *See York v. Morofsky*, 571 N.W.2d 524, 526 (Mich. Ct. App. 1997) (describing an equitable parent as one who is not biologically related to a child but has a parent-child relationship with the child and who wants to continue to have the rights and responsibilities of parentage even after the divorce).

Answer (C) is incorrect, because there is no requirement that the other parent supports the recognition of the parent-child relationship at the time the parents' relationship is dissolving. *See York v. Morofsky*, 571 N.W.2d 524, 526 (Mich. Ct. App. 1997).

Answer (D) is incorrect. Some states do not recognize equitable parent doctrine, possible interests of the child notwithstanding. *See*, for example, *In re Marriage of Halvorsen*, 521 N.W.2d 725, 728 (Iowa 1994) (rejecting that doctrine).

231. **Answer (D) is the best answer.** The agreement between the parties would be important to consider, although local law might impose additional conditions, e.g., that it be in writing. *See In re K.M.H.*, 169 P.3d 1025, 1030 (Kan. 2007) (rejecting that known sperm donor has parental rights when there no written agreement to that effect).

Answer (A) is incorrect. Bill's paternity would likely depend, at least in part, on the agreement between Bill and Ann at the time of the insemination. Depending upon the jurisdiction, such an agreement might have to be in writing to protect Bill's parental rights. *See In re K.M.H.*, 169 P.3d 1025, 1030 (Kan. 2007) (rejecting that known sperm donor has parental rights when there no written agreement to that effect).

Answer (B) is incorrect. Were there an agreement at the time of insemination between Ann and Bill that Bill would be the child's father, then Bill's parental rights might well be recognized. *See In Interest of R.C.*, 775 P.2d 27, 35 (Colo. 1989).

Answer (C) is incorrect. The relevant issue involves the (possibly written) agreement between Ann and Bill. If there had been an agreement that he would have parental rights, then her subsequent desire to raise the child alone might well not preclude Bill's establishing parental rights. *See In Interest of R.C.*, 775 P.2d 27 (Colo. 1989).

232. Even if Robert is not the twins' biological father, he may well be able to maintain his parental relationship with the children if the jurisdiction recognizes equitable parent doctrine. *See York v. Morofsky*, 571 N.W.2d 524, 526 (Mich. Ct. App. 1997). Even if the jurisdiction does not recognize equitable parent doctrine, there might be a statutory presumption that he is the father of the children born into the marriage. However, many states permit a party to the marriage to rebut the presumption of paternity, so it would be important to establish whether the jurisdiction requires that the challenge occurs within a

certain time frame. *See*, for example, West's Ann. Cal. Fam. Code § 7541(b) and (c) (specifying that the motion for blood tests to challenge paternity should be made within two years of the child's birth).

233.   **Answer (B) is the best answer.** Dissipation occurs when a party uses marital assets for his own purposes when the marriage is breaking down. *See Averitt v. Averitt*, 2009 Tenn. App. LEXIS 470, at *28 (July 24, 2009) ("A party dissipates marital property when he or she uses marital property frivolously and without justification for a purpose unrelated to the marriage at a time when the marriage is breaking down.") When a party dissipates marital assets, the dissipation can be credited against what he should receive in the distribution of the marital assets. *See Jones v. Jones*, 942 P.2d 1133, 1141 (Alaska 1997) ("The proper method for dealing with an unreasonable depletion of marital assets would be for the trial court to recapture the proven losses by adding their value to the marital estate before making the equitable division and then crediting that part of the value to the account of the party responsible for the unreasonable depletion.").

   Answer (A) is not the best answer. While gambling losses need not be viewed as involving dissipation if, for example, the parties go on a Las Vegas vacation together, the gambling losses are likely to be viewed as dissipation in this case. *See Lowrey v. Lowrey*, 25 So. 3d 274, 288 (Miss. 2009) ("gambling losses can be considered as dissipation in an equitable distribution of marital assets").

   Answer (C) is incorrect. The court might well suggest that it is Wayne's own fault that he is receiving few if any of the remaining marital assets. *See Tamba v. Tamba*, 1991 Del. Fam. Ct. LEXIS 47, at *39–*40 (Aug. 16, 1991) ("To the extent that the Husband has already squandered a portion of his aliquot share of the marital assets, that is a problem which he will have to live with since he has only himself to blame for the plight in which he finds himself.").

   Answer (D) is incorrect. Even if marital assets were used to purchase a gift for Wanda (perhaps at a happier time in the marriage), that gift might well be classified as Wanda's separate property. *See*, for example, *In re Marriage of Weiler*, 629 N.E.2d 1216, 1221 (Ill. Ct. App. 1994) (gift to wife was her separate property). But her separate property would not be used to offset the marital assets that he dissipated. *See Romano v. Romano*, 632 So. 2d 207, 210 (Fla. Dist. Ct. App. 1994) (dissipation of marital assets to be accounted for in the distribution of the marital assets).

234.   **Answer (C) is the best answer.** The necklace is likely to be viewed as Meredith's separate property if Agnes is understood to have made an interspousal gift. *See In re Marriage of Fenton*, 2010 Iowa App. LEXIS 809 (July 28, 2010) (interspousal gifts are separate property and not part of the divisible marital estate).

   Answer (A) is incorrect. The mere fact that the necklace was bought with marital funds would not make it marital property. *See Heineman v. Heineman*, 768 S.W.2d 130, 140 (Mo. Ct. App. 1989) (gift of necklace classified as separate property even though purchased with marital funds).

   Answer (B) is incorrect. Salary earned during the marriage is marital property. *See Flechas v. Flechas*, 791 So. 2d 295, 299 (Miss. Ct. App. 2001) ("Assets acquired during the course of marriage are marital assets and subject to equitable distribution unless it can be proven that such assets belonged to one of the separate estates prior to marriage.").

Answer (D) is incorrect. An interspousal gift of jewelry may well be viewed as separate property. *See In re Marriage of Fenton*, 2010 Iowa App. LEXIS 809 (July 28, 2010).

235. **Answer (C) is the best answer.** Because John's car was purchased with monies that he earned during the marriage, it is likely to be treated as marital property. *See Carnathan v. Carnathan*, 722 So. 2d 1248, 1253 (Miss. 1998) ("Assets acquired or accumulated during the course of a marriage are subject to equitable division unless it can be shown by proof that such assets are attributable to one of the parties' separate estates prior to the marriage or outside the marriage."). Because Mary's car was purchased and maintained with separate funds, it is likely to be viewed as her separate property. *See Deidun v. Deidun*, 606 S.E.2d 489, 495 (S.C. Ct. App. 2004) (car purchased with separate funds remained separate property).

Answer (A) is incorrect. A car purchased with marital assets is likely to be treated as marital property. *See Carnathan v. Carnathan*, 722 So. 2d 1248, 1253 (Miss. 1998).

Answer (B) is incorrect. If Mary's car was purchased and maintained with separate funds, it is likely to be treated as separate property. *See Deidun v. Deidun*, 606 S.E.2d 489, 495 (S.C. Ct. App. 2004).

Answer (D) is incorrect. While title might be relevant to determine whether property is marital or separate, *see Tinger v. Tinger*, 709 S.W.2d 123, 124 (Mo. Ct. App. 1986) ("The title, being in the names of the husband and wife, establishes that the car was marital property."), that will not be the only criterion. *See Jacobs v. Jacobs*, 2003-Ohio-3466 (Ohio Ct. App.) (car titled in names of husband and wife held to be wife's separate property).

236. **Answer (D) is the best answer.** If the increase in value was not due to the investment of marital resources, then the increase is not a marital asset. *See Pagano v. Pagano*, 665 So. 2d 370, 372 (Fla. Dist. Ct. App. 1996) ("purely passive increases in the value of a pre-marital asset caused by inflation are not subject to division"). However, the use of marital resource to increase the home's value would make the increase in value a marital asset subject to distribution. *Id.* ("asset appreciation constitutes a marital asset subject to equitable distribution where marital labor contributes to its value").

Answer (A) is incorrect. Merely because the home was used as the marital domicile would not without more make it marital property. *See*, for example, *Bridgewater v. Bridgewater*, 360 So. 2d 219, 219 (La. Ct. App. 1978) (noting that the marital domicile was the husband's separate property).

Answer (B) is not the best answer. The characterization of the separate property's increase in value during the marriage will depend upon whether that increase was due to the investment of marital time, energy or assets or, instead, to other factors. *See Mayhew v. Mayhew*, 519 S.E.2d 188, 194 (W. Va. 1999) ("increased value resulting from spousal efforts becomes the property of the marital partnership, [w]hereas increased value attributable to other sources remains separate property").

Answer (C) is incorrect. If the increase in value were due to the investment of marital resources, that increase in value would be a marital asset subject to distribution. *See Mayhew v. Mayhew*, 519 S.E.2d 188, 194 (W. Va. 1999).

237. **Answer (A) is the best answer.** The primary caretaker presumption suggests that the parent who has been primarily responsible for taking care of the child's daily needs will likely be awarded custody. *See Lewis v. Lewis*, 433 S.E.2d 536, 539 (W. Va. 1993) (noting that the "primary caretaker is that natural or adoptive parent who, until the initiation of divorce proceedings, has been primarily responsible for the caring and nurturing of the child") and that the primary caretaker will likely be awarded custody. *See id.*

Answer (B) is incorrect. The primary caretaker presumption does not favor one gender over the other. *See David M. v. Margaret M.*, 385 S.E.2d 912, 925–26 (W. Va. 1989) (explaining that the "role of primary caretaker, without regard to the sex of the parent, is a substantial factor which the trial judge must weigh in adjudicating a custody matter where the child is of tender years").

Answer (C) is incorrect. If the state employs a primary caretaker presumption, it is more likely to award custody to the parent who was the child's primary caretaker, *see Lewis v. Lewis*, 433 S.E.2d 536, 539 (W. Va. 1993), whether or not that parent was the primary caretaker as a result of the couple's agreeing that this was a good allocation of responsibilities.

Answer (D) is incorrect. The primary caretaker is the individual who is primarily responsible for taking care of the child's daily needs. *See*, for example, *Hogue v. Hogue*, 574 N.W.2d 579, 583 (N.D. 1998) ("the following have been held to be indicia of primary caretaker status: (1) preparing and planning meals; (2) bathing, grooming and dressing; (3) purchasing, cleaning and care of clothing; (4) medical care, including nursing and trips to physicians; (5) arranging for social interaction among peers; (6) arranging alternative care, i.e., babysitting, day-care; (7) putting child to bed at night, waking child in the morning; (8) disciplining child, i.e., teaching general manners and toilet training; (9) educating, i.e., religious, cultural, social, etc.; (10) teaching elementary skills, i.e., reading, writing, and arithmetic").

238. **Answer (B) is the best answer.** Nadia will likely be successful if she would have aborted had she had the relevant information and if she suffered emotional or financial harm as a result of the professional's negligence. *See Harbeson v. Parke-Davis, Inc.*, 656 P.2d 483, 488 (Wash. 1983) ("wrongful birth will refer to an action based on an alleged breach of the duty of a health care provider to impart information or perform medical procedures with due care, where the breach is a proximate cause of the birth of a defective child"). Most cases involve a claim by the mother that she would have aborted but for the negligence, *see Azzolino v. Dingfelder*, 337 S.E.2d 528, 533 (N.C. 1985) ("The jurisdictions which have reached the merits of claims for wrongful birth currently appear to be almost unanimous in their recognition of them when but for the defendants' negligence, the parents would have terminated the defective fetus by abortion."), and involve a claim for emotional or financial harm. *See Keel v. Banach*, 624 So. 2d 1022, 1030 (Ala. 1993) ("the following items are compensable, if proven: (1) any medical and hospital expenses incurred as a result of a physician's negligence; (2) the physical pain suffered by the wife; (3) loss of consortium; and (4) mental and emotional anguish the parents have suffered.").

Answer (A) is incorrect. A wrongful life action involves a claim by the child, Ophelia, that but for the medical professional's negligence she child would not have been born and that her having been born constituted a harm. *See Bruggeman by and through Bruggeman v.*

Schimke, 718 P.2d 635, 639 (Kan. 1986).

Answer (C) is incorrect. That is a condition of a wrongful life rather than a wrongful birth claim. *See Bruggeman by and through Bruggeman v. Schimke*, 718 P.2d 635, 639 (Kan. 1986).

Answer (D) is incorrect. The harm here was in the failure to provide the relevant information rather than in having caused the child to have Down's Syndrome. *See Harbeson v. Parke-Davis, Inc.*, 656 P.2d 483, 488 (Wash. 1983).

239.   While West Calixico can grant the divorce assuming that Trinity has met the domicile and residence requirement, *see Davis v. Davis*, 210 N.W.2d 221, 226 (Minn. 1973) (discussing the need to meet both the domicile and residency requirement to obtain a divorce), West Calixico would not have jurisdiction to distribute property located in New Caledonia when it does not have personal jurisdiction over Tomaso. *See Snider v. Snider*, 551 S.E.2d 693, 697 (W. Va. 2001) ("if a court has jurisdiction over only one spouse but not the other, the 'divisible divorce' concept permits the court to dissolve the marital relationship of the parties . . . without addressing the property rights and obligations of the parties.").

240.   While a noncustodial parent who suffers a substantial change in income may qualify to have her child support obligation reduced, *see Rome v. Rome*, 621 P.2d 1090, 1092 (Mont. 1981) ("a substantial change in the financial condition of the parent or child has been recognized as grounds for modification of a previously-entered child support order"), a parent who voluntarily brings about a reduction in her income may well not be able to have her child support obligation modified. *See Burdette v. Burdette*, 681 So. 2d 862, 863 (Fla. Dist. Ct. App. 1996) ("A change in circumstances does not exist when a parent obligated to pay child support attempts to avoid or reduce that obligation by voluntarily becoming unemployed or underemployed."). If the court were to find that Darlene took a different position at reduced pay so that she would not have to pay as much in support, it is unlikely that the court would reduce that support obligation. *See Sawicki v. Haxby*, 186 P.3d 546, 550 (Alaska 2008) (ex-wife's voluntarily taking lower-paying job did not justify reducing child support obligation).

241.   **Answer (B) is the best answer.** Because Alfredo and the two children continue to live in New Meriana, which is the state issuing the initial decree, New Meriana is the state that would have jurisdiction to modify the support obligation. *See McHale v. McHale*, 109 P.3d 89, 92 (Ariz. Ct. App. 2005).

Answer (A) is not the best answer. While it is true that Miguel might be rehired, a court might order a temporary reduction in support while Miguel was looking for work. *See Manning v. Manning*, 600 So. 2d 1274, 1276 (Fla. Dist. Ct. App. 1992) ("although the trial court did not err in refusing to modify the former husband's child support obligations because the reduction in income had not been shown to be permanent, it was nevertheless an abuse of discretion not to grant the former husband 'emergency' or temporary relief from that obligation"). The better answer is that the Colozona court likely did not have jurisdiction to reduce support and that Miguel should instead have filed in New Meriana. *See Lilly v. Lilly*, 2011 UT App 53 (noting the intent behind the Uniform Interstate Family Support Act is that there can only be one state that has jurisdiction to modify support). As long as the child or one of the parents remains in the initial decree-granting state, that state will continue to have exclusive jurisdiction to modify support. *See McHale v. McHale*, 109

P.3d 89, 92 (Ariz. Ct. App. 2005).

Answer (C) is not the best answer. While it is true that Miguel might not be able to have the support obligation modified if he was fired for cause, *see Lambert v. Lambert*, 617 N.W.2d 645, 650 (Neb. Ct. App. 2000) ("A petition for the modification of child support will be denied if the change in financial condition is due to fault or voluntary wastage or dissipation of one's talents and assets."), the better answer is that Colozona likely does not have jurisdiction to hear this case under its version of UIFSA. *See McHale v. McHale*, 109 P.3d 89, 92 (Ariz. Ct. App. 2005).

Answer (D) is incorrect. Colozona will likely be found not to have jurisdiction to hear this case under its version of UIFSA. *See McHale v. McHale*, 109 P.3d 89, 92 (Ariz. Ct. App. 2005).

242.   **Answer (B) is the best answer.** John will likely be able to rebut any presumption of paternity created by statute, given that he is doing this in a timely way, has never held Zachary out as his son, and has never bonded with Zachary. *See Kohler v. Bleem*, 654 A.2d 569, 575–76 (Pa. Super. Ct. 1995) (divorcing spouse permitted to rebut paternity of child when he could not have fathered child and had never held child out as his own).

Answer (A) is not the best answer. The presumption created by a child being born into a marriage is rebuttable. *See Moody v. Moody*, 822 A.2d 39, 43 (Pa. Super. Ct. 2003) (ex-husband permitted to challenge paternity of child whom he could not have fathered and whom he never held out as his own).

Answer (C) is incorrect. An undeceived ex-husband may be permitted to challenge paternity when he has never held the child out as his own and when he could not have fathered the child. *See Moody v. Moody*, 822 A.2d 39, 43 (Pa. Super. Ct. 2003); *Kohler v. Bleem*, 654 A.2d 569, 575–76 (Pa. Super. Ct. 1995).

Answer (D) is incorrect. A support obligation can be imposed on a non-genetically related father who has held the child out as his own. *See Kohler v. Bleem*, 654 A.2d 569, 578 (Pa. Super. Ct. 1995) ("Estoppel does apply, however, when the father has accepted the child and treated him as his own and he may not, upon separation, reject paternity and demand a blood test to rebut the presumption.").

243.   **Answer (C) is the best answer.** Of those jurisdictions recognizing a loss of consortium cause of action for children, some jurisdictions limit the cause of action to minors, *see Belcher v. Goins*, 400 S.E.2d 830, 840 (W. Va. 1990), whereas other jurisdictions permit adult children to maintain such a cause of action. *See Villareal v. State, Dept. of Transp.*, 774 P.2d 213, 216 (Ariz. 1989).

Answer (A) is incorrect. Claims by children for loss of consortium with their parents are recognized in many jurisdictions. *See Villareal v. State, Dept. of Transp.*, 774 P.2d 213, 216 (Ariz. 1989) ("children may recover for loss of consortium when a third party causes serious, permanent, and disabling injury to their parent").

Answer (B) is not the best answer. Even if the jurisdiction recognizes a loss of consortium action for children, that does not establish that such a cause of action will be recognized even if the child has reached majority. *See Belcher v. Goins*, 400 S.E.2d 830, 840 (W. Va. 1990) (refusing to recognize a loss of consortium action for adult children).

Answer (D) is incorrect. Some jurisdiction will not recognize a loss of consortium cause of action if the child has reached majority, close relationship with the parent notwithstanding. *See Belcher v. Goins*, 400 S.E.2d 830, 840 (W. Va. 1990).

244.   **Answer (C) is the best answer.** Depending upon the size of Mona's contribution compared to the value of the house, she might receive a credit for it, *see Horn v. Horn*, 445 So. 2d 717, 718 (Fla. Dist. Ct. App. 1984), or the house might be viewed as marital. *Cf. Martinez v. Martinez*, 556 So. 2d 668, 672–73 (La. Ct. App. 1990) ("the matrimonial domicile in the instant case should be classified as community property because it was purchased with separate and community things and the value of the community things . . . used was almost twice the value of the separate things used.").

   Answer (A) is incorrect. A number of factors in addition to title might be considered when deciding whether property is marital or, instead, is owned by the person in whose name it is titled. *See*, for example, *Nesci v. Nesci*, 1990 Del. Fam. Ct. LEXIS 106 (Feb. 5, 1990) (considering numerous factors to determine degree to which marital domicile was marital property).

   Answer (B) is incorrect. Merely because some separate property was contributed to the house would not make the house part of the marital estate. The separate property might be construed as a gift. *See Quinn v. Quinn*, 512 A.2d 848, 851 (R.I. 1986) (inheritance assets used to purchase marital domicile construed as gift to marital estate) or the individual making that contribution might receive a credit for it. *See Horn v. Horn*, 445 So. 2d 717, 718 (Fla. Dist. Ct. App. 1984) ("The court provided for appellee to receive from the proceeds a special equity in the amount of $10,000 as a result of her contribution to the improvement of the marital home from an inheritance (funds wholly unconnected with the marital relationship)").

   Answer (D) is incorrect. Separate funds might be used to purchase a house, which might later be treated as marital because of the intent of the parties. *See Quinn v. Quinn*, 512 A.2d 848, 851 (R.I. 1986).

245.   **Answer (C) is the best answer.** Such a marriage might be recognized if validly celebrated elsewhere, notwithstanding that it, if attempted within the state, would be treated as null and void. *See Ghassemi v. Ghassemi*, 998 So. 2d 731, 743 (La. Ct. App. 2008) (recognizing first cousin marriage validly celebrated elsewhere, although Louisiana treats such a marriage as void if individuals attempt to contract it within the state).

   Answer (A) is incorrect. Merely because they could not marry within the state does not establish that their marriage would not be recognized if validly celebrated elsewhere. *See Mazzolini v. Mazzolini*, 155 N.E.2d 206, 207 (Ohio 1958) (first cousin marriage prohibited locally nonetheless recognized because validly celebrated elsewhere).

   Answer (B) is incorrect. Even a marriage treated as void by a jurisdiction might nonetheless be recognized if validly celebrated elsewhere. *See Ghassemi v. Ghassemi*, 998 So. 2d 731, 743 (La. Ct. App. 2008) ("the mere fact that a marriage is absolutely null when contracted in Louisiana does not mean that such a marriage validly performed elsewhere is automatically invalid as violative of a strong public policy").

   Answer (D) is incorrect. When evasive marriages are discussed in the case law, they refer to individuals who evade the domicile's law by going to another state, marrying, and then returning to the domicile to live. *See In re Loughmiller's Estate*, 629 P.2d 156, 157 (Kan. 1981) (discussing couple who went to Colorado to marry to evade Kansas law precluding first cousin marriage). Here, Betty and Carl did not marry in Libertania and then move back to their domicile, East Pennio, to live. Instead, they simply made Libertania their new domicile, where they were permitted to marry.

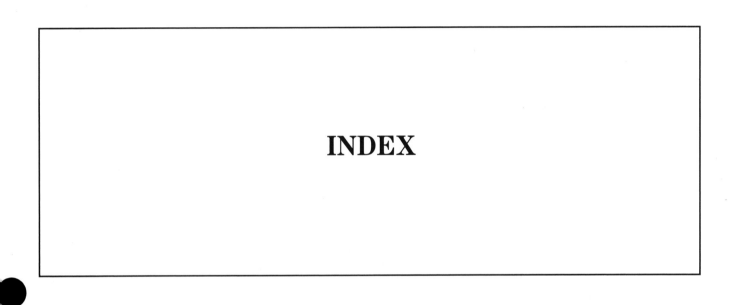

INDEX

INDEX